THE FORCE OF TIME

An Introduction to Deleuze through Proust

Keith W. Faulkner

University Press of America,® Inc.
Lanham · Boulder · New York · Toronto · Plymouth, UK

Copyright © 2008 by
University Press of America,® Inc.
4501 Forbes Boulevard
Suite 200
Lanham, Maryland 20706
UPA Acquisitions Department (301) 459-3366

Estover Road
Plymouth PL6 7PY
United Kingdom

Library of Congress Control Number: 2007933360
ISBN-13: 978-0-7618-3878-4 (paperback : alk. paper)
ISBN-10: 0-7618-3878-3 (paperback : alk. paper)

Table of Contents

Preface

À la recherché du temps perdu isn't about memory. Deleuze makes this claim on the first page of *Proust and Signs*. But if it isn't about memory, then what's it about? Against the grain of scholarship, he claims that Proust is more concerned with forgetting or with becoming than he is about the past, more concerned with the question: "What is a memory one does not recall?" He isn't just being contentious, for there's much in Proust's work to bear this out. But the reasons for his analysis of Proust have little to do with Proust himself. Instead, he faces an entire tradition of philosophy, which puts the self at the core of thought.

What's wrong with the self? To think with the unified self you must also think of the abstract unified object. This is Kant's claim. But what happens to the self when its object can't be unified in this way? That is, what happens when you face the void of time *itself*? In this book, I ask this question. Kant's answer, that empty time must be represented as a line, is just a cop-out. Yes, we can imagine this line, but it doesn't cover over time's force. Instead, it symbolizes the force that it represses. The timeline can't save self-representation, however. If the dissolved subject has any appeal at all, it isn't just because it defies Kant. Instead, it offers us a glimpse into the realms where memory and thought fail.

Why should we explore these vague limits of the self? Traditionally, thinkers have sought a firm basis for judgment. Their fear of error and illusion logically leads them to imagine a rational, unchanging soul. For me, however, this fear seems trivial compared to a new fear: the fear that judgment may limit my power to act, to create, and to perceive all the forces of this world. Yes, judgment brings security, but hasn't it also built us a prison-house? The only way to chip away at its walls is to see where thought and memory break down. This directly opposes the tradition that links Plato to Kant and reminiscence to representation. But this tradition must be overcome if we're to go beyond its image of thought. To do this, this study targets two philosophical dogmas: that

all of time is actively synthesized by the "I think" that attends every representation and that to think is merely to recall forgotten knowledge. Instead, I'll
show that thought is also an involuntary thought and that memory is also an
involuntary memory. My reading of Proust serves this end. Fascinated with the
involuntary, Proust evades the type of thought that Deleuze opposes. Thus, to
grasp *his* Proust is to see these two core ideas in *his* philosophy. And this is why
Proust makes a good introduction to Deleuze.

For too long the faculty of judgment has organized all perception. It has
served as the unquestioned basis of all synthesis. But what if there's a deeper
synthesis that bypasses the mind? What if there's a drive, well known to some,
that exiles us from the organized use of our faculties? A death instinct, perhaps?
And what would happen if, rather than facing an object for the mind to judge,
we face, instead, the empty formlessness of time and space itself? This is what
happens in Proust's *Recherche*. His hero faces a memory he cannot recall, an
empty time he cannot imagine, and an anonymous Other that he cannot place.
These three factors express the virtual in Proust's work.

In the pages that follow, I'll replace the Kantian "I think" with a dissolved
subject, and the "object = x" with an empty time. I'll do this by examining the
Kantian law and the temporal fragments that it engenders. I'll do this to find the
phenomenological subject's "outside." And, from that position, I hope to test the
unquestioned assumption of self-identity. But I'll also try to undo Plato's split
between *idea* and *appearance* by making the obscure internal to the clear and
vice versa. In this way, I'll seek the idea's genesis within our sensory limits, not
in mental categories where they're generally sought. This is this book's theoretical basis.

But this theoretical base will also bear a new type of practice. First, it will
engender new ways of thinking without active judgment. Against the practice of
interpretation, I'll set one of non-interpretation or of learning through signs.
Against the idea of artistic genius, I'll set a transversal style that emerges from
the artist's blind spot. In the end, the dissolved self opens up new creative paths.
Second, it will set out a new way to fight sad passions. That's why, against
depressive Platonism, I'll set schizoid joys; against fidelity to ideals, betrayal;
against envy, indifference. Furthermore, against Kant's categorical imperative,
which reveals the law when it's transgressed, I'll set profanation; against the
alienation it creates, a world without others; against guilt, nature's innocence.
With these transformations, we can change the way we dwell in time.

To do this, however, I will not take the usual routes of scholarship. Often,
scholars treat an idea as if it were a logical equation to be grasped abstractly.
With the aid of examples from Proust, however, I will dramatize ideas. That is,
I'll make abstract ideas concrete so that they can be visualized. In this way, I
resist the trend to scholasticism and return to the philosophical practice of
storytelling by way of Proust. Moreover, because the scholastic uses abstract
terms as a kind of shorthand, we can never be sure if everyone uses them in the
same way. But a story can draw its readers to a shared problem. That is, whereas
an abstract concept must be tested logically, a concrete one can only be tested in

our lives. A purely theoretical argument only changes ideas, but a practical approach can change our lives. That is, while many books try to define time, this one will give you tools to feel its force.

Because I seek the temporal forces that drive thought, however, I must delve beneath the superficial reading of Proust as a thinker of signs. Instead, I will read Deleuze in reverse. Though he begins with signs, Deleuze ends the third edition of *Proust and Signs* with madness. But madness has two regimes: the paranoid and the passional. The paranoid thinker obsesses over phantasms. The jealous man, who sees rivals everywhere, is paranoid. They are his phantasms. But the passional thinker obsesses over viewpoints. The artist, who encounters the obscurity of sensation, is passional. In the end, signs are the results of madness, not its cause. But madness isn't insanity. Rather, it's that which drives thought, one which stays perfectly logical. It's a breakthrough, not a breakdown.

How are we to explore this madness? We could be professorial, give lectures, and write journal articles about madness. Or we could engage in what Deleuze calls "guerilla warfare" and seek the forces of madness in ourselves. Proust's magnifying glass is the lens through which we can discover these forces—forces, however, *that are not* merely traumas, or mental conflicts of a disturbed mind. This would be too reductive. Instead, psychology springs from ontology. Traumas are divisions in time, not merely childhood events. Mental conflicts are the result of an encounter with the *being of sensation*, not merely a psychological imbalance. Certainly, psychoanalysis has a lot to offer. But it fails to open itself up to the outside, to the region of Being *that we are*. That's why, in this book, I explore *madness as ontology*. Literature, however, is the best way to do this, for, although I could give a theoretical exegesis about time's force, such an exegesis wouldn't arm you with tools to engage in guerilla warfare.

As a result, those looking for a simple exegesis of Deleuze's work may be disappointed. Instead, I examine a specific problem. Rather than debating well-known concepts, I'll attempt to break new ground to dissect his often neglected ideas. Mapping out their implications to fill in the blanks, I'll say what Deleuze left unsaid. That is, to say something one step beyond his reasoning, but still in harmony with his thought. Therefore, rather than sticking to one text and explaining it, I'll use bits of text from here and there as a toolbox. For example, I'll explore the "repetition and thought" of *Difference and Repetition*, "the depth and the surface," the "world without others," the Stoic and the Kleinian theories of *The Logic of Sense*, the "line of flight" and "faciality" of *A Thousand Plateaus*, as well as the "part objects" of *Anti-Oedipus*. Thus, I'll break the author's identity to double him with the aid of a Proustian lens.

You may ask, are these ideas mine? Or do they belong to Deleuze and Proust? Both and neither! Every problem creates it own conceptual plane with its own characters and dramas. That's why I use Deleuze's method of conceptual personas to insert Proust's characters into Deleuze's philosophy and vice versa. That is, this method will dramatize *and* characterize ideas. I'll not only argue for an interpretation (what *this* concept "is"), but will also test it with characters (*who* personifies this concept). To do this, however, I'll forgo the impersonal style, used to seek facts, and will use, instead, a personal tone, as Proust himself does, to seek what's interesting.

But what are the interesting points in this book? Temporal intuition is interesting because it makes us think through signs. But this intuition is rooted in two psychological positions: depressive and schizoid. The first traps time in closed vessels, which the second reopens. These positions, however, are rooted in sexuality. That's why Proust's *aesthetic* homosexuality is interesting: it springs from those primal myths that affect our sense of time. This mythical affect, in turn, is tied to a pre-human world of intensity. That's why part objects are interesting. They *are* intensity *itself*. Together, these themes form part one of this book.

In part two, the metaphysics of continuity and discontinuity is interesting because, without it, time and space would be indivisible. But the divisible implies that there's a virtual *difference* from which divisions spring. That's why the virtual is interesting: it permits moments to resonate passively. Creativity, in turn, springs from this resonance, from the transversal—creativity's true source, for, to create is to discover a blind spot within thought. That's why the clash between the represented and the repressed is interesting: it creates this blind spot's obscurity. This obscurity, in turn, forces us to think. And these forced movements are interesting because they rouse thought and memory. This, at last, is the question that I find *most* interesting: not "how can I be sure that my thought is true?", but "how can I enlarge my power to think?" How else, but through the force of time!

All in all, the topics in this introduction to Deleuze are in the air of the times. Many scholarly works written on Proust in the last twenty years mention Deleuze's reading of Proust. And the Bergsonian revival has come with a renewed interest in post-Heideggerian theories of time. Deleuze's *Difference and Repetition* is one of the most recent French revisions of these temporal theories. But despite their value for philosophy, Deleuze's theories are regularly studied in literature departments in North America. And though there have been several books on Deleuze *and* literature, no book has truly placed Deleuze theories *into* literature to personify his concepts. I wrote this book to remedy this, so that those who've read Proust can understand Deleuze.

Keith W. Faulkner
Hobe Sound, FL.
    April, 2007

Abbreviations

AO   Gilles Deleuze and Félix Guattari, *L'Anti-œdipe: Capitalisme et schizophrénie.* (Paris: Les Éditions de Minuit, 1972); *Anti-Oedipus: Capitalism and Schizophrenia.* Translated by R. Hurley, M. Seem, and H. R. Lane (Minneapolis: University of Minnesota Press, 1983).

DR   Gilles Deleuze, *Différence et repetition.* (Paris: Presses Universitaires de France, 1968); *Difference and Repetition.* Translated by P. Patton (New York: Columbia University Press, 1994).

LS   Gilles Deleuze, *Logique du sens.* (Paris: Les Éditions de Minuit, 1969); *The Logic of Sense.* Translated by M. Lester and C. Stivale, edited by C. Boundas (New York: Columbia University Press, 1990).

PS   Gilles Deleuze, *Proust et les signes.* (Paris: Presses Universitaires de France, 1964); *Proust and Signs: The Complete Text.* Translated by R. Howard (Minneapolis: University of Minnesota Press, 2000).

TP   Gilles Deleuze and Félix Guattari, *Mille plataux: Capitalisme et schizophrénie.* (Paris: Les Éditions de Minuit, 1980); *A Thousand Plateaus: Capitalism and Schizophrenia.* Translated by B. Massumi (Minneapolis: University of Minnesota Press, 1987).

RTP Marcel Proust, *À la recherché du temps perdu.* (Paris: Éditions Gallimard, 1999); *Remembrance of Things Past.* Translated by C. K. Scott Moncrieff, T. Kilmartin and A. Mayor, 3 vols. (New York: Vintage Books, 1981). All translations of this work are mine. I cite the page numbers of the Moncrieff translation, however, *only* so that those who have read Proust in translation may have a familiar point of reference.

General Introduction

The Story of N

When I ask Miss N to tell me a story, she says nothing since I haven't given her a context. So, I ask her about her day. But when she starts, she pegs events to people. Each spins a new temporal thread, a new world, fragmenting her story. Nevertheless, she always keeps *her* view. "Everything happens as if a universal storyteller existed, who registers all occurrences and who, seeing the impossibility of recounting everything at once, distributes information into numerous personas."[1] Each is an island in her story, and her journey—a sea voyage. It doesn't matter if she meets Peter or Paul on the road. Each is alike. Only an anonymous encounter and its fractured viewpoints are essential, for, without a theme, time breaks apart. Each event alters the whole. Thus, I can't call this *encountered time* "subjective" even though each event happens to her.

So I ask her to tell me something interesting, something vital to me as well, something extraordinary. But, as if she didn't hear me, she continues to unwind her tangled thread, which is so mixed up that she hesitates. That's why I still can't see how it connects: she went for a walk, it rained, Georges played in the garden, the postman came, and Miss A visited her. But her account doesn't reveal *time's order*, merely occurrences, "or rather a day of her life."[2] But its events resonate because, though differing, they parallel each other. For instance, while she walked, it rained, and while the postman came, Georges played. They all share some link. But she would have left these events unordered, *if I hadn't asked* about her day. Therefore, I force her to recall.

These events follow each other like a shopping-list that she recounts without embellishment, for time's unfolding doesn't resemble her narrative, that dramatic "something interesting." But what actually organizes her events? Indeed, some of them never find a place in her story. Why not? It only covers her life partly—as if, though she *obscurely* perceives events, she creates a personal place within time's larger expanse. So, when she recounts her day, she seems to see how "this anonymous and impersonal time, in which things always occur, takes form, finds a beginning and an end within her life, within a day of her life, which makes sense in relation to a universal time, which each of us calls our life, as if each of us had our own time."[3] It's as if time had multiple narrative threads, which Miss N must pull to find *the one* that best represents her day. Therefore, as time unfolds its eternal combinations, each thread touches her—so that her life inhabits a point in history's unfolding—an *impersonal* time.

So, when I ask her to recount something *really* interesting, not just her day, it's as if she presents a menu of events. But she also follows a line of flight: as if she seeks to justify something, as if something compels her to speak. Or, perhaps she's expecting judgment. Perhaps, that's why her story seems to coalesce. At first, the walk, the rain, her friend's visit, and Georges playing in the garden seem detached. "The events that she relates in succession do not seem to have any relation.... When she tells me that it began to rain and that George stopped playing in the garden, I understand perfectly that the first event causes the second.... Their succession is not marked by a simple 'then,' but by a 'because.'"[4] Now events make sense *because* she arranges them causally: I say to myself, "Of course Georges stopped playing if it rained." But, given time's impersonal nature, events cannot order themselves naturally. Only a force can do this. With it, she reads time's signs, goes beyond the universe's *impersonal* time, and arranges her life by steps: Back from her walk, she saw the postman, and it began to rain. So she called Georges in from the garden, and her friend, Miss A, who also came out of the rain, visited her. The rain is key. Without this *crisis point*, her narrative would lack shape. This proves that she neither controls the story, nor that events have intrinsic meaning, nor does she give them one. The *problem* does; the drama demands it. But if she recounts events objectively, it fades. Hence, Miss N occupies time by living them causally, not randomly. "Therefore we rediscover in Miss N's account what we can call preformed lines.... Before all accounts, the human spirit has already written its work, and preordained facts in time."[5] Miss N inhabits these preformed lines that "the human spirit," according to this narrator, sets down. On the line, she counts the hours and the days. But she also occupies time's emotional depths, which magnifies her intensity, for any machine can record events, but only the human heart can feel their passage. That's why *any* account would be incomplete without emotion. So, if she didn't care about Georges playing in the rain, the sequence would stand still. This, in itself, gives it a *force*. Without emotions, Miss N would lack not only a reason to act, but to recall her story as well.

So, when she tells me it rained and Georges fell ill, I feel that *this* event has a cause. Though I may have seen the rain and then noticed Georges falling ill, I never *actually* perceived their link. My brain composed it. But is there not also something more fundamental? Without *presupposing* an associating mind, I ask myself, "Doesn't the situation dictate it?" In fact, when Miss N recounts her day, she sees its sequence and unfolds its viewpoint, not her own. She imagines and untangles its strange standpoints, and then asks herself "Why should the postman arrive then, and why should her friend enter the house?" These questions all concern time, not her *personal* viewpoint (which she always has), but that of a day. For this reason, "all of humanity's efforts consist in replacing the infinite variety of actual series... by an ordered series representing a common text."[6] In this way, a fictional series replaces an objective one. Now she abridges her story to include only interesting things. She bars the nightmarish complexity of possibilities, which now grow coherent.

She isn't alone in her story. When others visit her, they share her events. In fact, most of them make up that memorable "something interesting." Vital to her day, Miss N's visitors do more than make her self-aware. Like surveyor-poles, they map out space and time. Without them, her day would be shapeless. So, when I ask her what happened when her neighbor left, "she tells me that nothing happened until the point when she received another visit. Until then, she stayed alone. There is, therefore, a gap in her account. But there was no gap in her day. Her life continued. She must have lived something outside of these events."[7] She can't recall those lonely hours. But what is a memory one cannot recall?

Life's most powerful events are not the revived ones, but the forgotten ones. If the repressed returns, then did the events in Miss N's day occur accidentally? Or *could there be some moments she forgot* that explain her day better? After all, the events she recalls are only ones that she dares confess. The others appear as the empty times filling the vast regions *forgotten within memory itself.* They represent a mental power-failure breaking up her story like a bad tape recording. But since these temporal gaps lack that "something interesting," she ignores them unless someone demands an account. Obviously, she continues to live and breathe in these vacant moments that make every *interesting* event stand out. "These empty times have great importance for the account. There is something that occurs before and after this empty time.... This allows us to better understand the character of an actual series.... All her accounts relate each time to time's unity. And one day Miss N. will write her memoirs, and these unities will form part of the great unity of her life."[8] When she will write it, she will represent her entire life. But, because she will organize it around interesting occurrences, she will leave out all these empty moments. Thus, between a vast *impersonal* time and her small *personal* time-islands lies an ontological gap— Being and psychology—for neither psychology, nor phenomenology fully explain this emptiness. This ontological desert is *the* virtual. Though she's oblivious to this *outland*ish region, she certainly feels it, just as every neurotic feels that something bad happened, albeit something unknown. As a result, Miss N can't call her memoir "whole," for it merely includes events that the "I think" qualifies. Thus, Miss N occupies time by *repressing.*

Since Miss N is only one of her story's characters, when the scene empties, nothing occurs: "Her day continues. She continues outside the spectacle."[9] Like a playwright, Miss N, can mix up the scenes to build a drama, or a comedy of errors, for those who lived these events with her will feel that they've been mischaracterized, almost to a comic-strip-like cartoonishness. That is, her ego cuts down other people to build up her own self-worth. But such egotistical narratives never record people and places exactly. Thus, time's malleable blocks can be rearranged and distorted at will. But she doesn't do this maliciously; rather, to highlight the dramatic scenes, some must fall on the scrap-heap.

Therefore, in a single day, she lives through empty time. But Miss N will only grasp this once she expands her account to cover a lifetime:

> But now suppose Miss N. goes over her notes while composing her Memoirs. She finds, in revisiting these different accounts, each of which relates to a particular day, that she mistook the "chronological" order that was unjustified. In fact, different days do not resemble each other and events that she thought she lived have found their natural place in each of these days. By now envisioning her whole past, she recognizes that events cannot be displaced in time without the life she lived changing... it seems, therefore, that her whole life was composed of many times, each of these like a life in itself, having a beginning and an end.... Time's divisions are not, therefore, the work of the intellect. Time itself seems to divide within a lifetime.... We have abandoned phenomenal time, where everything occurs without beginning or end. But outside of this universal time, there is, for each of us, *our* time, organized time, life's time, biographical time.... This constitutes the time of our accounts. But every account is a composition; each account presupposes a narrator, which is in a way outside of the accounted time.[10]

With this story, Bernard Groethuysen points out something strange, which Deleuze depicts in "Occupying Without Counting": "We perceive easily and sometimes painfully what is in time, we perceive also the form, unities and relations of chronometry, but not time as *force*, time itself, 'a little time in the pure state.'"[11] By describing her day, Miss N buries *time itself* in this interstitial fold. Nonetheless, in it, time goes uncounted, unmeasured, but not unsensed. In fact, its very existence, as we've seen, troubles Miss N. After all, like Kafka's Joseph K, she might have done something *truly wrong*. And, even if she were a saint, she could never remove all doubt. Therefore, guilt haunts empty time. In it, she finds time's force, not its occurrences. And, on this level, she touches something beyond her personal or psychological time—she touches its ontological core, its abyss: a liquid sea solidifying iceberg-events. As a temporal being, she measures these floating time-chunks that Eros saves. But death's greater force, once again, smashes them. Hence, every time Miss N finds something her narrative contradicts, she senses this death: as if, in these moments, her entire being is questioned. She must recalculate her life. But, in the brief interval, she senses something her narrative can't explain: the world's thickness, its "becoming." But this *becoming* isn't *in* the fragments; it's *between them*, in empty time. That's why, as Groethuysen noted, when time is measured, it cracks—just as Miss N, inhabits an unmeasured time and detaches remarkable points that shine against an unremarkable background. As a result, during these wasted hours, she can obscurely sense time's force.

PART ONE

Love is Space and Time
Made Perceptible to the Heart

Introduction

"Love is space and time made perceptible to the heart" (*RTP* 1893; III, 392). With these words Proust opens a door of emotion through which the forces of time may enter. And yet, with all its abstract and technical definitions, time, and the involuntary reactions that vivify it, get buried. But Proust's work, more than any other, unearths this emotional plane. That is, unlike a stone, you must find what, in fact, makes you temporally unique. This is my first task. In this part, I examine the guilt, the envy, the idealization, and the alienation that comes with time: intense changes, past dimensions, complications and limits.

Normally, *guilt* debases. Though Deleuze, Nietzsche, and others have fought against theological guilt, they never stop it entirely. In fact, it persists, even in those who fight against it. Perhaps, then, direct repression isn't the right way. After all, the repressed returns. The trick, then, is to alter it, to make it light, affirmative, and productive, not soul-crushing. This, above all, affirms life. In chapter one, you'll learn how to view this normally crushing guilt *humorously*, thereby making it superficial. With this, time becomes sublime.

Then again, *envy* diminishes you by keeping you from achieving anything That's why faultless ideals need to be ridiculed. And that's why ambitious people need laughter. With it, every ideal becomes something to surpass. In chapter two, you'll learn how sadistic irony destroys envy: this superficial, humorous aggression weakens ideals, sentiments, and nostalgias.

On the other hand, *fidelity* is perhaps mankind's most deeply held virtue. But fidelity to a belief limits thought. And fidelity to an aesthetic vision limits the world's beauty. And, for Proust's hero, fidelity to one woman means giving up all hope of becoming a writer. But is it really worth giving up all this, in the end, just to feel safe? After all, the creative need to betray, not only to enter new possible worlds and new lives, but new aesthetic visions and new loves as well. Given this, should there not be a categorical imperative to betray? In chapter three, you'll learn how to evade fidelity by profaning, not by transgressing, which, in the end, only reaffirms its idols.

Finally, *alienation* hands your world over to Others, so that, in the end, you desire *only* what they desire, see *only* what they see, and observe a world that's no longer yours. The timid, who retreat into alienation, find it hard to live immanently. But can they really be said to live if they ignore immanence and view their whole lives from a distance? In chapter four, you'll learn how to abolish these sentimental distances by naturalizing the Other.

With these four emotions, which begin in love and in frustration, time is perceived. For instance, guilt propels you into a line of flight in which you can feel time move. Envy induces nostalgia in which you sense the past *as a dimension*. Fidelity and its idols, to which you can submit or rebel, cut time into segments that you can traverse by betraying, *or* can be trapped in by remaining loyal. Alienation and obligation limit time and space and split moments and places. All in all, by moving it forward, by moving it back, by segmenting it, and by limiting it, these emotions add a perceptible force to time.

Chapter 1

A Sort of Magnifying Glass

In the *Critique of Pure Reason*, Kant limits intensive magnitudes to an empirical consciousness and extensive magnitudes to an abstract line. But, in this chapter, I'll show how the *intensive* begins in repetition and how the *extensive* begins in a line of flight. Using Proust's magnifying glass, I'll undercut the "I think" and will replace it with a more complex mode of thought.

The Proustian Lens

What does literature do? What is its use? Deleuze asks these questions.[1] Unlike philosophy, which divides the well-founded from the misleading, literature, such as Proust's, dramatizes problems and, thus, treats time differently. For instance, Kant's time is linear. Like Plato's cave allegory and Descartes' clear thought analogy, he relies on a vision metaphor. Literature, on the other hand, explores time by repeating. For Proust, the novel is like a magnifying glass through which his readers can see their own temporal rhythms, inner resonances, and passing lives. That's why Proust says that his book "would be a means for them to read themselves" (*RTP* 2390; III, 1089). Regret, nostalgia, lost childhoods—in short, all the passions this literary machine churns out make them feel life, emotion, and time—not a linear time's marble icons, of course, but its emotional lava-beds. In this way, the *Recherche* mangles them, not by a dyslexic logical argument, but by exhibiting the stray fragments of a wrecked identity.

In your life, for example, you feel these fragments when you move to a new place, take a new job, or make new friends—changes often ignored, until one day you wake up and realize how different the world has become. Proust reveals time-splinters and the work of oblivion called "the intermittences of the heart."

But why do you need an optical device to see them? Modern minds have become so enthralled by time's symbolic chain and by an enduring sense of self that, despite all contrary evidence, few feel it pass. For many, the past is a series of days, of weeks, or of years inhabited like so many hotel rooms. But these segments have become cliché. From Plato, "the revolutions of the years have created number and have given us a conception of time," time has become a number of movement; from Descartes, time is "a mode under which we conceive of the thing in so far as it continues to exist," time has become a medium which things inhabit; from Kant, "time is a necessary representation that underlies all intuitions," time has become an unfolding medium; and from Husserl, time is "a continuous chain of retentions of retentions," time has become expectation and memory.[2] They all solidify bad habits.

Unlike philosophical argument, however, drama reveals such fragments. Not dividing the true and the false dialectically, it doesn't *challenge* your sense of permanence, it merely renders it intensely uninteresting. But some readers don't react to his magnifying glass since "sometimes the reader's eyes are not those for which my book is suitable" (*RTP* 2390; III, 1089). Sometimes it fails to resonate. That's why it doesn't reveal universal truth as philosophy claims to.

Those philosophers who claim universal truth deny an inequality of reason. When Descartes declares "good sense" to be "equally distributed," he acts as if, in Proust's words, it were "instantly detectable by the interlocutor through an intuitive faculty" (*RTP* 1863; III, 353). Plato also fools himself, believing intellects can "rise to that which requires no assumption and is the starting point of all." And, though avowing a lack of memory or of imagination, "they always find themselves well served with regard to intelligence and thought" (*DR* 173; 132). After all, who claims that their beliefs are based on faulty reasoning? In short, "clear and distinct ideas" stand on the sand of an old saying, not on the rock of experience, for, without denying that physical strengths differ, everyone assumes that mental ones are potentially the same. In fact, democracy must homogenize via this "equal reason" to ensure the rights of citizens. Thus, equal reason is enforced for the benefit of an abstract humanity. That's how society *purges* individuals to make way for citizens. Such is the bedpan of democracy.

Yet, remember that each individual, despite this homogenization, maintains a unique outlook. Literature, for instance, appeals to differing powers: eyes that see their own colors, ears that hear their own sounds, skin that feels its own textures, each perceiving the world using, not the homogenized mind, but differing senses. Under these circumstances, the intellect neglects time's force.

The mind only sees decaying monuments: in a cracked, yellowed statue, for example. Time seems to unfold in those changes that only time-lapse photos reveal. Juxtaposing such snapshots, you represent it linearly. This film-logic supports the law of non-contradiction: a single rock cannot ascend and descend at the same time. Only an idea links them (I=I supports object=object). This logic must be weakened to uncover real changes. Though this rock appears successively, no one perceives its sameness. Eyes only see change. However, the temporally sensitive feel this flux organically even if the mind ignores it.[3] That is to say, the mind makes you aware of change without portraying time *as it is* as *a pure intuition*. But Proust does this by capturing time in a pure state.

The Discovery of Intuition

In the history of philosophy, islands of time in a pure state surface only to succumb to the intellect. Despite this, Kant and others foster this abstract *image of thought*, while Deleuze stresses intuitive leaps. But if learning is truly empirical, then you can only know yourself in this unfolding Dionysian medium.

But a radical empiricism such as this hasn't been seen since the birth of rationalism: when Leibniz and Kant ordered time and change differently. For Leibniz, time "consists in the successive order of things" in a temporal nexus. But for Kant, who thought that it needed an underpinning, time precedes this nexus.[4] This seems to be an unhatchable chicken-and-egg question since the mind can neither link moments without an underlying plane of time, nor can it sense an underlying time without its linking moments. Kant, however, reaches a conceptual turning point in which "time itself unfolds... instead of things unfolding within it" (*DR* 120; 88). Now, it becomes an *a priori* intuition of a historic expanse on which you're like a small cork, *a pure form of changeless change*—its currents swirl, but its mass persists. And yet, it lacks vivacity since this static time calls for a force to give it life—namely, a dynamic genesis.

But the Kant-Leibniz conflict weakens, Deleuze writes, if "one takes account of the dynamic factors present in the two doctrines" (*DR* 40; 26). When it forms an intensive chain, time extends because "all reality in perception has a degree."[5] Stretched beyond their ephemeral existence, intensive blips become like signposts, stretching to the horizon, that divide light from dark, near from far, hard from soft, that contrast moments, and that make change permanent.

Time isn't merely a concept, however. As an intuition, Kant writes, it "yields no shape," thus the mind must "represent the time-sequence by a line progressing to infinity."[6] In other words, faced with a formless abyss, your mind must impose limits to count the days, the weeks, and the years so that you can steer your way through time. Only with a line can you picture time as a whole. On it, moments coexist even though intuitions of them may differ. Though the mind represents time extensively, the body *lives* time intensively.

Kant favors linear time since, for him, it "acquires a magnitude, which can be entitled *duration*," without which "existence is always vanishing and recommencing."[7] But is duration merely what we *add to time* to save it? The intensive now filtered out, only the intellect remains. Deleuze resists this because, without intensity, moments would fall into the dark night that blackens all cows. An extended space, has many equal parts: one mile seems like every other mile, and one hour seems like every other hour. But when intensities strike this darkness, they ignite a furrow that sets apart its colors, weights, and temperatures. That's why a marathon's first and last mile differ. And, in the final steps, the ground gets harder; legs, heavier; and vision, vertiginous. So, although inhabiting an extended domain measured cardinally, the runner lives in this intense domain when he moves by degrees: that is to say, ordinally. With these numbers, he occupies time in one of two ways: "counting in order to occupy space-time, or occupying without counting."[8] Without *repetition*, however, all events would feel alike. Time would end. Extended space would kill off difference (the marathon's last mile), not those identical units called hours, days, and weeks.

But such repetition is unconscious. Evolution, for example, produces species blindly. It repeats without recognition. That's why Darwin made evolution "the blunders of numerous workmen."[9] Words are another example of repetition: though having discreet meanings, when spoken, they become unique. The Beatitudes, for example, repeats "blessed are," which builds to a crescendo. Each rebirth, in each new sentence, intensifies the phrase like the musical one Proust depicts: "to the phrase's many recurrences, such or such sonata, returns, but changed each time, with a rhythm, with different accompaniments, the same yet different, just as things reoccur in life" (*RTP* 1798; III, 261). This echo renews similar colors, sounds, and scents with different accents without which the repeated would seem as dull as the water that washes so many theoretical dishes. Thus, its rhythms enjoy more force, more power, than any abstract idea. To sense them, you must occupy them *without counting*.

But this requires a passive intuition—intensities flowing into the body's every tendril, stimulating it, bathing it in the electric seas of a nebulous universe. But on this sea, the mind shields itself like a boat upon these waters, fixing instead on stable landmarks of its own making. So, when referring to Bergson's intuition, Deleuze means "the movement by which we emerge from our own duration."[10] On it, these temporal seafarers forsake their safe, tranquil cabins and encounter these blasts of time from without.

While we wait on the dissolving sugar lump, for instance, intensity shows us "a way of being in time... partially revealed in the process of its dissolving." Though its shape may be mentally constructed, the lump's actual *dissolving*, nonetheless, shows us something exterior: a degree, which, as Kant writes, "can diminish to nothing (the void) through infinite graduations without in any way altering the extensive magnitude of the appearance." Yet while its intensity fizzles, you sense something that overflows the dissolving body: a change that infuses you, little by little, with the world's other rhythms.[11]

Of course, time is an inner sense, *as Kant insists*, but an intuitive faculty *also* undergoes shocks externally *as Bergson insists*. That's why an hour spent with a friend over dinner *will not seem as long as* an hour in a doctor's office. As waiting-room prisoners, we sense an intensity beyond the extended world.

Bergson and Plato also split the world along these extensive and intensive lines. On one hand, Plato divides intellectually, splitting the essential from the inessential, unlike the Sophist, who "takes refuge in the darkness of not-being." But when is the essential reached? Because one could chisel away without end, a firm base is needed: the intellect's circular course, which parallels that of the universe, from which all rational beings partake "of the natural truth of reason," so that they "might imitate the absolutely unerring courses of God and regulate our own vagaries." Plato's ideal forms measure the world, such as a justice that excludes the unjust, a mother that excludes the daughter or the wife, as if they were spread among worldly forms based on their likeness to their ideals. And, because the sophist never measures up to that ideal lover of wisdom named "Socrates," naturally, this method is very popular among philosopher-kings.[12]

On the other hand, like Bergson, Spinoza divides according to natural powers: "bodies are distinguished from one another in respect of motion and rest, quickness and slowness, and not in respect of substance."[13] This type of thought is no longer Platonic. Now problems are resolved in their colored thicknesses, not in their cold truth. Thus, a philosophical monkey, seeking food in colored boxes, encounters "a paradoxical period during which the number of 'errors' diminishes even though the monkey does not yet possess the 'knowledge' or 'truth' of a solution in each case" (*DR* 214; 164–165). This banana-eating thinker finds truth unconsciously. This cogitating primate enters real problems temporally, not those hidden in the chorus of clouds, for learning follows a sign's natural contours, not those of abstract ideas.

Returning to the main point, it's now clear that Proust's magnifying glass, found in his hero's failures and frustrations, and that Bergson's intuition both defy this image of thought. That's why his hero complains, "I sensed I was not a genius or perhaps some malady of the brain was hindering it" (*RTP* 143; I, 188-189). These mental diseases, these fated disasters, drive the *Recherche*. These are the physical and psychological barriers upon which the mind teethes.

Readers, who learn painfully, know this. Even after many years, despite any pretence to enlightenment, they feel that they still learn in the dark. In defiance of Platonic optimism, the hero cannot go from darkness into reason's light. Instead, Proust leads them down these paths to a new model of thought. And, with it, he exposes unending problems, not revelations that triumph over your earthly state. You can't simply say "Hallelujah," for, unlike such tokenistic answers, his problems continue, but with an ever-renewed meaning. In this process, salvation is forsaken and worldly problems become more appealing *because you've learned how to encounter them.*

So far, we've seen how intensive-time unfolds, but have not yet explained *how* or *why* it turns into a line. In fact, Kant leaves its genesis unexplained. And representation without explanation is mystification, for there's more to the force of time than these intense repetitions. There's also a force holding it open. Next, we'll see how a perverted categorical imperative extends it.

Time and the Law

The hero lives time's force through an ironic Kantian guilt: in pleasant feelings (his falling in love) and in negative feelings (his falling out of love). That is, he feels inferior to the law, feels a painful, but sublime, durational flux as if he were traipsing amid those invisible landmines on time's moral landscape.

Unlike empirical laws, such as "keep off the grass," a transcendental one, which lacks "as its base any law prescribing particular actions,"[14] remains *unknown* until it's broken. That's why the hero feels guilt when his parents let him go to the theater because "their consent made me cherish them so much that the thought of causing them pain stabbed me with a pain... and life seemed good or evil only insofar as my parents were happy or sad" (*RTP* 356; I, 478). Such crossed limits mark the hours of his life since memories focus on events that break them. Such events not only punctuate his life, they come to embody his slow breakdown in time, for no force affects his temporal sense more than guilt.

In a Kafkaesque world, the Kantian law replaces the Good. But its well-intended nature backfires. Of course, it would be preferable to *know* the law and to attain virtue. But this is impossible, for *the more* people curb their baser instincts and resist gratification, the more draconian their superegos become.[15] In fact, the more they scrutinize, the more caches of gluttony are found by those who grumble about society's self-indulgence because it mirrors their own.

Why do people submit to this self-defeating bondage? Deleuze says that they find it strangely satisfying: "a kind of negative enjoyment expressing our independence from sensible inclinations."[16] By denying them, they flee the cannibalistic cesspool of their corporeal confines. But this *isn't* the mind's way of shedding the body's shackles. Indeed, not a soul's spiritualization, but the pleasure of sickness, which liberates the feverish mind.

When I fall ill, for example, my libido wanes, my hunger dwindles, and my interest in the world fades. But I also feel aware of "a life." As its poisonous and phantasmal allure dries up, I feel the world's thickness. Paradoxically, the law brings about this intense-dwindling. While it purges pleasures, it also produces *negative ones that fill time*, which Deleuze calls "a progress that continues to infinity in its ever increasing conformity with the law."[17] This "increasing conformity" is the decline from a lustful childhood to a detached old age. But why stop there? Even death doesn't leave me frigid enough! I must eternally be dying, forever growing colder and yet more alive. Deleuze espouses this austere and sober joy, this negative pleasure that expands into the future.

So when mankind is abandoned to its pain and when its laws become infinite, the gods no longer issue lots to mortals, punish them, or send supernatural signs. Now, mortals must judge themselves. *But this isn't easy.* Their judgment failing them, they only know their guilt in pain. Now, debts become infinite. Formerly, when the gods tallied your bill, you knew when the tab was paid. But *now*, without these divine bartenders, all you have left is another person's eyes—those abysses toward which debts seem to flow. Once supplications were offered to Apollo's Temple, now they're offered to these human orbs, which, paradoxically, grow more otherworldly as they extend an infinite line of credit. This is the anxious freedom that Sartre depicts. No god forbids, so we freely condemn ourselves to jump from an unseen precipice.

An innocent actor marches onto the stage of life and is abruptly accused of crossing a line. Oh, how dull would life be without such abrupt reversals! From the theater's birth, with the sudden misfortunes enacted in Greek tragedies, such dramatic limits have been explored—like the mortal limits overstepped when Clytemnestra kills Agamemnon. Only death restores balance to the cycle of destiny, "for everything that has come into being destruction is appointed."[18] In these cycles, a judging god consigns mortals to perpetual servitude.

For Hölderlin, the Oedipus trilogy changes this. Not atoning for patricide with instant death, Oedipus flees, exiles himself, and thereby defers judgment. The gods don't punish him, so he must punish himself. Duty forsaken, the gods, themselves betrayed, betray mortals. Echoing this dramatic turn, Kant makes the avoidance of punishment a betrayal of rational principles.[19] That is, ethics only truly exists when lightning bolts no longer fall from Olympus. So, when the gods spare the rod, they *do not* actually spoil the child. Instead, the unpunished guilt only deepens as it does for Dostoevsky's Raskolnikov.

Now the force of duty comes *from* within and, unfortunately, *to* nothing. No longer able to pay my tab and go, I'm charged an infinite interest rate because holiness is "attainable only in an eternity." Thanks to Kant's moral law, "we have to renounce the ancient cycle of faults and expiations in order to follow the infinite route of the slow death, the deferred judgment, or the infinite debt." What better way to make this line straight than eternal self-denial! Thus, the superego makes me sense time *as a force* as I face an "indefinite prolongation." Before, time was internal. Now it has a second force: an external or extended time. Modern time-consciousness, therefore, is one of waiting: Beckett's *Waiting for Godot* and Kafka's "Before the Law."[20]

As we wait, inner-time unfolds. And, as it passes, moments start to differ. Though the oscillation of pleasure and pain *is* inner-time, for Spinoza and Kant, however, this occurs differently. For Spinoza, the mind only knows itself "in so far as it perceives ideas of affections of the body." This self-knowledge spans the flesh and sparks a duration: "from one state to another... there are transitions, passages that are experienced, durations through which we pass to a greater or lesser perfection." And, when these changes leave traces, they leave behind "purely transitive" signs that are "not indicative or representative." That is, the mind doesn't record them. Though they're felt, their causes are not understood. They're mixed. The depressed, for example, will repaint the past with bleak colors and will see only darkness up ahead, for the melancholic mind doesn't synthesize, represent, or compare these states.[21] They're pointillistic blips on a line, "an unlimited number of stationary, metastable states through which the subject passes. The Kantian theory according to which intensive quanta fill up, to varying degrees, *matter that has no empty spaces*, is profoundly schizoid" (*AO* 26; 19). Deleuze and Guattari applaud Kant's schizophrenic *spatium* that overleaps any abstract space or time. Kant links these states on a line as if it were a photosensitive plate, which starts with the empty intuition = 0, and builds shades of color, degrees of heat, and pounds of weight.

But this intuition can also shrivel until, like Leibniz's monads devolving into a plutonian state after death, they become empty intuitions.[22] *There would be no duration without this empty expanse* that Deleuze and Guattari call "the body without organs," a *tabula rasa* that "serves as a surface for the recording of the entire process" (*AO* 17; 11). In the end, *only this surface preserves traces* as if it were stringing intensive beads together on a thread of time.

These intense shifts crop up all throughout the *Recherche*, when the hero, ignoring the world, feels only his flittering body. His internal world having drowned out the monuments that last beyond his lifetime, he finally reaches a point where he can no longer feel anything else: "how could the world have outlived me... since it was enclosed in me?" (*RTP* 729; I, 996). In these instants, the real world is immersed in his viscera, which "had so shifted the world's reality away from nature into my torrential sensations... it had broken the equilibrium between the immense and indestructible life which circulated in my being and life of the universe" (*RTP* 729; I, 995). The outer world ignored, history descends and his inner kingdom ascends. But this is only half of time's force. Another one swings him back to history.

At the *Recherche's* end, the hero senses a distant past that extends time: "one could hardly believe that the thirteenth century was so distant from the present, it's hard to believe that churches of that century can still exist" (*RTP* 2314; III, 976). But he only feels this larger expanse because his loving-self has died. He therefore seeks a distant future from which to reflect on it objectively. In fact, he sabotages his love affairs to grow detached, to go beyond pain and pleasure, so that he can sense history's vastness once more. This is repression: an imperative that shrinks intensity and that expands *negative enjoyment*.

Negative enjoyment, or the Kantian feeling of "respect," is more pleasant than hedonism since "reason is the source of the feeling of pleasure." It's "a purely intellectual contentment immediately expressing the formal accord of our understanding with our reason." It's a death instinct, which represses intensity without abolishing it as Freud thought, for, with it, you can begin life anew.[23] That's why the hero swaps his *positive* state for this equally intense *negative* one when he oscillates between love's anxious pleasures and the calming ones of an illness. In the latter, he also senses empty time filling the interstitial void: "we find between them, thanks to a lacunae, to vast stretches of the forgotten, something like the abyss of a difference in altitude" (*RTP* 1053; II, 413). This black hole absorbs all content, and leaves behind an unmeasured, sublime abyss.

To feel this sublimity, Kant says, the law's moral force must also be felt, for only it can allow you to keep your wits in a collapsing world. Only it can draw you out of yourself and allow you to embrace world history. That is why, by the novel's end, the worn-down hero senses vast temporal landscapes and unbridgeable distances. The law having crushed him, he feels this expanse.

But this law cannot be captured since it recedes the faster you chase it. Nowhere is this more darkly apparent than in Kafka's parable, "Before the Law," in which a man comes *from* the countryside and, ultimately, *to* despair as he waits for the law in an act of Sisyphean futility. What does he gain by waiting? Nothing! This seems strange: "the Law, he thinks, should be accessible to every man and at all times." The law is a negative presentation, which only seems to hide beyond the guard, when, in fact, it lies in his repressive force.[24] Law, desire, and time form a trinity. *Law* represses intensities, replacing them with extensive qualities. *Desire* seeks a degree = 0. *Time* deploys them on an empty line stretching toward the unattainable for which we all reach.

But all is not lost. Even life's harshest aspects reveal a sublime joy. Even a dim light shines from the door in Kafka's story. The man waits his whole life as he grows sober. This clarifies his vision. In this trial, "the verdict is not suddenly arrived at, the proceedings only gradually merge into the verdict." The humor of this postponement *grimly* fascinates Deleuze.[25] For him, it weakens the law.

In fact, this simple Kafkaesque joke rises above the law to such an extent that, for Freud, "the pleasure from the joke" succeeds "in making its way through, perhaps without any diminution."[26] Repression is a dam, the joke is a floodgate, and the water is pleasure. Normally, without the dam, the pleasure-water would flow. But when you open the floodgates of humor, the pleasure-water surges more than it would without repression. Thus, the law's restraint yields a more intense *negative* pleasure than the one it denied. Kafka's humor is sublime because it entails this kind of waiting and strips time of its measure.

Normally, *logos* measures a star's course, a chronometric *number of movement*, a legion (*legein*) that splits it into the astrological quadrants of fate. These measures impose ideal proportions on time—a Greek idea changed, but continued by Kant. For example, the *I think* synthesizes days, months, and years into a single, personal viewpoint that sets events apart. But apperception is only the folly of the first critique. In the "Analytic of the Sublime," he depicts an amorphous event. When I contemplate Niagara Falls or Alpha Centauri, measure collapses and a negative presentation "expands the soul." That is to say, my mental powers expand as I shrink. And I fail to grasp anything but a force. Unmeasured time has stripped bare the illusion of measure that syntheses presume. Without them, my faculties would break, discords would emerge, but reason would still maintain a *measureless* totality, for my frenzied mind, reaching into the darkness, forsakes reason (*logos*) and embarks on a *line of flight* (*pathos*).[27]

These two temporal modes parallel *Oedipus Rex's* two halves. In its first half, Oedipus personifies the "I think," the synthetic truth-seeker, the despotic interpreter, the cerebral tyrant crossing many bounds with each new disclosure, thereby casting his pearly light on the oracle's swinish prophecy. But the play's second half lacks this synthesizing "I," for *the order of time* vanishes once Oedipus finds his origins. He leaves the *logos* of time-space, and enters the nomadic countryside where his steps go uncounted.[28] Kant is also a thinker of nomadic spaces when, in the "Analytic of the Sublime," he opens the door to the unmeasured from which time springs forth in a pure state.

Having witnessed the negative pleasure of waiting, we see how time expands linearly. Now, we'll see how we can *dwell* on its line of flight.

The Line of Flight

In his line of flight, Cain, that archetypical fugitive, inhabits a boundless time, a temporal freefall in which *time-consciousness develops*. This partly explains Deleuze's interest in nomads and scapegoats, for they inhabit a harsh, but fantastic, unmapped region in which they lose themselves.

But those who doubt this, read the *Recherche's* opening scene—where the hero's father lets his mother sleep in his room—as a sign of an Oedipus complex. Of course, he has one! Not the one Freud depicts, but the one described by Hölderlin, who fixates on the character split *before* and *after* the crime is revealed. Applied to the *Recherche*, it's clear that, unlike Freud, who bars maternal contact, Proust actually *allows it*. The father seems to say: "Please sleep with your mother." This saps his power to judge space and time. Thus, the hero eerily resembles a blind and fleeing Oedipus. The hero flees what he calls "a sin so deadly that I expected to be banished from the house" (*RTP* 39; I, 40). Yet he isn't. If he were, his debt would be *finite*. But, betrayed by paternal apathy, he embarks on the flight that Proust depicts: "for the first time my unhappiness was no longer regarded as a punishable fault but as an involuntary illness which one could officially recognize" (*RTP* 39; I, 41). This incurable illness is more misfortune than transgression. Still, he's eternally guilty.

Though the novel seems to begin sadly with the words "this evening marks a new era, laying like a black date on the calendar" (*RTP* 40; I, 41), it's more comedy than tragedy. As a masochist, the hero easily turns misfortune into a farce in which punishment is postponed. Hölderlin sees, in this delay, an empty time cutting the "I" off from intuition. Kant buries, but can't deny, this rift:

> At the extreme limit of the rift nothing in fact remains any more except the conditions of time and space. At this limit man forgets himself because he is wholly inside the moment. God forgets because he is nothing but time. And there is infidelity on both sides, time because it is such a moment lived categorically, and in it the beginning and the end do not let themselves agree as in a rhyme; man... can no longer resemble the initial situation.[29]

In this rift, this changeless synthesis, "man" becomes a "pure consciousness" that makes "the real" (shape and form) vanish as if you were flying into a cloud. Dreamed, drugged, and schizophrenic states duplicate this. And, in this silver-lined cloud, a mountain looms ahead. But you don't care. After all, it can't hurt you—or can it? Now the self falls asleep, but nobody takes the wheel to guide the mind. Kant briefly sees this driverless mind, but buries it under the "I think."

But unlike Hölderlin's "infidelity on both sides," Deleuze's "turning away" links psychoanalysis with the Kantian law. For instance, he says that "anorexics do not confront death but save themselves by betraying food, which is equally a traitor since it is suspected of containing larvae, worms, and microbes" (*TP* 161; 129). Under the death instinct's sway, the anorexic recoils from food as if from bees. To escape these stinging part objects, the *body without organs* remakes the body *to renounce* introjection and projection—or, more to the point, to make it reject itself and food. With this betrayal, however, bodies don't seek to die, or to return to matter, but to live indefinitely. This injects the categorical imperative with the death instinct's embalming fluid. Now intensity replaces objects.

The hero, at first blurs signs with that which embodies them. This upsets him, for "we are disappointed when the object does not give us the secret we were expecting" (*PS* 46; 34). He seeks *material* beauty. But intensity is beauty, not matter. And, like Kant, he initially places intensity within a physical form.[30] But, then, Deleuze says, a body without organs drives him to involuntary memory: "the narrator has no organs insofar as he is deprived of any voluntary and organized use... a faculty functions within him when constrained... and the corresponding organ wakens... an *intensive outline*" (*PS* 218; 182). Now aimless, organs run wild. Each finds its limits in a *formless* intuition. This quote invokes Kant's "Anticipations of Perception" and his "Analytic of the Sublime": in the *Anticipations*, an intensity; in the *Analytic*, a discord.

But let's expand these principles and cast off the noumenal. Focus instead on *inter sense* and give up *self-control*, as the hero does when he rejects his *active* faculties and accepts a "glorification of Passion or passivity" (*TP* 157; 125). Passivity pulls him by a passionate thread into the Daedalian labyrinth. This other path isn't a *transcendental subject*, actively synthesized, but a *sublime or passive* path on which Deleuze built his own philosophy.

Now that Kantian representation has been broken, we must ask: "How can one think without representing?" That is to say, "How can one escape the abstract?" In the rest of this chapter, we'll look for a type of thought that unfolds in time, not outside it as Kant and so many others have claimed.

Methods of Thought

Interpreters often overlook the world's *real* textures. Against them, Deleuze champions a Proustian apprenticeship, a non-interpretation that examines how things *work*, not what they *mean*. For Proust, thought calls for worldly, not just theoretical problems. That's why he "counters observation with sensibility, philosophy with thought, reflection with translation" (*PS* 128–129; 106). Though favoring a passive, passionate thought, he's not an anti-intellectual romantic, for, neither Proust, nor Deleuze, call for an end to philosophy.

So, what, in particular, do they object to? They object to the spirit of Kant for whom observation makes us seek the object; reflection, truth; and philosophy, answers. For Kant, every real change needs a formal unity. The self, God, and the world, in his philosophy, provide it. Each needs to embrace every changing fragment; each needs "an ideal foci outside experience toward which the concepts of the understanding converge (maximum unity)." But this *maximum unity* not only extracts a subject from the *category of substance*, it also encloses everything like a Robinson Crusoe on an island of the "I think."[31]

Against this island, Nietzsche objects that the laws of identity under it "are not forms of knowledge at all! They are regulative articles of belief." Kant still longs for a rule to reduce the multiple to the one.[32] But Proust temporalizes fragments: "Sometimes a landscape-fragment transported into the present will become so detached and isolated that it would float uncertainly in my mind like a flowering Delos, without which I could not say from what place, from what time—perhaps, quite simply, from what dream—it comes" (*RTP* 151; I, 201). The move from fragments to unity, from doubt to certainty, from the darkness of Erebus into the light of Phoebus, unravels as a new method replaces it.

Though we learn empirically, philosophers make mind active and matter passive. Even after the mind/body is made internal (as concepts/intuitions), Kant left their link in doubt. Indeed, we never know, given this theory, if our heads might not leave our bodies and just walk off. But Maïmon returns thought to the senses, places mind and nature on one plane, and, by reviving Leibniz, mixes the obscure and the clear. And presto, the head returns to the body. And we can think with our senses again. No doubt, merging the conceptual and the concrete is worthwhile given that theory tends to the abstract. That's why every clear idea retains obscurity; and every thought, an unthought. A math example shows this:

Draw an infinite number of straight lines around a point and you'll have a circle. Ostensibly, you *could* do this, but only if you lived forever! Failing this, the mind only would grasp it abstractly and fill it in as it would any incomplete picture: by imagining it. But this means that, while abstractly *clear*, the circle can still be concretely *obscure* (like the monad, which only knows itself partly). Such a concept can't be otherworldly. Every garden leaf has one. You think and feel it *at once*, for just as a concept *is* an obscure sensation, a sensation *is* an obscure concept. Thus, in this mind-nature identity, you learn by encounters, not by categories.[33] Are not, then, "types" just abstract impressions and individuals just imperfect concepts? By fusing them, the mind forms a clear-but-obscure idea. And, in an added feat of abstraction, it analogizes this already abstract image with others to form a mega-abstract category—the epitome of obscurity.

Fortunately, in Deleuze's work, Leibniz's monads lose their theological overtones and become a differential unthought-in-thought. It's the problem, the remainder, the fragment that keeps it concrete. Thus, the world's real thinkers, nature's true philosophers, refuse to flee sensory problems into conceptual safety. Their concepts stay partial. They add the transcendental *real* to thought.

But where is the real in daily life? It's in stupidity—the unthought's place in the swamp of human squalor. Lacking an ideal from the start, stupidity is naturally a failure of thought. And Proust's novel paints vast landscapes of it, like the "transcendental landscape" Deleuze depicts, in which "places for the tyrant, the slave and the imbecile must be found" (*DR* 196; 151). Indeed, Proust adds stupidity to his novel because thought, itself, *must battle* the stupid.

For instance, one of Proust's most intelligent characters, Swann, is engrossed in society's mental flatulence at the Verdurin's, where social codes go unquestioned. As if descending into Dante's inferno, he is subjected to stupidity, to suffering, and to the ironic punishments of baseness and cruelty, for they are "on the social ladder's lowest rung, the inner circle of Dante" (RTP 233; I, 313). *Logos* their only sin, they depend too much on ideas, which, Deleuze writes, "are valid only because of their explicit, hence conventional, signification" (*PS* 24; 16). But, for Proust, these superficial truths forever change with the winds of fashion. Indeed, aren't most philosophical truths just as superficial? They work by a "dialectical trick by which we discover only what we have already given ourselves" (*PS* 128; 105–106). But the hero's disgust with the present, his personal Nineveh, leads him to flee from these truths like a modern-day Jonah, hoping that, perhaps, art or literature will defy the eternal-present when it's *always* teatime with Madam Verdurin. That's why the hero slides into stupidity, into madness, to use Deleuze's words, "to the point that it can no longer stand itself" (*DR* 198; 152). He must pull back (into stupidity's realm) like a slingshot, so that, when he lets go, he'll be flung into a *negative enjoyment* (purging stupidity). The categorical imperative is now one to question, to battle idiocy on its own monstrous ground—within its Grendel's lair.

Though countering "philosophy with thought," Proust doesn't defy all philosophers. In fact, his questioning parallels that of Bergson, who ignores words and goes right to a concept's real components. Both attack philosophy's received ideas—ones that omit things themselves. "But if one claims to be doing more, to be grasping realities and not to be re-examining conventions, why should one expect terms... to state a problem which concerns the very nature of things?" One might ask if pleasure and happiness are the same. Seeming similar, humans "found them of the same practical interest and reacted toward all of them in the same way." But often, such opinions seem strong, not because they're true, but because a strong metaphysical bias is embedded in language. In fact, if you reason this way, why not reduce philosophy to a word-association game? For to do so, Bergson writes, you only need "to collect thought ready to hand and phrases ready-made." But is this truly philosophy?[34]

In the *Recherche*, Proust relegates this type of thought to high-society—to the true "philosopher-kings" of our modern world. In the Verdurin clan, for instance, all of the phrases, all of the opinions, all the little platitudes that make up their conversations, are changeable—they change truths as often as they change their dirty undergarments. That's why, after the Dreyfus trial, a former truth now seems an outrageous lie: "everything Jewish, even the elegant lady herself, fell, and obscure nationalists rose to take her place" (*RTP* 412; I, 557). Such conventional meaning hardly rises above the buzz of gossip. But, unlike these gossips, a real philosopher would feel compelled to say something interesting, something concerning how the world actually works, not to say something *merely* "true" by way of a superficial interpretation.

Neither interpreting, nor seeking mere answers, Proust and Bergson deepen problems. And, as the *Recherche* progresses, these problems change. Like an unsolvable mathematical equation, they continue even to the end where, in time's vast depth, the two ways form "a rich network of memories... an infinite variety of communicating paths from which to choose" (*RTP* 2388; III, 1086), but fail to synthesize. Instead, they offer riddles that disrupt and that *open* the once balanced structures of thought. Interpretation, on the other hand, *closes* them and solidifies new orthodoxies. But how can this be avoided?

In their Kafka book, for example, Deleuze and Guattari use a non-interpretation to deride the court and to "extract from social representations assemblages of enunciation and mechanic assemblages and to dismantle these assemblages."[35] Non-interpretation merely shows the court's perverse, conflicted nature by attacking its flanks. Thus, it thwarts a soul-crushing bureaucracy. Now the law is exposed. Rather than ask "what does it mean," they ask "what does it do?" That's why, while examining the pornographic law book, Joseph K finds the judges' perversity, the law's true motive: its guilty confessions, dirty secrets, and obscene spectacles. And, by analyzing these power-assemblages, they not only detect symptoms, but transform, analyze, and clarify problems as well.

Using signs, non-interpretation tests the tangible thickness of love, of strife, and of freedom, for signs are only mental effects of flying particles. These are the natural articulations of problems Bergson depicts: "Whoever has freed himself from words in order to turn to things, to find once more their natural articulations and to probe a problem experimentally, is perfectly well aware of what surprises await the mind."[36] With this, existence goes beyond any imposed text. Proof of this is everywhere: aphasia and analphabetism testify to *a natural force* limiting thought. That's why, once his muddled mind forsakes conventional signs, the hero obsesses over these natural ones: "Words themselves taught me something only on the condition that they be interpreted in the manner of a rush of blood to the face of a person who is disturbed, or in the manner of a sudden silence" (*RTP* 1668; III, 83). Such natural signs force him to seek "what is implicated or complicated" (*PS* 129; 107), not what is clear. Thus, like a feverish gold miner, he must seek these precious nuggets in the depths.

This is unlike the dialectical method in which, as Bergson writes, "one sought to agree upon the meaning of the word and a distribution of things according to the indications of language."[37] By inspiring the most *abstract* image of thought possible, it forces the friends of wisdom to set up an ultimate truth, enslaves the individual to the group, and thereby subjects philosophy to etiquette. If you disagree, its superficial accord easily proves you wrong. Sadly, such a smothering atmosphere kills independent thought.

Still, the greatest insights occur *not* in dialogue, but in silence. Whether in sleep, or in quiet moments alone, insights arise beyond the banter. Perhaps that's why answers come only *after* debate ends. And that's why the hero doesn't find truth in a salon, but on a natural, artistic, or amorous road. And, on these less traveled roads, he meets three people who guide him to a new type of thought.

A Matter of Interpretation

In Proust's novel, Cottard, Norpois, and Saint-Loup encounter violent signs. For instance, in the Verdurin clan, harmony is as nasty as a lover's quarrel. In their home, they endure a battle of wits—barbs and insults their only weapons, they duel to the death. And, if they can't endure, they leave. In this veritable *Symposium*, fashionable pretenders, like sophists, are expelled when they fall short of an ideal—a *conventional* one forever limited to their group, but which, nevertheless, they suppose to be universal. Thus, experiment is scorned.

For instance, in this group, readers find an odd character, Doctor Cottard, who struggles with language, who stutters, who finds himself confused by the conversation's general bearing, but who, nevertheless, possesses a keener mind, a greater power to diagnose those silent signs of illness, than anyone in the room. In this case, the true wise-man, the true philosopher, exercises his talents as a physician, not as a dialectician who persuades with his finesse:

> Placed in the presence of symptoms that could be those of three or four different diseases, it is finally his flair, his instinctive judgment that decides, despite their close resemblance, which of them he can deal with. This mysterious gift doesn't imply any superiority in other parts of his intelligence, and despite being a person of great vulgarity, who admires the worst paintings and music, lacking curiosity, he can perfectly well possess it. (*RTP* 397; I, 536).

Though having strong intuition for signs, Cottard has a weak social intellect since "one may be illiterate, and make stupid puns, and yet possess a particular gift which no amount of general culture can replace" (*RTP* 348; I, 467). Culture cannot replace instinct. Since his critical faculties fail to extend to society, he is openly blocked by the Verdurin reign of terror particularly, and the restraint of *logos* generally. After all, who can truly think when a group of baboons critique every diagnosis? Doesn't such tyranny lead to mediocrity? But his vast powers flourish in his little space outside the little clan where they're suffocated. So he delves into his patients' flesh, like a diviner examining a dead goat, to read those signs of future health. Pursuing a "silent interpretation" (*PS* 129; 106), he wrings confessions from entrails. His experiments rely on use, not on meaning, for a doctor doesn't ask what a symptom means, only what can be done to correct it. He's a mechanic, not an interpreter: he works with problems, not with truths.

In the diplomatic sphere, Norpois deciphers signs buried under a diplomatic veneer. Like Cottard, he carefully ignores a word's manifest meaning, seeking, instead, its natural articulations, its deceptive power, and its hidden forces:

> Norpois... knew well that it is not by the word "peace," or by the word "war" that they would be signified, but by another, apparently banal word, terrible or beneficent, that the diplomat, aided by a cipher, would know immediately how to read, and with which, to safeguard France's dignity, he would respond with another word just as banal, but one which the enemy nation's minister would immediately decipher as: "War." (*RTP* 944–945; II, 268)

Norpois ignores recognition since, for him, a manifest meaning masks an intent. He ironically says, "This is 'true,' if you know what I mean?" The faculties no longer work together—as do the writing hand and the reading eye—to fathom an enemy-diplomat's meaning. Instead, Norpois freely depends upon his linguistic intuition, which "makes diplomats like Norpois go mad over some official wording which is almost meaningless" (*RTP* 944; II, 267). Unlike a Socratic, diplomats don't seek the truth. They hide it. They start with the true and end with the false. They break the chains holding them in the sun so that they can flee to the Platonic cave. To do this, diplomats must remake language: "because words have more value, offer more nuances in the eyes of men who try for over a decade to bring two countries together, to understand, to translate... into a seemingly simple adjective, which means everything to them" (*RTP* 350–351; I, 470). For Bergson, this is thought's true nature: "Invention gives being to what did not exist."[38] Thus, Norpois must invent meaning for meaningless signs.

Saint-Loup uses signs to make war, "false signs intended to deceive the adversary" (*PS* 130; 107). Unlike diplomacy, warriors decipher false acts, not false words: "But even for the interpretation of what the enemy *may* do, what he actually does is only a symptom that can signify many different things" (*RTP* 833; II, 113). If the enemy attacks your right flank, it may be a ruse to hide his plan to attack you from the left. Indeed, the sign may divert you from the real battleground (the enemy yells "look behind you!" and smacks you as you turn). As a result, a sign is always a surprise. It only shows a partial picture, hiding all sorts of dangers, which can never be seen, for war lacks a dictionary. Its first rule is *war has no rules*. Thus, surprise will always disrupt plans made dialectically. And a good dialectician may fail at strategy. Then why favor dialectic? The strategic art requires an intuition of problems and a power to pose the right questions. That's why historic battles will never reveal *preset answers*, for answers only follow each battle, as signs do each problem.

A problem, therefore, has three parts. The first is translation: Norpois must translate diplomatic signs. The second is use: Cottard must know what method to use to cure. The last is deception: Saint-Loup must develop strategies based on deceptive acts. Thus, translation, use, and deception are its three parts. But, unlike linguistic ones, problematic signs unwillingly show their truth, which only a self-betraying lie can reveal: "I had been brought... to attach importance only to a testimony that does not find a rational or an analytical expression of the truth" (*RTP* 1668; III, 83). Such signs are exposed *against your will* like a symptom. Indeed, while analytical truth can always lie, symptoms, which begin deep in *Being*, cannot. Only practical problems animate signs.

By training yourself to read natural signs, you undo the damage that education inflicts. What better revenge than to discard the breeding your schoolmarms have wrought! I'm talking about the damage Bergson depicts when he likens a philosopher to a schoolboy "who seeks the solution persuaded that if he had the boldness to risk a glance at the master's book, he would find it there, set down opposite the question."[39] Alas, the Socratic method persuades us that every question reaches into a grab-bag of ancestral knowledge. And, students, after many exams, start to think that each problem has *its own* preordained answer. Like laboratory rats, each correct one is rewarded by a diploma down the pellet-shoot of their academic cages, and independence automatically gets a bad mark.

Proust's signs, by contrast, reveal wordless problems which Norpois, Cottard, and Saint-Loup face, ignoring solutions that could satisfy an examiner. Thus, a diagnostician may use words to explain a solution, but an actual one rests on a bodily result—a cure, a treaty, or a victory. With this, Proust hands a branch to those drowning in abstraction to pull them back to the *terra firma* where senses and intellects mix in a *problematic* world, not in a mental one. Bergson bemoans this mental world when he writes, "the human mind imposes its form upon a 'sensible diversity'... the order we find in things is the order we ourselves put in them." But, if I only see in them what I give them, how can I learn? If Kant is right, I can't. Against him, Deleuze upholds an intensity that makes you think. Such thinking, Bergson writes, "is perhaps more painful, but no philosopher will work at it for long at a stretch; he will have quickly perceived each time what he is capable of perceiving." Since this learning is instant, the Kantian time, in which the mind bestows order, is inverted. But, remove apperception's unity and "space and time themselves would vanish." If true, then they'd only exist during human history. Before that, an ameba *couldn't* evolve! Unlike Darwin, Kant takes time's *subjective* nature for granted. To fix this, Proust, Bergson, and Maïmon put thought into encounters.[40]

This chapter showed how signs make time visible. And, though, Deleuze writes, "each sign has its privileged temporal dimension," (*PS* 34; 24) signs are not *time itself*. They merely express its force.[41] So, in symptoms, it is found in a pure state. And, in the later chapters, if I don't approach it directly, I'll do so indirectly through involuntary forces, through Proust's magnifying glass.

Chapter 2

The Two Sexes will Die, Each on its Own Side

For Plato, the lover seeks the Good and the Beautiful; for Sartre, he seeks to bind; and, for Lacan, he merely demands. Each fosters an image of enslaved desire, which Deleuze refutes. For him, the Good and the Beautiful hide the *formless repressed*, the wellspring of jealousy, which bears the ideal. And, with this feeling, one not only foresees, but welcomes love's end in advance. Therefore, the lover doesn't enchain the beloved, he destroys her. And, for him, unlike for Lacan, language sings. Each of these counter-desires involves time: The decaying present fosters a beautiful past; the jealous lover straddles two moments and destroys not only the suspected past, but the beloved's face as well; and, finally, like an attribute of substance, laughter echoes across the infinite. In Proust's novel, these are time's forces: the desires that split the sexes.

The Machines

Vast machines toil under the surface. Like a loom, they unite and bind. But they also disrupt and fragment like a plow. Called bachelor, literary, or unconscious machines, they all work with two or three parts. The most active ones, the ones penetrating the deepest, are resonance and forced movement (a.k.a. "Eros" and "Thanatos").[1] And, while Eros synthesizes in a lost paradise (Platonic Good), Thanatos, awakened from a nightmarish Kantian law, *fragments* and *forgets*.

Deleuze expands these two parts, using Klein's depressive and schizoid positions, to which he gives a philosophical sense. The *depressive position* only revives the lost Good through forgetting. And the *schizoid position* "teaches us what [the law] is only by marking our flesh" (*PS* 159; 132). It dismembers, divides, and destroys. And while the Good entails reparations (finite payments for finite debts), the law entails guilt (infinite debt). These two parts of the One, the lost union *and* the fragmenting law, mark not only flesh, but time as well.

As a result, two conceptual personas drive philosophy: an injured god abandoning mortals who, in turn, plead for his return, *and* an angry god hurling thunderbolts. Both haunt every thought. Menacing our self-image, as well as our being-in-time, they invade our minds as a disorder, as an illness, or a symptom, which infects both head and heart with its refrain. For us, such refrains are *signs*.

Before the Law

The law's division is a symptom of a deeper split in time. At the heart of Proust's novel, it resists the self and memory's unquestioned link to a past. Both serve an unseen morality, which Deleuze disputes, by which we are judged.

Time's division mirrors the sexual division that Alfred de Vigny's *La Colère de Samson* depicts: "The two sexes will die, each on its own side" (*Les deux sexes mourront chacun de son côté*). This is the Proustian split. But the word "*côté*" gets lost in translation: not only translating as "side" and as "way," as in Swann's *way* or Guermantes' *way*, but also resonating the two *ways* the hero cannot visit in a single day since they inhabit "closed compartments of different afternoons" (*RTP* 114; I, 147). These *côtés* can't meet, for they belong to "mental distances that are not only separate, but placed on another plane" (*RTP* 114; I, 147). And why should these spatiotemporal planes *ever* meet? In fact, sexual division engenders all others—a drive to divide called "Thanatos" that negates the uniting drive as if it were an ice-pick splitting Eros. In short, old ruin leads to new mixtures. Thus, the teeth serve death; the stomach, life.

This severing drive hides in Vigny's next line: "And glancing with irritation at each other from afar" (*Et se jetant de loin un regard irriré*). So, the two sexes not only divide, but divide from afar—not only divide, but divide with rancor. Indeed, they'll die apart without ever knowing each other since they find themselves, to use Proust's words, "driven from every lodging, unable to find a pillow upon which to lay their head" (*RTP* 1220; II, 638). Now that each sex will only know itself, heterosexuality vanishes—for when they see each other, the sexes merely detect their mirror image. That is, in this pool of Narcissus, every Romeo sees himself mirrored in his Juliet. Each sex, facing an unknown, conjures the other's image from this repressed pool of self-love.

Without common ground, sexual intercourse is impossible. And each sex ends up making love to itself. Like Guermantes' way and Swann's way, love has no bridge. Like the hero's partition, "which served as a morning messenger," (*RTP* 1332; II, 790) this screen bisects, leaving only emotional scars, for—since they invest in their beloveds as they would their own body—lovers find that, when the beloved dies, they feel as if a limb has been severed, not knowing, of course, that when they mourn for others, they really mourn for themselves. Such pain seems futile, but if they really knew its temporal nature, it would free them. Time not only rips your body from you, but memories, places, and loved ones as well. This theme recurs in the novel: no total sex, total place, or total time. Absolutely divided: "Women will have Gomorrah and Men will have Sodom."[2]

Most people stop here, not daring to penetrate this Eleusinian mystery deeper. For them, the two sides divide, time splits, and the two ways part. But, questioning further, Deleuze hands us a guiding thread to this mystery when he asserts "the law is applied to parts only as disjunct, and by disjoining them still further, by dismembering bodies, by tearing their members from them" (*PS* 159;

132). In countless texts, this theme recurs: in Freud's *Totem and Taboo*, brothers kill and eat their father, in Foucault's *Discipline and Punish*, condemned men praise the law's justice while they're lacerated, and in Kafka's "The Penal Colony," the harrow cuts the sin into their flesh. Though unpleasant, these tortures reveal the law's coldness without actually guiding its victims. None divulge an exact crime. According to Kafka, the law is only felt: "How difficult it is to decipher the script with one's eyes; but our man deciphers it with his wounds."[3] So, like the death instinct, the law observes a deadly silence.

While depicting the law's force, Deleuze inverts Kant's categorical imperative, for, without setting any new rules, it replaces Plato's Good, which "no possession... is of any avail without." After all, only those who're ignorant of it need laws. This reversed, however, Kant places the formless law *above* it and strips us of its benefits. After Kant, the Good becomes an idealized ego. In vain moments, each person gazes into the mirror and asks "who is the fairest of them all?" But, for the modern troubled conscience, fragments disrupt this ideal.[4] And, if anyone dares ignore these demons, by self-ignorance, these repressed fragments will take their revenge, as they do with Freud's patients, who not only defend time's unity by repressing themselves, but the *I think's* power to synthesize as well. This active synthesis goes on *nonstop*, but only if we posit a Kantian unity of apperception, which supports our sense of full self-transparency. But, like so many conjectures, it ultimately fails, for he omits those silent witnesses, those accusers, who dislodge self-knowledge from its honored place by exposing the ego's hidden crimes.

For instance, while easily noting the mote in your neighbor's eye, you "beholdest not the beam that is in thine own." Indeed, you *are* this "beam," this inexorable darkness. Therefore, by casting the "Other thinks" from the ego's courtroom, Kant sustains the "I think." How can such a view be avowed in the face of the Other! Indeed, at the end of the day, it seems that Kant's so-called "unity of apperception" reigns *only* because it flatters a hollow sense of autonomy. But who's he fooling? After all, when Freud returns the splinters of the repressed "beam" to the ego, the *cogito* fractures and the Good fades. Now, the alienated must face an unknown law that defies their sense of self-ownership.

With a good self-image, who doesn't yield to egotism? After all, "am I my brother's keeper?" This egotistic legacy haunts the children of Cain. Suddenly, their *actively* rejected acts return *passively* as unsynthesized fragments (such as God who's unable to find Abel). But, however deeply buried, these dark thoughts ultimately return to attack the ego. In dreams, even the most devilish devil only sees his good self. But accusers openly deny the accused of a sense of self-transparency. For instance, *The Trial* begins: "Someone must have been telling lies about Joseph K., for without having done anything wrong he was arrested one fine morning."[5] Accused, he faces an anonymous Other.

Though, with its vague charges and unknown judges, this guilt seems superficial, if you plead innocence, you may hear the same reply Joseph K did: "'But I am not guilty... it's a mistake. And, if it comes to that, how can any man be called guilty? We are all simply men here, one as much as the other.' 'That is true,' said the priest, 'but that's how all guilty men talk.'"[6] Indeed, latent attacks at any moment, from any corner, typify a paranoid position in which "persecutor and persecuted are always the same" (*LS* 218; 187). That's why the ego's worst enemies are always internal. Every hostile thought threatens to return as a voice that yells, "I condemn you in the name of the law!"

As a result, innocence unites and guilt fragments. Hence, when the hero ignores Albertine's guilt, his love apparently has cataracts. Blind to guilt (despite his certainty of it), his love is only a self-love (Eros). And his unconscious hate (Thanatos) projects Albertine into remote worlds. This manifestation of Kant's law in its extreme formality, however, lacks form.[7] The law forcefully decrees, but what? Almost anything! In fact, for Proust, this voice decrees: "The two sexes will die, each on its own side." You can sense this force that cuts into bodies and memories, but cannot deafen yourself to the maternal bidding of this Salome, which bars all common measure, without losing your head.

For Kant, this unmeasured *formlessness* triggers the sublime feelings *The Critique of Judgment* depicts: "Perhaps there is no sublimer passage in the Jewish law than the command, 'Thou shalt not make to thyself any graven image, nor the likeness of anything which is in heaven or in the earth or under the earth.'"[8] This Old Testament passage rips thought's inside (its power to represent) from its outside (its formlessness). But note how it treats the void— how *The Anger of Samson* bids: "Do not form an image of the opposite sex!"

Thus, *jealousy must be formless*, for any image would kill it. In fact, the clearer the image, the weaker the jealousy. How un-Platonic! After all, Plato makes beauty *distant*: "the quest for the universal beauty must find him ever mounting the heavenly ladder."[9] But if the hero actually saw Albertine this way, his *jealousy* would fade. So, to stay in *love*, she *must*, by her very nature, be in "an unknown and infinitely more interesting universe," from which he finds himself cut off "by a clear boundary" (*RTP* 707; I, 707). So, *love* needs a distantly clear shape (Plato); *jealousy*, a sublime formlessness (Kant).

Indeed, Gomorrah, that unknown city of the plain, eludes his grasp. Its *formlessness* recurs under Combray (the non-place) and under the pure past (a non-time). It's unrepresentable. That's why, on a timeline, odd gaps emerge—a force-filled no-man's-land through which the law, the Other, and the fragment enter. Through them, you find your formless unconscious symbolically. And one of the most potent symbols of it, as we shall now see, is the hermaphrodite.

The Hermaphrodite

Is hermaphroditism the pure past's myth? Deleuze asserts that Eros (or the hermaphrodite myth) is the immemorial of love (or the pure past). Not only does Aristophanes portray this total-being in the *Symposium*, but Freud re-portrays it as an *idealized* unity. When idealized, however, a never-lived past is born from memory's base—an alluring image assumed to be prehistoric, but which, because it hides, leaves the mind to reminisce eternally. This theory explains why we remember. Though it binds the heart *to* the now-lost One (the Good), if ignored, it causes amnesia; if obsessed over, nostalgia. But, as we shall see,

Proust's vegetal hermaphrodite (the innocence of flowers) topples the Greek unity-as-logos and its organism-centric, zygotic metaphor because, outside the social world, neither purity, nor impurity can exist.[10] Perhaps that's why bees never call each other "sluts" for visiting too many flowers. And perhaps that's why animal guilt is the weakest, least evolved, notion of unity. Yet it persists.

In this unity, readers may see the *Symposium*'s "lost animal totality," but may not see its unpleasant Kleinian-Freudian overtones. So let's consider them:

In the *Symposium*, Aristophanes projects this *whole* into the past to rid it of its Frankensteinian aspects and to cut it off from the hermaphrodite that "is only used nowadays as a term of contempt." For instance, imagine your dreamed-of beauty with four arms, four legs, and two heads. Beautiful or unsettling? Aristophanes and Freud find ambiguity in this: given that the gods feel menaced by "their strength and energy," such beings echo the Freudian "primal scene."[11]

For half-beings, a whole entices when the heart seeks oneness, but repulses when it seems as cannibalistic as a Hieronymus Bosch devil. For Aristophanes, it attracts since "love is always trying to reintegrate our former nature, to make two into one." But it also repels: "if we neglect the worship of the gods, they will split us up again, and then we shall have to go about with our noses sawed asunder." This penis-nose castration joke briefly eases the myth's repression.[12]

By making it prehistoric, however, Aristophanes changes this *cannibalistic* unity into a Platonic one that seems realer by way of nostalgia. After all, who can explain the "beauty" of birth, with its amniotic fluids, its placentas, its blissful contractions—or the "beauty" of a caesarian section, with its bloody scars? Indeed, what a "keen" eye we must have for our origins! Clearly, in this case, unless memory loses this so-called "good object," it would be too awful to recall. Perhaps that's why Deleuze says the ego *only* revives it as lost:

> Only as lost, the good object confers its love on the one who is able to find it for the first time as "found again"... it confers its hate on the one who approaches it aggressively as something "discovered" or "exposed" and yet already there. (*LS* 222; 191)

In their wrath, the gods threaten to destroy those who *too boldly* reach for this completeness in the same way children fear their father's wrath when they hog their mother's attention. Luckily, this doesn't occur. After all, what mother would prefer a cute baby to a fat old man? Nonetheless, love and hate both spring from this "hypothetical" struggle. And this drama, as I'll soon show, sustains memory.[13] Deleuze calls this hermaphroditic state, which frustrates, a "depressive consciousness of the law" (*PS* 160; 132) that fills its victims' dreams, thoughts, and desires, and then places them under one aim: Platonic reminiscence. Why? Quite simply, memory, by driving them to restore the immemorial *as lost*, also stirs up a bittersweet sadness: the past's sweet truth mixes with the present's bitter reality. Deleuze calls this a Platonic past-perfect:

> Schizophrenic pre-Socratic philosophy is thus followed by depressive Platonism: the Good is reached only as the object of a reminiscence, uncovered as essentially veiled; the One gives only what it does not have, since it is supe-

rior to what it gives, withdrawn into height.... These, as we have seen, are the characteristics of the depressive past perfect. (*LS* 223; 191–192)

Though Plato and Proust both stress *lost time* and *time regained*, they ultimately differ. Unlike for Plato, for Proust, lost time flees the more you seek it: As the ego proceeds, the ideal recedes. Indeed, the harder you chase the golden egg, the faster the goose runs. But Socrates cheats by stopping too soon. When they tire, his interlocutors mindlessly repeat "Yes, Socrates." Instead of finding real problems, they agree on words. Their mental wrestling-match must end in a tie.

Though Socratics still cling to dialectical synthesis, experience shows that ideas resist. For Deleuze, such clarity is fantasy. Perhaps that's why he says "philosophers hate discussions." After all, no one thinks during them. They only waste time. Though this may upset a brash young thinker, an old sage actually unmasks more truths *in his private nightmares* than in all humanity's shared dreams. Indeed, if the force *driving* thought were unmasked, you'd find the same horror that Oedipus found: the *immanent* ideas that break the intellect and the returning gods that split you again so that you'd have to hop on one leg.

How does the depressive past-perfect block this unmasking? It splits time into a painful present and an ideal past and thereby forms a past-perfect conjugation: "I have-loved, I have-done, I have-seen" (*LS* 185; 158).[14] Once an isolated, ideal past is saved, however, alcoholics can deny their ruin. *The Great Gatsby* depicts this type of identification: Gatsby couldn't grasp *being-rich* or *being-in-love* when he was truly rich or in love. Only when lost are they ideal:

> He hardens this present with all of his might and wishes to bring it to enclose the most tender identification—namely, that with a past perfect in which we would have been loved absolutely, exclusively, and without rival by the same woman.... It is at this summit of identification... that he loses everything, his recent love, his old love, and his fantastic love. (*LS* 187; 160)

In this pure past, he lives a perfect love, without rivals, problems, or breakdowns. This ideal love fosters that which is unmixed with anything *complicated*, which Plato depicts: A justice that's only just, a wife who is only a "wife," not a daughter, a mother, or a sister. Using them, Gatsby can make his past wealth into one *unrelated to any amount of money*. In short, ideals are only actualized *in* Gatsby's forgetfulness and *in* his slow "demolition."[15] Both stop Platonism's changeless world, for those in *our* world, here below, only dream of an eternal one out of fear. Therefore, in the depressive position, mourners, like Fitzgerald's Gatsby, self-destruct, reminisce, and realize that they've wasted so much time.

"My God, drunk for ten years!" With these words, Gatsby assumes a depressive position and realizes what he has lost. Unlike sober empiricists, idealists of his ilk imbibe. Unlike Socrates, who stays sober in the *Symposium*, true ideas are only open to the self-destructive wretch. Though, for the Platonist, the lucid ideas seem to stop worldly becoming, for Deleuze, ideas come from the same worldly demolition that Plato shuns. *Thus Platonism falls from within.* Its ideas aren't some castle in the clouds, but a worldly loss developing *in* time.

Though it topples many philosophical apple carts, this actually implies a re-birth. That is, this new philosophy would study thought's passive synthesis, not its manifest ideas; its causes, not its results. After all, innate ideas haven't lived up to their promise: they claim to end forgetting by evoking the immemorial. But they can't. As Aristophanes hints, the hermaphroditic state can't be restored without danger. Reviving it only destroys thought without removing forgetting.

To grasp this thought-destruction, let's consider the Freudian model that splits the child. In the essay, "On the Sexual Theories of Children," Freud dubs the hermaphrodite the "primal scene"—what Klein calls a "combined parent figure"—which holds out the promise of primal unity. In it, *logos* vanishes and leaves only *pathos* in its wake, for the child now faces the same unbounded truth as did Oedipus: a scene that drowns the child in a violent parental bed.

During this Freudian scenario, a child, feigning sleep, hears noises, sees quarrels by day, and with foreboding, imagines them lasting into the night. Are they roughhousing—which, as Proust writes, had "another object than the one avowed" (*RTP* 395; I, 532)—like his hero does with Gilberte? Envisioning this only rouses paranoia: a fear that, if he intrudes, he *too* will be attacked. Though, if he holds back, he fears for his mother's safety. But when he acts, his heroic rescue backfires, for his inner demons now return as a voice from on high.[16]

This child, who can't detach this voice from his masochistic desire, thinks, "if I don't behave, my father's anger will turn on me." But, then again, "How tempting," he unconsciously thinks, "to share in such a brutal love!" Thus, children, such as he, "adopt what may be called a *sadistic view of coition*" that links violence with oedipal desire.[17] Though it repels, it *seduces* even in non-oedipal events—such as when Charlus and Jupien are heard in the tailor's shop:

> These sounds were so violent that, if they had not repeatedly been ratcheted up an octave by parallel cry, I might have believed that one was cutting the other's throat near me and that the murderer and his revived victim were then bathing to efface the crime. From this I later concluded that if there were something as loud as suffering, it's pleasure. (*RTP* 1215; II, 631)

The hero at once hates, fears, and desires this scene. He must resist its pull since it's too close, but he also draws near as a voyeur, and profanes it, not to join in it (hence the shop's partition or the window at Montjeuvin), but to distance himself from it. Such an abhorrent *seduction* only feeds his voyeurism further.

This seduction fantasy, like the one Freud found in the Wolf-man's dream, spawns an *aftereffect*, a sentimental distance from a primal scene (a dark precursor). Even if baseless, it enjoys a resonance that spans a latency period: a) The trauma (in the paranoid position) recurs in the depressive position as a newborn desire to be seduced; b) the latency period, between the two positions, sublimates an infantile homosexuality into a paternal identification; c) paranoia recurs in regression and drives denegation: "that's not what I wanted" (*LS* 242; 208). In the end, this *delay in Platonic reminiscence engenders a pure event.*[18]

Indeed, this new Plato-Freud combination explains Platonic reminiscence *even better* than Plato did! For instance, in the *Phaedo*, Plato conjures an immemorial past in which the mind learned ideas:

> So before we began to see and hear and use our other senses we must somewhere have acquired the knowledge that there is such a thing as absolute equality. Otherwise we could never have realized... that all equal objects of sense are desirous of being like it, but are only imperfect copies.[19]

Remarkably, Freud orders seduction scenes in a way that corresponds, point by point, with Platonic reminiscence: a) you undergo the original scene, b) you forget it, and c) you revive it. But *this* new kind isn't at all what Plato imagined. In fact, in Freud's work, the order differs: a) children know nothing of an original violent struggle since it traumatizes them, b) repression not only stifles ideas, like a Platonic forgetting, but also changes them; then, when they crop up a second time, they differ, and c) because this memory is unlike the original, it's an ideal *engendered by* change. Thus, Plato's *Phaedo* can be critiqued using Freud's "idealization," a process whereby children feel like flawed copies under their ideal. Indeed, it crushes those who think Platonically since, under its sway, they condemn themselves.[20] This is the very heart of depressive Platonism.

Platonic guilt subjects the child to an image that rises from these violent ashes. That is, what starts as a noisy primal scene turns into a distant, forbidding voice.[21] This scene's axis rotated, the depressive position's *vertical* height-depth *grows out of* the paranoid position's *horizontal* partition-partitioned. By rotating this axis again, we shall see how schizoid regression subverts Platonism.

Schizoid Aggression

With their schizoid banter, Proust's characters deny hermaphroditic pleasure and thereby do away with *ressentiment* and bad conscience. For them, a "divorced parent," this time "partitioned and not communicating" (*PS* 163; 135), replaces the Platonic "combined parent." Now, rather than seeking a lost oneness, Proust splits the sexes into different cities on the plain.

But why abolish this unity? If the combined parent enjoys itself, the infant barred from it thinks, "If I feel lack, it must feel fullness." In greed, the infant feels an almost Nietzschean *ressentiment*, which a division would relieve. But the drama goes on *even* after this little lawyer divorces them. True, *ressentiment* goes away, but *bad conscience* soon takes its place. These angry gods must now be appeased with love. Rather than attack them, he attacks himself and assumes a depressive position. His debt now beyond his wealth, he makes his paranoid-aggressive drives internal; he feels indebted. How comforting this must be! But is there no alternative? Debt can't simply be wished away.[22]

Though learned at a very young age, there are always ways to escape this voluntary slavery. And Deleuze and Guattari find these ways in schizoid regressions—not in those of clinical schizophrenics, of course, but in the every-day ones we unknowingly undergo—those thwarting the depressive position: "the fixation or the regression to the schizoid position implies a resistance to the depressive position, such that the surface would not be able to be formed" (*LS* 230; 198). The basis of *ressentiment* and *bad conscience* would never form, for the pre-oedipal stage conquers these domestic slave masters. Oedipus must die!

This sounds like a good idea, but Deleuze and Guattari must first prove that this non-oedipal position can be used this way without making you go mad or, for that matter, back to an infantile state. Proust's novel is proof. As "a schizoid work par excellence," it annuls the depressive position: "it is almost as though the author's guilt, his confessions of guilt are merely a sort of joke. (In Kleinian terms, it might be said that the depressive position is only a cover-up for a more deeply rooted schizoid attitude)" (*AO* 51; 43). Proust's characters *save* their original aggressive nature, though they remain aristocratic. Indeed, you couldn't ask for better house guests since their *projected* attack suspends guilt. But this playful attack is tentative, for, at any second, the veil of good humor can lift and earnest hostility can return in full force. Though they enjoy another's pain, "like cannibals for whom a wounded white man has roused their blood-fever" (*RTP* 1459; II, 965), they embody the most "evolved" sensibilities of polite society.

For these reasons, real schizoids inhabit high-society, which lacks center or hierarchy, not the mad houses.[23] After all, such groups differ from families. Such creatures snub the central hub and ban the schlubs from their club. Naturally, those snobs who seek better groups must go, leaving behind only a few "faithful" members. In fact, only by attacking "bores," to whom they feel superior, do the schizoids manage to briefly harmonize.

Even those who condemn such acts, while fleeing their own inner despots, regress to a sadistic, schizoid stage, for despite its puffed-up stupidity, this anarchic clan appeals to the reader's egalitarian nature—even if its so-called "justice" treats its scapegoats unjustly. As in any "civilized" democracy, they bar some while they claim to be "the equal and betters of all the world's 'bores'" (*RTP* 211; I, 282). In their passive-aggression, they're united by a denial of authority. Listening to their tittering snipes, we seem to hear a chorus of angels—fallen ones, of course. That's why Deleuze and Guattari set them apart.

One thing surely threatens those in the Verdurin clan—a higher society. Thus, when they hear that Swann dines with the president, they belittle him, call him a "bore," as if "invitations from M. Grévy were very little sought after" (*RTP* 179; I, 236). This is an obvious lie that the clan easily accepts because the lie disavows a primal scene. Following the motto, "one's reach should *recede* from one's grasp," they succumb to the egalitarian's self-satisfied madness, for its soft pillow aids their intellectual slumbers and saves their schizoid-paranoid position, their innocent madness.

What is this sadistic madness? Normally, the libido *fuses* sex and violence. But when they "defuse," *Eros* desexualizes and flows backwards. Freud calls this "sadism" since it forsakes procreation and serves the schizoid mechanisms instead.[24] Normally, in a combined parent phase, sadism *is* sex, love *is* violence, but perversion changes this. Outside the family, violence becomes creative on an intensive body without organs. But it almost never reaches a ferocious pitch, for it's more like an adolescent joke, a friendly ribbing to weaken juvenile anxiety.

For these reasons, Deleuze breaks with Melanie Klein, who confuses these cruel part objects with an attack on *the mother herself.* He does this because, during the schizoid stage, mothers have not yet formed. In fact, they don't appear until the depressive stage. And, without these whole objects, guilt vanishes.[25] When they overlook this underlying intensive realm, however, psychoanalysts like Klein seem trapped not only by the male-female distinction, but by the heterosexual-homosexual one as well. They miss sex's deeper realm: neither man, nor woman, sex *is* truly cosmic. Here is where the real part objects lie, not in a personal body, but in a body without organs—*deus sive natura.*

Homosexuality and Transsexuality

Deleuze calls the *Recherche's* three levels: heterosexual, homosexual, and transsexual. On the heterosexual level, the sexes feel the mutual lack of Aristophanes' split-beings. But Freud barely permits one sex: the phallus, which he crowns even before he'd finished mapping its kingdom. In essence, he fails to see how *delayed action*, from the depressive primal scene, channels its forces.[26]

This heterosexual level, however, conceals a homosexual one. Deleuze and Guattari write that homosexuality comes with barter: "Whenever men meet and assemble to take wives for themselves... one recognizes the perverse tie of a primary homosexuality between local groups" (*AO* 194; 164–165). These "lucky" women mediate men's desires (the more *other men* desire them, the more they entice). But once rival groups are allied, this trade of limited-debts produces a "perverse group desire" totally unlike the oedipal one of unlimited-ancestral-debt.[27] In our "enlightened" society, however, the latter predominates.

In turn, this alliance-paranoia forms a homosexual underground "numbering its adherents everywhere, among the people, in the army, in the church, in prison, on the throne" (*RTP* 1221; II, 640). That is, while vying for women, and while hesitating between friend and foe, heterosexuals unwittingly take part in a paranoia that proves that *jealousy is homosexual*. In fact, the ambiguity of their innuendo reveals the paranoia around their quasi-sexual friendships.

Unlike a filiative homosexual (infinite debt), or negative Oedipus complex, which favors *pater*sexual desire, Proust's alliance model *only has finite debts*: non-connecting, fungible blocks. For instance, Proust lists those who seek women "who love women, who can procure them a young man, to add to the pleasure that they find with him; moreover, they can likewise enjoy with her the same pleasure as they would with a man" (*RTP* 1225; II, 645). Two options arise. The homosexual can ally Sodom and Gomorrah, the divided sexes, using Gomorrah-women to connect Sodom-men (a bumble-bee linking flowers) or he can enjoy his own sex's *intensive* part objects in women and can bathe in deeper transsexual waters. The first links human sexes; the second, non-human ones.[28]

But Melanie Klein stops short. She traps the sexes in their *human* cages and limits them to two *positive* traits, to non-communicating vessels in which each child is modeled on the same-sex parent. She thereby isolates them by making homosexuality filiative. Her part objects castrate and, thus, anthropomorphize. For all these Kleinian reasons, the *Recherche's* homosexual level is an "accursed race" from a filiative, moral standpoint. But, beyond this, a non-human third level, the transsexual flower, evades castration and guilt.

On this transsexual level, sex is a spatiotemporal force, not anatomy. As we will now see, Deleuze not only filters his theory through Spinoza's philosophical lens-grinder, but through Kant's sublime organ grinder as well. In chapter one, we saw how time starts in an intensity = 0. But now this influx recurs in those non-spatial part objects that Deleuze and Guattari liken to Spinoza's attributes:

> The body without organs is the matter that always fills space to given degrees of intensity, and the partial objects are these degrees, these intensive parts that produce the real in space starting from matter as intensity=0. The body without organs is the immanent substance, in the most Spinozist sense of the word; and the partial objects are like its ultimate attributes, which belong to it precisely insofar as they are really distinct and cannot on this account exclude or oppose one another. (*AO* 390; 326–327)

Now, thumb sucking or a mother's caress can span the infant's flesh like the attributes of Spinoza's substance. But unlike those who reduce part objects to games, Deleuze's schizoid theory places their *real aim* in the intensities they *produce*, not in the sexual aims they merely *symbolize*. But it's Spinoza who first portrayed this becoming-susceptible in which intensities penetrate you, alter your states, and, by bypassing the mind, make you a body without organs.

Deleuze and Guattari, insisting that men contain as many women as women do men, rise above platitudes of bisexuality. They measure a creature's sex as a scientist does white light, which contains all the rainbow's colors, by its intensity or frequency. Clearly, this molecular sexual-theory eludes castration:

> The molecular unconscious... knows nothing of castration, because partial objects lack nothing... everywhere a microscopic Transsexuality, resulting in the woman containing as many men as the man, and the man as many women, all capable of entering... into relations of production of desire that overturn the statistical order of the sexes. (*AO* 351–352; 295–296)

By getting rid of the combined parent image that withholds pleasure, resentment and alienation fade. Now, rather than thinking of marriage like Kant, who mystifies desire's *labor-value*, "as the tie that makes a person the owner of the sexual organs of another person" (*AO* 85; 72), Deleuze and Guattari think you *own your own intensity*. They spurn the belief that "I desire the other sex," holding instead to "I desire intensity = 0" that's open to a world without lack.

Normally, the idea that lovers desire a fantasy *is* castration. But desiring-production annuls such muddled thinking. After all, where would romantic love be without the "superb" void, the "beautiful" resentment, and the "elating" depression of desiring-lack? Indeed, as Deleuze and Guattari write, this illusion is "an idea originating in bad conscience, and not in the unconscious" (*AO* 351; 295). That is, when the object of desire is felt to be out of reach, mediocre people repair an oedipalized mother-father image as do workers who're grateful to their bosses for giving them low-pay jobs. But why serve such masters?

Doesn't this sexual ownership smell of voluntary slavery? It's a lasting belief, born in a depressive Platonism, that you need another's tools to work when you have all that you need at home within yourself.

Such idols, however, are only saved from afar, for the lover can only live *true* love, or *perfect* love, in reminiscence. That's why the hero sabotages his loves to idealize them once more through memory's telescope: "it was such anticipated forgetfulness that I preferred" (*RTP* 492; I, 669). But, with Deleuze and Guattari's part objects, desire no longer has to be oedipal: "Partial objects unquestionably have a sufficient charge in and of themselves to blow up all of Oedipus and totally demolish its ridiculous claim to represent the unconscious" (*AO* 53; 44). They can derail *ressentiment* and *bad conscience* at their origins.

Platonic Cages

In line with Proust's Janus-faced desire, the forces that chain the hero also free him—a route whereby the lover kills the self-that-loves to spawn a loveless-self—a route opposed to those depicted by Sartre and Lacan, who ignore its transversal potential, who confine it to a *thwarted* demand, to the beloved's slavery. That's why the hero enchains *himself, not* his beloved. As we'll see, this vicious drama supplants desire-as-possession and breaks love's Platonic cage.

Just as capital shifts labor's products to capitalists, language shifts desire to other people, leaving us to demand *their* desire. But what if the reverse were true? What if love really *expels* its object? Didn't Plato's hermaphrodite myth show this? After all, it tries to remove desire by merging a lover and a beloved.

But Lacan inflicts a linguistic desire upon us. For instance, infants cry for no reason, but when they speak, their cries turn into a depressive demand "from on high" like one that yells: "Hey you, stop!" Hearing this, you stop. Thus, desire-as-slavery confuses love with dictatorship. Yet no descriptive account can dismiss it. In this light, Sartre reads Proustian love in *Being and Nothingness*:

> Proust's hero, for example, who installs his mistress in his home, who can see her and possess her at any hour of the day, who has been able to make her completely dependent on him economically, ought to be free from worry. Yet we know that he is, on the contrary, continually gnawed by anxiety. Through her consciousness Albertine escapes Marcel even when he is at her side, and that is why he knows relief only when he gazes on her while she sleeps. It is certain then that the lover wishes to capture a "consciousness."[29]

For Sartre, lovers want to capture their beloveds, not to objectify them, but to force a pledge from them. But is this *truly* Proustian desire? If it were, the hero would be a master of *logos*, who subjugates others and spreads lack. But not even Albertine's total assent could fulfill him since, like an Othello, he can always suspect her in her dreams. And who can fight a dream? Thus, Sartre's reading remains partial, for the hero is torn between her continued house arrest and her eventual freedom, which, in turn, would free him to write and to travel. By exploring a painful struggle to end love, however, Proust exceeds Sartre's reading of him and thereby avoids the bad conscience that it would entail.

But his fear of killing a loving-self, to spawn a loveless one, binds the hero to a depressive position. At first, he'd "rather bear those ills we have than fly to others." But then, his jealousy ends with his beloved's death. But don't mistake this death of desire for a mental nirvana, for desire's death is actually intensity's rebirth. After all, when you love, everything else grows less important. But when love fades and mourning passes, the world *regains* vivacity as object-desire returns to nature. Though he *seems* to desire his beloved's slavery, the jealous man actually endures a slow demolition.

Thus, Albertine is freer than her captor. She can go; he cannot. His freedom only comes with self-destruction, for he, like the warrior, never feels more alive than when he fights. But this is unclear. On one hand, his jealousy drains him of love. On the other, his inner Kantian voice tells him to "act through duty," to seek Albertine's truth, to destroy her vice—her transversal nature.

These transversal links, passing within her, only fade when she falls into an Endymion sleep and becomes "that expressionless body lying there" (*RTP* 1874; III, 366). Only then does he escape his paranoid demons, who demand an account for her every gesture, whose voices stifle her transsexual level.[30] Perhaps that's why Sartre and Lacan mistake *logos* for desire—a mistake that makes lovers into fools. Deleuze's desire, however, belongs to the beloved's transversal flesh, not to the jealous lover who denies it. Thus, while jealousy drives us to seek depressive truth, the schizoid transversal level does not.

The Role of Language

Language not only gives orders, it also sings. In *L'Abecedaire de Gilles Deleuze*, for instance, Deleuze depicts how priests and prophets use language differently. The priest says, "Repent in the name of infinite debt."[31] But, after all, how far can infinite debt crush you? *Never enough for the priest!* After all, his power, as Nietzsche says, *grows* the more he stifles you. But he doesn't name your sin. He merely "forbids without our knowing what is forbidden" (*LS* 226; 194). In Proust's work, this is the jealous voice that extracts confessions.

But language also sings and cries like a prophet: "The prophet wails, why did God choose me? And what is happening to me is too much for me."[32] The prophet's cry, no longer shouting orders, expresses his inner forces. Neither inflicting debt, nor griping about injustice, nor seeking revenge, which would evoke *ressentiment,* he says, "don't take on my complaint, don't touch me, don't feel sorry for me, I'm taking care of it."[33] In joyful pain, such prophets regress to a schizoid position, or to what Deleuze calls a "schizophrenic" language, which changes a "painful passion of the body into a triumphant action" (*LS* 108; 88).

Charlus does this when, during a quarrel, he throws words like a heavy vase. By affecting his listeners rather than commanding them, his words sting, slander, and reproach—not to shame, but to offend. That's why his relatives fear him, for when a friend asks to be introduced, they try to dissuade him: "you'd run the risk of his being rude to you, and I shouldn't like that" (*RTP* 592; I, 805). Deleuze, thus, calls Charlus's language a nonlanguage: "his verbal interpretative madness masks the more mysterious signs of the nonlanguage working within him" (*PS* 215; 179–180). In fact, language and bodies mix when Charlus throws words as a monkey does its feces.[34] That is to say, he throws ordure, not orders.

In the end, Proust's characters don't *demand* anything with their worldly signs since high society communicates immanently, in cruel and stupid ways, to evade the depressive position's prohibiting voice. In their salons, barbs and witticisms fly without serious malice. Indeed, everyone at Madam Verdurin's takes them lightly. For her guests, the cruelest attack seems normal, for it transmits, not Hermes' messages, but the Furies' affects, "ones capable of causing a kind of nervous exaltation" (*PS* 13; 7). And this sadistic language fatigues them and gives them a prophet's joy. In fact, Charlus's vicious attack conveys love, not anger. So, when he calls the hero to his home to reproach him, he does so with love—the only kind sadists know. Alas, only this can truly satisfy Charlus's desire: "I am never satisfied until I have touched them, not physically, but touched a responsive chord" (*RTP* 1217; II, 634). Sadism demands nothing of its victims. The sadist merely notes distress. But since language only communicates conventionally, you can never truly confirm if your listener understands you. An attack, however, can always be verified by the victim's screams, in the violent signs that bridge these two worlds—for, unlike equivocal language, these intensive signs equally affect all creatures that inhabit a single, univocal Being. Now, closed-vessels unfold in this profane space, one of high society in which words become violent and ironic.

Philosophy also endures this ironic reversal that demystifies and profanes the law. Plato's *Phaedo*, for instance, handles grave events ironically when Socrates tries to assure his listeners that his death serves a greater good. By willingly swallowing the poison, he weakens the law's voice that declares, "Socrates, you must die!" Indeed, his irony pursues an end greater than that of the law: "an infinitely superior Good." That's why, in the *Phaedo*, one partici-pant declares, "I felt an absolutely incomprehensible emotion, a sort of curious blend of pleasure and pain combined, as my mind took it in that in a little while my friend was going to die." Indeed, irony, with its *reductio ad absurdum*, frees these repressed emotions that logic normally straightjackets. That is, now that the depressive search for truth recedes, irony frees philosophy and draws it nearer to language's schizoid force, nearer to *pathos* than to *logos*.[35]

Under these circumstances, Socratic irony brings about encounters. But unlike Socrates' characters, who know what's coming, Proust's characters don't. In this way, they reverse Platonism. Proust's humor is a "Jewish humor as opposed to Greek irony. One must be endowed for the signs, ready to encounter them, one must open oneself to their violence. The intelligence always comes after" (*PS* 123; 101). If the philosopher-midwife delivers truths, then the philosophical-birth-canal always delivers them to the right place, unlike in Proust's work, where they must be cultivated in a schizoid aggression. Then again, they may not be that different—for ideas circulate as violently in Socratic dialogue as they do at the Verdurin's. In the end, both secretly employ an immanent, but cruel language. But language isn't the only way to communicate intensively. Art also turns schizoid, but only if it breaks its depressive chains.

Art and Love

Since Swann, as a collector of ideals, is immersed in the depressive position, he will never be an artist, nor will he ever grasp art's schizoid essence since he only sees its outer form. Enchained to love, he can't create art. And he can only love through Zipporah's portrait. This depressive idealization frames the fragmented present, projecting it into two lost objects: Vinteuil's little phrase and Zipporah's image. For him, the only paradises are the lost ones, which he thinks that his collection gives him. Thus, he thinks that, by possessing Odette, he owns Zipporah's beauty. But even this doesn't satisfy him, for these graven-images that inflame him mentally never satisfy him physically. This pains him. Seeming to be otherworldly, beauty's secrets elude him. He feasts on spiritual ambrosia while his body starves. In Swann's Platonic madness, these false images seem to refer to true ones when he weighs their artistic nobility against Odette's flesh:

> The words "Florentine work of art" served Swann well. Like the title, they let Odette's image enter a dream world, from which she had been formerly barred, and where nobility infused her. And, while the purely carnal view he had had of this woman, by perpetually renewing his doubts about her facial, bodily, or all her beauteous qualities, weakened his love, now these doubts vanished, for this love was confirmed when he had instead, for a basis, the makings of an un-questioned aesthetic. (*RTP* 185; I, 244–245)

Swann uses his power to idealize to reduce, to almost erase, Odette's flaws, since "he no longer judged Odette's face by her cheek's doubtful quality, by the purely fleshy softness which he supposed would find his lips... but as a skein of beautiful, delicate lines his eyes unraveled... as though in a portrait of her in which her type became clearly intelligible" (*RTP* 184; I, 244). His unquestioned faith in art belies her body's falseness. But his friends, who lack his artistic association, overlook her beauty, just as the hero does with Saint-Loup's mistress: "No doubt it was the same thin and narrow face... but we arrived at it by two opposed ways which never communicate" (*RTP* 867; II, 161). Depressive Platonism is a lover's *private* truth, which no dialogue can convey.

Unlike love's *private* truths, those of jealousy come from rivals, who bolster the beauty of their "Venus emerging from a seashell"—just as the Trojan War did Helen's beauty—because it leads the lover to imagine her with his foes.[36] At the same time, the lover desires *himself* as the chosen or most desired one. For both these reasons, the two sexes will die, each on its own side: in love, they only seeks ideals without knowing their real beloved; in jealousy, they only know their rival's sexual appeal without knowing their beloved's real charm. Thus, lovers are doomed to misrecognition, to a *private* midsummer night's dream, for neither love's private truth, nor rivalry's shared truths unite the sexes.

Even art can't unite them, for, bound to memory, it merely symbolizes something alien to life. The hero, while asking why Swann never became an artist, notes this: "Was this the happiness that the sonata's little phrase gave Swann, which he failed to find in artistic creation and thus incorporated into love's pleasures... anyway, it wouldn't have served him, for the phrase could well have symbolized an appeal, but not generate the forces to make Swann the writer he wasn't" (*RTP* 2271; III, 911). Depressive pleasures are of love and idolatry; schizoid ones are of art and sensation.[37] But the romantic dreamer, the depressed Goethean, refuses to dirty his hands, fools himself about his muse, and sublimates his inner forces. But love is inspired physically, not mentally.

The depressive thinker individualizes the beloved. Therefore, although Odette's flaws increase like Tithonus, her ideal stays the same like Adonis. And, as they draw apart, Swann's struggle grows. But, blind to the physical causes inspiring his love, he seeks them in images, which, as quasi-causes, only *seem* to arouse love. This simple Stoic distinction corrects a profound Platonic error: bodies engender real causes, and since Platonic ideals lack bodies, they cannot cause minds to think, nor Swann to love. So, as he contemplates Zipporah's portrait, he ignores the solid clay under his feet. But Odette is only a territory, not an ideal, for she infuses places, clothing, and landscapes *into* herself.[38] That's why, at first, the hero thinks that Albertine contains Balbec's waves. But, as she loses her individuality, the regions she encapsulates unfold again.

So, love territorializes, art deterritorializes, and Swann's depressive Platonism *reduces* the ambient world around him down to Vinteuil's little phrase, to Swann's little territory: "as if it reassured Swann that the Bois de Boulogne was indeed his territory, and Odette his possession" (*TP* 392; 319). In effect, Swann reterritorializes music's forces back onto Odette as if the musical refrain and his love were combined. And, unless he quits his love, these forces will live forever-entombed within her. Only art can free them. And, the more abstract the art, the more they unfold their disembodied motifs:

> Proust was among the first to underscore this life of the Wagnerian motif. Instead of the motif being tied to a character who appears, the appearance of the motif itself constitutes a rhythmic character in "the plenitude of a music that is indeed filled with so many strains, each of which is a being." It is not by chance that the apprenticeship of the *Recherche* pursues an analogous discovery in relation to Vinteuil's little phrases: they do not refer to a landscape; they carry and develop within themselves landscapes that do not exist on the outside. (*TP* 392–393; 319)

This landscape forms part of music itself, just as Mondrain paints landscapes—not by linking them mentally, but by Elstir's method that mixes landscapes and seascapes and by Vinteuil's method that mixes musical sounds with non-objective soundscapes. These landscapes and soundscapes, as involuntary memory's viewpoints, are blocs of becoming, combining Combray's assemblages with those of the tea and the madeleine, *not with recollections*. But this "becoming" isn't linear, for you can easily place your birthday on a timeline, but you can't place your pains or your fears.[39]

So, if the two sexes communicate at all, they do so through the transversal, through intensive states that are synthesized passively, with a language beyond any human text, of which the body's forces know nothing. And that's why transversals belong to the being of the sensible. Transversals belong to art.

Chapter 3

The Original Sin of Women

How can you demythologize the original sin of women, which philosophers and theologians vilify, and extol its aesthetic aspects instead? Freud's phallus and Plato's homosexual ideal oppose femininity. In fact, many of our mythical roots reject feminine becoming. But Deleuze naturalizes it and blunts these theological phantasms. Instead, he values its "sinful outside": an anti-oedipal, deterritorializing betrayal that cuts time into segments. Once this original sin is probed, difference can be made internal, the fragment can be restored to its natural splendor, and the myths that make us reminisce can finally be crushed. In this original sin, you can, at length, find out what it means "to become."

The Aesthetic Outside

After Albertines dies, the hero loses the depressive position that chained him to her. Grief passes. Memory breaks.[1] Its cloak now shed, and the lost object now made internal, he yields to an identification stage. To disavow her death, he tries to become her: "the idea that a woman had perhaps had relations with Albertine no longer caused me to desire anything but to have them myself with that woman. I told Andrée this while caressing her" (*RTP* 2055; III, 612). But Andrée's reply thwarts him: "Ah! Yes, but you are a man. And so we can't do together at all the same things I did with Albertine" (*RTP* 2056; III, 612). Unable to move to a new stage, his grief returns, for he lacks a *thing* to mimic. As a man, he can't know her pleasure. This *outside* blocks, but opens his mind.

Consider how Freud reacts to this dilemma. By asking what woman wants, he posits an aim—a false problem, rooted in language, which *threads* desire to a being. But the thread frays because he misses desire's real source.

This is why the hero cannot know Albertine's becoming (her sensation). Like an oily fish, it slips from his grasp. For Elisabeth Ladenson, this failure "becomes a key obsession in the book, the locus of female specificity and narratorial anxiety." For her, Proust and Freud react differently: "Where Freud sees lack, then, Proust's hero imagines plenitude"[2] Blind to desire's other forms, the hero says that it "seemed like contacting the unknown" (*RTP* 691; I, 942). Indeed, men *obviously* know feminine desire—don't they?

Still, when Freud studies feminine desire, he masculinizes the girl: "This 'masculinity complex' in women can also result in a manifest homosexual choice of object." For him, all girls start life as boys: "to the change in her own sex there must correspond a change in the sex of her object."[3] This magical sex-change comes when they admit to castration. Ignoring the soil of femininity, he favors a masculine, orgasmic end. Hence, his bias against "perversity." Though he sees it in the infant, he deems its seedlings to be *but a brief anomaly* that adult, phallic-sexuality overcomes. But, in the end, even this seems insufficient.

Why can't Freud know women? Poor Freud has a phallus fixation. This leads him to make a boy's status no less bizarre. His desire is homosexual since, for him, his mother has a penis. He loves her when she turns masculine—just as an actress does when she dons a beard to play a male part. This gender-confused Freud only knows male homosexuals, in the end, because, for him, not only do women love one another as men, but men only love women *as if they were men.*

Homosexual desire and narcissism now linked, Freud equates them with a man's love for "what he himself is… what he himself was… what he himself would like to be."[4] In effect, when a man loves a woman, he *actually* loves the infantile narcissism that she symbolizes. But, realizing that it would tread *far too closely* to what he represses, he reacts homophobically. And yet, this repressed infant is projected onto his loves. (Hence, the strange synecdoche of the word "baby.") In this way, desires are like the mirroring pool of Narcissus, which reflect a beautiful childhood, a youthful innocence he has lost internally.

Given Freud's gender-confusion, he seems to make himself an honorary lesbian, since he can't tell his desire apart from hers. After all, he asks, is not her narcissism like his, masculine? Moreover, doesn't this narcissistic Freud ultimately see the infantile Sigmund in these women—as if he confused himself with the girl in the looking glass? Though simple-minded, his must be the final word! After all, who could know women better than a nineteenth-century male?

So, in Freud's phallic stone-age economy, lesbians need a mediator or a translator, who not only inserts a masculine tongue between two women, but also a *phallo*-centrism that engulfs all desire, merely spitting out morsels of it to the lover. But why feed off these leftovers when Freud gives us another option? Though he subjugates women to lack, he also admits to an essential ignorance.

With this ignorance, Proust evades this phallic trap and draws nearer to *another* Freudian model of narcissism. As such, Proust could have written his words: "The great charm of narcissistic women has, however, its reverse side; a large part of the lover's dissatisfaction, of his doubts of the woman's love, of his complaints of her enigmatic nature, has its roots in this incongruity between the types of object-choice."[5] Though he gripes about her mystery, the hero is drawn to Albertine because her *lesbian world* echoes his childhood-narcissism, his repressed past. But if Freud's phallic-lack were right, Albertine would lack this mystery, her allure would fade, and male desire wouldn't differ from hers. Since they desire women *as women*, lesbians aren't linked by a penile magnet. Isn't this a better choice since it abandons mediation in favor of a feminine mystique?

Since his obsessed hero is built upon this narcissism, Proust can sexualize thought. This thrusts him far deeper than any logic ever could. By swinging him like a sling, this narcissistic woman echoes his feminine self-love. That's why, Elisabeth Ladenson writes that Proust "situates true *homo*sexuality only in women."[6] Freud's concept now reversed, he cuts out the lesbian mediator, while, in effect, mediating the *male* homosexual via *feminine* narcissism. His budding theories are replanted in a looking-glass in which Freud becomes-woman.

For instance, Proust says that Charlus must become a woman to love other men since "he has a woman's heart" (*RTP* 1135; II, 527). As such, this masked woman *alone* needs a mediator. Thus, he desires a *real* man, "who lacks anything feminine about him" (*RTP* 1220; II, 638). Female-identified, he is changed as if by alchemy. As we shall see, this has philosophical consequences: Proust parts company with Gide, who sides with the *unmediated* homosexuality of the ancient Greeks, whose pederasty rests on the morality of manliness.[7] But this limits them. While their sexuality values turgid symbols, on one hand, Charlus, by becoming-woman, on the other, is exiled from *logos*. In simulacra's sinful domain, *beyond* virtue's light, Charlus flees Platonic forms. And, in his flight, he leads a richer, more sensual life than the Greeks ever could.

In the *Symposium*, for example, the homosexual bond trains young men to value identity.[8] But to seek the non-phallic, Proust swaps "Greek homosexuality with the Biblical and accursed variety" (*PS* 129; 106). Indeed, Proust identifies with the happy sodomites that the Bible extols: in fact, they're so happy that, when the angels revel with Lot in Sodom, God literally crashes the party.

But, for Deleuze, this Biblical homosexuality's *apparent* sinfulness topples the salt-pillar of Greek *logos* and leaves behind the brimstone of simulacra—forsaking "moral existence in order to enter into aesthetic existence" (*LS* 297; 257). Though morality doesn't end, at least it no longer thwarts the aesthetic.

So, while Gide defends homosexuality *morally*, Proust gives artistic reasons for it. He shifts from the moral to the metaphorical. For Gide, the homosexual saves man's self-resemblance, unlike Proust's Charlus, who loses it—just as one loses a likeness to God in sin—and, thus, arrives at the simulacra that the Bible depicts: "changed the glory of the uncorruptible God into an image made like to corruptible man." With these words, Augustine built his two cities, a heavenly and an earthly realm—the second, whose earthy hues only a Rothko can create.

In this worldly realm, homosexuality becomes aesthetic, since, in Proust's words, "this sexual mistake is a source of poetical imaginings" (*RTP* 1224; II, 644). Freed from a *logos* that bars poetic vagueness, he can play with metaphor. That's why Charlus rides an emotional rollercoaster when his suggestive signs spin allusions. This way, only women are truly *homo*sexual. Without models to copy from the start, in Freudian logic, they live a "perverse" aesthetic life naturally. And, with this logic, Freud's theories take an unexpected turn.

In effect, by tying sex to the biological tracks of procreating, Freud eventually condemns all those who refuse to admit their "lack" to the perverse netherworld. In fact, anyone who fails to project his or her desires *onto* another person, *of* another sex, *for* procreation, falls under his curse. And if you dare oppose him, he merely has to say, "You're crazy!" For your "perverse desire" would destroy the Platonic Good. Clearly, the lunatics have now taken over the Freudian asylum since the world now offers many goods, for modern perversity no longer cuts the *authentic* off from the *inauthentic.*[9] That is to say, *once upon a time* the Olympic Games divided the pretenders from the real athletes, but *now* its judges have been bought and paid for in advance. That's why, in this primal Greek-alphabet-soup that is philosophy, the *agon* ended in a victor asserting, "I am the inspired one." But, now, how do we *really* select our inspired ones? Just look at our election results. O blessed be our modern perversity!

As this method's descendents, heterosexuals use its *moral* principles to select "real" men or women, thereby distinguishing Adonis and Aphrodite from Vulcan and Medusa. In the end, this puts all pretenders-to-perfection on a ladder on which each sex vies for its ideal—a truly Platonic sex with an otherworldly arbitrator. And this ideal is the mold in which each must lie. If the mold fits, claims can either be verified, or tossed on the pile. And, in fact, pretenders almost always end on that pile, left to dream of what they might have been.

As a result, these ideals trap the lover in a phantasmal cinema—a Marilyn Monroe on the silver screens of the mind. All assignations subliminally encoded, these ideals cut off each side, so that no one loves this-man-here or that-woman-there. Instead, the starstruck dream their lives away. After all, who marries a ditch digger when young girls only dream of movie stars? In this way, these ideals pave the way for jealousies on both sides since, when all is said and done, the lover's self-worth is a mere ideal: his or her allure. Indeed, if you lack it, jealousy will soon follow since the fear it inspires begins in *a failure to be this ideal* (a "true" man or woman). This is the lover's tormented choice.

In light of this, Deleuze names *two jealousies* heterosexual and homosexual: the first, upholds the *agon*, a rivalry measuring men and women; the second, a perverse world that denies rivalry. The second is essential. In the first jealousy, the beloved cheats with the opposite sex; in the second, she cheats with her own. But the second rarely rouses jealousy.[10] Indeed, in male fantasy, women poorly replace men—just as a childless woman replaces a baby with a dog. How badly explained! Is Lesbos really a result of a shortage? When its mystery is ignored, such fantasies swap women for men. But is she really so flimsy?

The hero, however, sees her enigma. That's why, for Deleuze, his jealousy is no longer "the explication of *possible worlds* enveloped in the beloved (where others, like myself, can be seen and chosen), but the discovery of the *unknowable world* that... develops within the beloved's homosexual series" (*PS* 168;139). Lesbians flub the rule that puts rivals, like two boxers, in the same ring. With no canvas-mediator, however, the sexes only box their own shadows. He *can never* gauge her sensation by his own, for no analogy reveals her world.

This new discovery added to an earlier one, we can now see how Freud almost finds this unknown world when he sees, before the oedipal stage, a girl's pre-oedipal one, which, in his words, is like "the Minoan-Mycenaean civilization behind the civilization of Greece."[11] Of course, he knows the world of Oedipus well, but cannot unearth it, for, before the Electra complex, the father has *not yet* split daughters off from mothers. And yet, Freud inserts a phallus.

Saving her mystery, Proust offers a better solution that neither tries to symbolize, nor to know, but to treat her like a glass-encased statue to preserve her charm—a child's charm, which Freud says "lies to a great extent in his narcissism, his self-contentment and inaccessibility."[12] That's why her coldness mesmerizes. But that's also why he must isolate her to make her heterosexual by expelling her narcissistic sin. If he truly purged it, however, he'd annul her charm and his love for her as well. But perhaps that's what he really wants.

Proust says that this "original sin" endears men to women: "That which makes such loves painful, in effect, is that a kind of original sin of women preexisted them, a sin that makes us love them, the kind that when we forget it, we feel less need of them, and to start to love again we must start suffering again" (*RTP* 1716; III, 147). In other words, simulacra's "sin" shorts-out reason, torments men, and, for Proust, inspires love.

Clearly, without narcissism, her charm would fade as a dream does upon awakening. It's an *outside*, a remainder that *logos* can't absorb.[13] In fact, he expends all his energy trying to wipe it out. But he can't find its reason. And why should he? After all, by an odd twist, she who does not kill him makes his life *stranger*. So, he preserves some mystery by not asking: "What does woman want?" This trap evaded, he forgets desire's "what," which, like life, lacks aims.

If you seek a non-*logoscentric* sex, therefore, don't look for it among the Greeks, who ponder restoration. Instead, seek it, like Proust, in the "sin" of biblical homosexuality. Only there will sex's aesthetic *non-aims* be found.

Guilty *A Priori*

In Proust's novel, the beloved is not only guilty, she is guilty twice over. She is not only guilty, she is guilty *a priori*. Indeed, she enjoys all the innocence of a primordial Eve. Nevertheless, he can't cast her out since, all things considered, he makes "a judgment of innocence rendered upon the being one knows nonetheless to be guilty" (*PS* 160; 132). This illusion begins in reparations—like a contrite lover, who atones with flowers, or like a child, who heals a wounded mother "with his restorative phallus" (*LS* 238; 204). That is, the child must deny her lack to restore her to a blended Hermes-Aphrodite. Thus, a woman is only deemed innocent when restored. But such children seek a majoritarian complete-being that inspires hate against those (including oneself) who fail to resemble it.

But note how, in Albertine's case, this strategy fails because, despite all his efforts, she defies the phallic. In short, she takes her Sir Galahad for a Simple Simon. Then why does she stay with him? Perhaps, social opinion, money, or a good marriage, which "would be the joy of her aunt's life" (*RTP* 1454; II, 958). Indeed, with such "good" reasons, what a devotion she must have had for him!

But, returning to the first point, we saw how Albertine's fragmentary nature is to blame for her first sin. But this first sin, in the end, interests Proust less than a second one: her betrayal, which reveals an excluding-universe. In other words, she casts doubt upon his world. Thus, to avoid despair, he must deny her sin. But he's torn between anguish and delusion, for no matter how innocent she seems, her betrayals testify, like so many witnesses, to divergent worlds:

> For was it not, in effect, despite all my rational denials, knowing Albertine in all her hideousness, actually to choose her, to love her? ... It is certainly among the charm of a being, in her eyes, in her mouth, in her figure, unknown elements that put us at risk, that make us the most forlorn, so much so that to feel attracted to this being, to begin to love her, is, however innocent we may pretend it to be, to read already, in a different version, all of her betrayals and her faults. (*RTP* 2064; III, 624)

This different version, in the long run, grips him as much as a child is gripped by an illicit toy. Before, he tried to restore her to *his* ideal, but love and nature sometimes disagree—making her as mysterious as a mythological creature.

In this mystery, a second, more sinister guilt emerges: no longer a Platonic one, which forever falls short of the ideal, but a Leibnizian one, which disrupts compossible storylines. The second, however, shames only those who *desire the good*, not those who, too weary to uphold a personality, say "Go ahead; make of me what you will." Barring this, most cling to their imagined goodness.

A Platonic storyline now replaced by a Leibnizian one, the hero faces a new problem: no matter how acute his senses, he'll never know Albertine. Rival *ideas* now become opposed *worlds* that vie for coherency, not for ideality.[14] Like Swann, the jealous thinker quickly jumps from possibility to possibility to restore unity to thought and, ultimately, to the self—for dissimilitude makes him inferior, but an inconsistency makes him uncertain, even of his own existence.

His obsessive reason brings about new accords. Now, harmony occurs in the result, without a preset end. For Plato, because the Good *is* harmony, a noble cause can even sanctify a lie. For Kant, however, it cannot. So what is virtue? For us moderns, it's the coherent story, not the best (in the Platonic sense). But, like Kant, Leibniz makes "the principle of the best" one of harmony, because, "one recognizes therein... the marks of the first substance, whose productions bear the stamp of a supreme wisdom and make the most perfect of harmonies." Kant echoes this: "Act as if the maxim of your action were to become through your will a universal law of nature." And, without harmony, no universality.[15]

As a result, Proust's jealous men seek truth in a Kantian-Leibnizian accord. But, without a Leibnizian God to preset it, they must restore their *own* image. In the process, even a single slip will stir a jealous man, such as Swann, into a mental frenzy: "he thought that, if left to herself, Odette might produce some deceit which would faintly indicate the truth" (*RTP* 226; I, 304). In Proust's words, it opens unknown worlds: "The perfect lie... is one of the few things that can open windows for us onto the new and the unknown, that can open in us sleeping senses to contemplate universes that otherwise we would never know" (*RTP* 1765–1766; III, 213). Perfect lies set up such a *compelling* truth that humanity ultimately shrouds itself within it. The novel's coherent lie is an alluring hyper-reality, for the faculty of reason makes the reader seek harmony everywhere. And, on balance, isn't love *itself* the most truthful lie?

But imperfect lies drive us to restore order. Thus, the hero *can* imagine that Albertine loves another man, just as a reader might imagine Proust's Paris, but not her *other nature*. Why? It's like Kant's formless whole in that it no longer lets itself "be held back by anything empirical, and indeed... goes right to Ideas, where examples themselves fail." Naturally formless, she's beyond all discord.[16]

Though dreams of travel expand the hero's mental harmonies, Albertine's remoteness breaks them. In fact, twelve-tone musical harmony, by analogy, creates *knowable* discords. But Albertine's tones lie as far beyond his range as do tones only dogs can hear. Indeed, this Sapphic music can't be dissonant since it exceeds all bounds, perhaps as far as ultraviolet light does human vision.

So, unable to forgive what he cannot imagine, this outside sin exceeds that of simulacra. It doesn't transgress; it merely baffles. Perhaps he forms the pornographic image Cottard's remark about the dancing girls suggests: "they are certainly keenly roused" (*RTP* 1356; II, 824). But he can't know what they feel. Alas, if only he had a woman's skin. But he cannot know their pure becoming.

But what is "becoming?" While not a simulacra, becoming has "a model of the Other from which there flows an internalized dissemblance" (*LS* 297; 258). Therefore, the mind *can* represent an outer difference, but not an inner one, for what shifts can't be measured: "Once you give definite quantity to 'hotter' and 'colder' they cease to be; 'hotter' never stops where it is but is always going a point further, and the same applies to 'colder.'"[17] Milestones make differences external, but *becoming* makes them internal as they flee to the horizon. Thus, when I touch fire or ice, I feel them differ. But when temperatures exceed such limits, "hotter" and "colder" *themselves* become ideals—differing *from themselves*—"hotter" goes beyond hot as "colder" does cold.

When this principle is applied to Freud, it's clear that he stops *becoming* when he limits desire to penis envy since he confuses it with a satiable hunger. That's why Albertine's lesbian desires break limits, even the sublime ones Kant depicts. But what can Freud do? He faces a choice: being or becoming, known or unknown. Only the latter, like Escher's optical illusions, can create problems.

But what is a problem? It's the unmeasured in thought. It's the ineffable. In fact, warning his readers of it, Plato writes, "there are two patterns... in the unchangeable nature of things, one of divine happiness, the other of godless misery," and those who neglect the unchangeable grow "less like one of these patterns and more like the other." The hero falls into this anti-Platonic misery when he ponders Albertine's formless depths. For him, she *is* an "outside," beyond space's bounds or before time's beginning—those found in *mental antinomies*, not in *real* encounters. It's the remainder, which nothing assimilates, that appears, not in the dawn of knowledge, but in the dusk of *pathos*. That's why the hero is gripped by the formless, the limitless, and the different.[18]

But the negativity he finds there is not that of negative theology. Albertine's *other nature* isn't a *far* being, but a *near* one—she's too close to him. Thus, the remote doesn't elude him as much as the nearby does. Drawn close, the hero's phantasms lose their mythical basis, for a proximate encounter can destroy persons, since Albertine lacks a clear form; can destroy bodies, since Swann's vision of faces fragment; and can destroy language, since the hero only grasps the words Albertine let slip. In fact, he can only demystify them once he sees Rachel up close. Only when he maintains a distance does he see a thing. When too close, unknowable worlds fade since the mind can't aim without *distance*— for the same reason that a vague pain, Sartre writes, forms "the translucent matter of consciousness."[19] And this translucency is, *in itself,* a becoming.

The Kantian Law and the Platonic Good defy this becoming. But what if the *becoming* that the Good and the Law defy were *only* a reaction? Inspired by Deleuze and Guattari's nomadic/sedentary dichotomy, I now suggest that, just as nomads caused the Wall of China to be built, Kant and Plato build their ideals to throw up a wall against becoming. That is to say, while opposing the suffering that thought entails, the Kantian law seems to say, "act only within harmony," and the Platonic Good seems to say, "imitate only the self-identical." These moral precepts, as reason's sentries, bar the sage from painful thoughts. But, against these guards, Deleuze foists suffering-as-discovery.[20] The hero rams their gates when he sees Albertine lying face. In fatigue, at the novel's end, he feels his age, time's vastness, and the slow death that beats him down.

Though the suffering Deleuze espouses may weaken you physically, it supports you mentally. Proust, for example, when asked what he'd do if the world were to end tomorrow, said that life would seem dearer. More than any other attitude, Deleuze embodies this one because, only at this far limit, can you feel time's force—the force of "a life." Thus, the hero's Promethean suffering seems larger than his theoretical musings. The impatient philosopher, however, overlooks his long journey. Such sophists fall prey to the cuts of Occam's overzealous razor, which, if it cuts too deep, bleeds all life from theory.

Only literature's conceptual personas, I argue, can expose this struggle. Ignorance and suffering, wrong turns and errors spanning over years, hold more treasures, more vivid lessons than any grand theory. Indeed, Deleuze says that the novel's "meanwhile" reveals time's force.[21] While, for traditional philosophy, on one hand, chessboard-like concepts clearly define logical moves, on the other, literature, like music, blends refrains, and differs them as it unfolds.

Ethics, by marking the harmony of mutual limits, and aesthetics, by internalizing these limits, differ along the same lines as traditional philosophy and modern literature. Kantian ethics makes limited moves, while aesthetics makes infinite ones.[22] And, while the moral law can be formalized, the sensible "totality" and the "sinful" world cannot. Ultimately, Deleuze and Proust use the words "sin" and "guilt," not to condemn, but to mark an outside that overpowers reason and that demythologizes the false infinite.

The False Infinite

Deleuze builds a genealogy of the subject across different works, ranging from the encoding rituals, explored with Guattari, to his critique of Lucretius' false infinity. Through them, he questions how the subject has come to be subjugated.

With this, comes an antidote to the infinite that poisons us. Thus, the myths that form us as individuals *collectively* and that haunt us as humans *individually*, make up our *most* basic truths, which develop in five steps:

Nietzsche identified *the first step* in *On the Genealogy of Morals*, where he tells us how punishment initiates "the making of a memory."[23] Bodily needs now repressed, memory begins to include other people. This serves a collective. Though, in nature, we all have an object-memory (of shapes), in civilization, language-memory must repress this earlier one. Unlike the physical need to recall an object, society makes you recall your words. But without a "festival of punishment" to mark us, *wouldn't we be left with only object memory*? After all, such vague threats still haunt us. Could memory be as vivid without them? *Inscribed* like Marsyas, we're left with their indelible marks.

This leads to the *second step*: a communal image-memory that engenders value, equality, and symbolic exchange. Coming to us neither by nature, nor by barter, nor by artifice, myths over-code everything. For example, the value of gold, whose prestige comes to symbolize universal exchange, begins with the myths of the first kings. Barter now uprooted, a universal standard comes to replace a *personal* one. And, the king's gold now prized above their needs, the masses protest, "less bread, more taxes!" Now, *only* what the king wants has symbolic value. Such myths guarantee public debts by "marking bodies, which are the earth's products" (*AO* 169; 144). The gift now marks the receiver, who can only annul debt by giving more. Such debt leads to shared memories.

The *third step*—the indebted self's internalization—occurs when this gift becomes the gift of life, and "the debt becomes a *debt of existence*" (*AO* 234; 197). Beholden to the gods, the subjugated, rather than forming alliances, pay tribute to a *State*, sanctioned, not by armies or by tax collectors, but by its *magical* powers—an eye of God that records debts and that equalizes exchange. Conscience now internal, the despot distributes individuals with his symbols.

Reaching into their vacant minds, this new indebtedness extracts a *personal* debt from their individual lives. And, if they don't pay, they fear that "the stork" that brought them into this world might come back to take them out again. As a result, people now recall themselves, not just their debts. Not merely fearing their neighbors, who really see their acts, they now fear a god who records sins as well. They now build a self-account. And their *attack and defense* mindset gives rise to a superego, an *inner lawyer*, who always anticipates the next trial. This is how personal memories develop—the condition for the judgment of God.

The *fourth step* sets up ideals (infinite debts) that stir up resentment. That's why, when he portrays mortals' envy toward the gods, Lucretius writes, though "they thought them pre-eminent in happiness," they suffer "because they do not know what is the *proper* limit to acquisition, and how far real pleasure extends." In other words, a Supreme Being's pleasure is a phallus-myth, the pleasure-symbol each sex reciprocally lacks.[24] Where they once envied the gods, mortals now feel mediocre. Each sex envies the other. Now that their greed overreaches their indebtedness, the dyslexic protestors chant "more bread, less taxes." For the despot has *now* so enriched himself that they can no longer live through him vicariously. Now that their wretched state is reflected in the gods, they suffer "the double illusion of an infinite capacity for pleasure and an infinite possibility of torment" (*LS* 321; 277). Envy and guilt begin in this illusion. And because it's inseparable from communal and individual memory, the community starts to seem more oppressive; and the individual, more degraded. Thus, modern isolation begins with inaccessible ideals. It begins with the depressive position.

The *fifth step* is responsible for the answerless, man-made problems each of which not only endows symbolic value to the poor man's treasures, but sets up lack in him as well. Thus, origins always seem richer.[25] For instance, the past's leaders seem stronger; its philosophers, wiser; its times, simpler. But, without the symbolic, thought would wane; personal contact, subside; and selfhood, fade away. Hence, contrary to popular opinion, values *set up* the self; the self doesn't set up values. For, without them, who'd reflect on themselves?

Overall, these myths constitute and destroy us with their clashing levels, for, no matter how high we climb, our betters always stifle us. Thus, our greatest curse begins in the doubt tied to our pleasures and pains. People no longer know what they *should* prefer, bread or taxes—for, their myth-filled phantasms, from one moment to the next, inspire regret and dread. Such problems persist.

These five steps mystify the modern mind. Through them, the modern-day harlequin not only overlooks her misery's source, but also clings to unfounded truths, to misguided faiths, and to unhealthy illusions, each of which needs mending. But this seamstress can only mend them by blunting the unhealthy myths that cloud her head and that trip her philosophical feet.

From this, I infer that thought is impossible without *real* problems, and that theological entities (such as an apodictic One or a *summum bonum*) condemn us to mediocrity. The fragmentary universe, however, rids us of mental wholes. That's why, against the theological philosophers, Lucretius revalues fragments. He thereby ends eternal lack of an imperfect world.[26] The world's finite parts now analyzed, the fragmented can be affirmed. In this way, he renews the philosopher's demystifying role. To grasp this, consider this scenario:

When I face injustice, I invent a foe, who I can only dismantle by seeing his physical forces, which, unlike bread or taxes, are not abstract. Spinoza suggests this approach when he writes "the essence of the mind is nothing else but the idea of a body actually existing." But sometimes non-existent things affect the mind more: "As long as a man is affected by the image of a thing, he will regard the thing as present even though it may not exist." Thus, such non-existing, metaphysical entities, lead only to bitterness. And though the mind *thinks* the whole, the body *senses* the fragment. Only through these senses can the world attain an immanent worth.[27]

When he depicts the flower's innocent sexuality, unlike that of humans, Proust revalues nature—therefore, "Less bread, more pollen!" Knowing nothing of debt, nature's finite blocs, unlike Plato's hermaphrodites, lack a *whole*. That's why Proust contrasts Sodom and Gomorrah's guilty myths to the bee's innocent flight. His naturalist's views weaken such myths, for a misanthrope blames humans for what he finds beautiful in nature. A social creature can be viewed in this floral light. Embodied in their sensitive pedals, the shadows obscuring nature dispel the myths that bring pain and perplexity to mankind.

However, though he assures himself that truths and myths differ, even the old sage cannot fully dispel a myth as he could an error. Paradoxically, these false myths empower truth as if it were a flasher who enjoys *exposing* himself. But *can* what is exposed *be truly bared without* a mystery? After all, isn't grave digging a myth-metaphor? For, while excavating the truth, the thinker unearths secrets. Every new mask carves out *its* truth, as every problem does *its* answers. Could one flourish without the other? Despite the simplistic *faith* that truth *simplifies* thought, the philosopher-surgeon cannot abolish the repressed without killing truth: for, in the end, myth and truth enter into an intimate congress like the bumble-bee and the flower. Hence, the Oedipus myth is symbolized *because* it represses a drive. It makes us fixate on a *mental construct* (driven by a boundless libido) and *infinitely* expands it, as the real world grows mundane. But such infinities are false: the Platonic hermaphrodite, Klein's combined parent, and Freud's primal scene. Nevertheless, these myths, rather than hiding truths, spawn those beliefs that are accepted true and that are found problems.

The Problem of Memory

Having explored myths and problems, it is time to return to the myth-memory nexus in Proust's work. To do this, I contrast Bergson's memory with Proust's involuntary type. They clearly clash. Since they have a role in reminiscence, memory unfolds in the myths I just described. But who knows them better?

Unlike those of problems, Bergson and Proust's philosophies of memory differ. Bergson, by clinging to the clear and distinct, stresses recognition and recollection. By delving into its dark passages, however, Proust stresses distorted memory. Though he doesn't go as far as Plato or Descartes down clarity's path, Bergson favors useful memory over daydreams, on one hand. On the other, by leading a writer's leisurely life, Proust need not recall like a doctor, a lawyer, or a bookkeeper. This frees him to study memory's other sides. And because useful recall is *but a thin spectrum* on memory's rainbow, Proust easily expands his sensitivity to its other colors—unlike Bergson, who still devalues dreams and, as Deleuze says, misrepresents pure memory.[28] By undervaluing this distortion, however, Bergson resembles Plato, who erected memory upon a saved-but-forgotten past. But does Bergson's insightful analysis forget forgetting's power? Forgetting, as an essential problem, must now be considered.

First, consider how Bergson's and Proust's ideas about recall differ. While Bergson's recall clears the fog of dreams, Proust ignores this and asks "What is a memory that one does not recall?" (*PS* 74; 59). This issue is well suited for Deleuze and Proust. For them, what voluntary memory does is clear. But what can an involuntary one do? In short, it revives a past that hides myths. Second, consider how Bergson and Proust's ideas about problems merge. In *Matter and Memory*, Bergson says that the intellect mediates, in Proust's words, "as though life were a picture gallery and all the portraits of one period had a distinct family likeness" (*RTP* 25; 1, 21). Here, they differ.[29] But, elsewhere, in *The Creative*

Mind, Bergson sets up a problem-question dialectic, unlike the particular-general one (a *perceptual* image to a *general* idea), which invents *new* ideas and finds *false problems* rather than uncovering or polishing existing ones. For instance, if an exam asked a student to find the false problem, would this not foster critical thinking better than the dialectical method? Third, consider how it's used. With it, I can inquire about a question's fecundity and ask, "Does it have results?" If not, I can remake it. Great philosophers have always done this.

Fourth, consider how this differs from dialectic. In the *Meno*, Socrates questions a slave boy who thinks with him. But he claims that the boy recalls the answer. Only, today, if the student does *too* well, the teacher asks: "Did you get the answers before the test?" Does he extol what modern sophists condemn? How shocking! The father of western philosophy actually sanctions cheating! But given Bergson's critique, I need not infer, as Socrates did, that all answers come from a primordial cheat-sheet. Instead, these problems resolve *themselves* with each step. So, as the slave boy solves the equation, he shows his work.

Fifth, consider how, by appealing to essences, the hero faces problems. While commonplace memory only sets up a flat, *intellectual* type of recognition, Proust's memory has a new power. If I subordinate involuntary to *personal* memory, then how can the euphoria in the novel be explained? After all, no man ever screamed excitedly when he recalls, "I ate bread last night!"

But what sets Proust's memory apart? By way of symbolic myths, the hero pursues something stretched across time's expanse, not something buried in memory. That's why the myth of Swann's love trumps the real memories of his mother's love.[30] This timeless myth, symbolic of the pure past, predates all the events he *can* recall. It's as if it were immemorial, like those castles built long before his birth, not like those Disney-castles put up last week.

Finally, consider how thinkers obsess over origins: of humanity, of fire, of the first state, all of which lay out an archeological roadmap to the present. Since they predate your life, you can't recall them. This is Proust's myth-memory. By testing memory's subsoil, he carries his analysis further than anyone else has dared. And, while Bergson still struggles with perceptions and memories, Proust delves into a timeless past. For all these reasons, Proust draws near to Bergson's theory of problems, while distancing himself from his theory of memory.

All in all, these considerations implicate the lost object, the forgotten past's alluring mirror that stirs up memory. As a reader of Proust, I can see the "search for truth," which Deleuze says is the novel's true point. But while I dig for it, I unearth my *own* life. I study *my* memory, *my* shifting sentiments, and *my* thoughts—each partake of the truth's mythical past. The pure past, as a mythic glue, hardens my splintered recollections. Without it, they'd be protozoan. What a narrow, short, and dull life I'd live under those conditions!

For all these reasons, the phallus "signifies no less the erotic mode of the pure past than the immemorial of sexuality" (*DR* 136; 103). Such myths make you aware of the past. That is, recall normally seizes past events. But without an initial fantasy, this faculty *wouldn't have begun*. Indeed, did you not, after all, practice a primal type of remembering in your cradle as you sucked your thumbs? Deleuze thinks you did: "Sucking occurs only in order to provide a virtual object to contemplate" (*DR* 132; 99). In short, for him, what starts with *fantasy*, ends with *memory*. That's why myth *predates* every lived past.

Ultimately, this shift to the mythical past starts in Nietzsche's "making a memory for man," whose cruel festivals are unrecalled because, as Freud noted, extreme pain creates amnesia. As repressed, it is recalled as *immemorial*. Thus, before the festival of cruelty, I must imagine a pre-human race without a past because only "giving man a memory" can initiate it. Coming from a vague guilt, this timeless event makes me recall because I, like others, use memory to fend off blame or to accept penalty—and by my memory, by my debts, I shall be judged. The divine eye unites the account that I may be asked to *render* at any moment. Even the most unselfconscious yield to it. Even atheists feels judgment's sore eye sighting them from a pupillary blackness.

As a result, Nietzsche's "festival of pain" (or its Freudian cousin, "castration") flees the more it is pursued. This narcissistic wound spurs the mind to heal it with its mental antibodies—or with Dr. Freud's placebo: the "talking cure."[31] The mind resorts to this graphic overlay, which, though it doesn't heal, gathers the past into a bloc. In effect, by reacting to this pain, the mind creates a *reaction formation* that hides an unrepresented abyss with a temporal dimension.

Memory's mythological origins now clarified, the question arises: "How can you demythologize or weaken these myths?" Myths are responsible for a depressive link to the past that only schizoid humor can break. Insisting that Proust's work isn't about memory, Deleuze shows how comedy is vital to memory's subversion. Now, the role of profanation and humor can be explored.

Profanation and Humor

With profanation, Proust embarks on a humorous adventure that overthrows freedom's roadblocks: the holy family, the sacred mother, and the loyal spouse. Certainly, they offer safety, but is safety really the best type of freedom? Against them, Deleuze upholds a kind of risk-taking. In place of these safe and sacred idols, Proust offers the underworld, the prostitute, and the loose women, attached to families as maids or to the countryside as milkmaids. These sullied creatures typify deterritorialization and bring out his perverse humor.

With its schizoid humor, Proust's novel takes apart the depressive position. That is, with his ironic guilt, the hero extracts confessions, applies tortures, escapes conjugal traps, evades oedipal complexes, and forsakes idols. But many commentators don't get the joke, believing instead in the hero's Oedipus complex.[32] But the hero uses *only* non-maternal women, such as the country girl and the milkmaid that link him to possible worlds, to unknown lands, or to social circles that he can only imagine. And, with their many borders, these places segment his world. Therefore, rather than substituting his forbidden mother, the hero's women link him to mysterious places.

Though the *Recherche* seemingly begins as a family romance, the story of Swann's love is actually an antidote to this maternal poison. And, though Albertine seems to be a substitute for the mother, by planning to leave her, the hero avoids this substitution. That is, by profaning her, he restores his freedom, ends his conjugal bliss, and evades maternal characters to seek, instead, such minor ones as whores or lesbians (anti-mothers). In fact, by entering a brothel, he leaves the mother and seeks the underworld's milieu instead—an anti-family zone smothering all oedipal desire under the Pompeian lava of vice.[33]

Unlike transgression, however, profanation shuns oedipal guilt. Consider, for instance, how a mustached Mona Lisa incites transgressive humor, while one drawn on a devil image does nothing. Clearly, transgression cannot occur unless the mocker esteems what's mocked. But profanation neither values nor disvalues its object.[34] In point of fact, unlike transgression, which forcibly takes the mother, profanation kills, repels, and deserts her. Proust's early stories share this theme: "A Young Girl's Confession" ends when a girl's profane acts kill her mother, another girl does this in "Violante." And, in the *Recherche*, the scene at Montjouvain profanes a father's memory. In each case, a clear anti-family and anti-oedipal theme recurs, while hiding its schizoid joys behind a mask of guilt.

Because they relieve kinship pressures, these joys cannot be called "evil," for they aid and abet those whom the oedipal laws weaken. Transgression, on the other hand, upholds these laws by reproducing the family: by substituting the mother with a wife, by seducing, or by playing house. The hero comes close to this when he ponders marriage.[35] But, because she's so unmaternal, he picks Albertine. As a lesbian, a liar, and a cheater, her underworld qualities dismiss the family. And, by bringing her into his home, he makes it into a bordello and Françoise into the head madam or the policewoman who raids the joint.

Nevertheless, his vague marriage promises continue to entrap him as she grows more and more conjugal, as she begins to block the underworld he so desires: "my life with Albertine was depriving me precisely of that unknown midinette who was passing at that moment" (*RTP* 1731; III, 169). Unlike migratory birds that fly south, the hero is caged by Albertine, who keeps him from warmer climates—for a marriage would foil his plans to travel or to write. No doubt Albertine seems beautiful to him now, but can he imagine her with curlers and a rolling-pin after they're married? To escape this threat, he must flee to a new segment: hence, betrayal's essential role.

Betrayal connects. And Proust's women connect to places or to social groups—Albertine (Balbec), Swann's Odette (the Verdurin clan), Gilberte (the Champs-Élysées), Madame Germantes (Combray). The disloyal hero abandons them, mourns them, and moves on. Each feminine territory expresses a new possible world. But if oedipal fantasies were his prison guards that safeguard segments, infinite debt would return to entrap him. The schizoid series, however, inhibit the neurotic signifier: "Schizo-incest with a maximum of connection, a polyvocal extension, that uses as an intermediary maids and whores and the place they occupy in the social series—in opposition to neurotic incest, defined by its suppression of connection, its single signifier, its holding of everything within the limits of the family."[36] They defy the Oedipus complex just as some primitive tribes select a false king to ward off real ones.

Such schizoid lovers innocently flee each other as do two restless children eager to find new adventures. But *really*, should such childish "betrayal" be in the same class as a Judas or a Brutus? Where would Dante place them? Only those who romantically idealize their Beatrice could so harshly condemn such betrayal. But the hero doesn't idolize his mother this way. Her curtain falls in the first act. And, like a dead and forgotten childhood friend, she slips into the obscure past. Clearly, his love doesn't begin there.

Proust's wolfish women stay in their guarded territory. That is, they inhabit a territory like Lorenz's fish, "whose charm lies in the delicacy of their designs, the harmony of their soft coloring, and the careful 'attention to detail.'"[37] Passing from one woman to the next is like crossing aesthetic borders. After all, the Renoir territory never enters the Picasso one.

Thus, when he falls in love, the hero foresees its end. His prescience deterritorializes. It cancels debts, in a segmental amnesia, which loyalty or duty would destroy, for they bolster depressive Platonism.[38] But the hero denies such feelings. Peasants, maids, and whores neither inspire, nor expect them, given that, at the end of the day, they obey the dictates of a harsh and ugly reality.

Hence, Proust uses guilt as desire's lure and as betrayal's anti-oedipal guarantee. Making it a universal law or a categorical imperative, he subverts its moral aim without actually contradicting it, for, while no one can make a lie a universal principle, according to Kant, betrayal has no such restriction—hence Morel's "universal treachery" (*RTP* 1533; II, 1067).[39] In short, while deception is still a transgression (a principled lie affirming what it denies), betrayal bears no such inconsistency. Fragments separated *as fragments*, it offers no *deniable* principle. As a result, deception dwells in *logos* while betrayal explores *pathos.*

More than from anywhere else, the hero learns betrayal from a womanizing Swann, who survived until he met Odette; that is, until his desires entrapped him. This youthful Swann would suddenly betray the families that he befriended: "The cook had been his mistress, and on breaking off relations she was the only member of the household whom he had thought it was necessary to inform" (*RTP* 162; I, 212). These social ties mask his erotic interest in servants, maids, and whores. And, like a cat, he enters the family's home knowing that he'll leave this family once he tires of his secret tryst with its mousy maid.

Therefore, Swann avoids society women, who expect fidelity and chases those of the *demimonde*, who don't. While they satisfy him, he doesn't find them beautiful: "they were women whose beauty was of a distinctly 'common' type, for the physical qualities which he instinctively sought were the direct opposite of those he admired in the women painted or sculpted by his favorite masters" (*RTP* 160; I, 209). In short, his love isn't of an Oedipal or idealizing type. He only profanes ugly women since a beautiful one would make his profanation a transgression. Hence, the rule: one transgresses idols; one profanes bodies. With this, his Casanova-ish desire swings from one encounter to the next. Romantic ideals ignored, his narcissistic desire stays home, within himself.

The hero mimics the young Swann after Saint-Loup calls the Putbus's maid "easy" (*RTP* 1302; II, 749). Despite his ignorance, she intrigues him: "I was to wear myself out in vain trying to picture... what the one Saint-Loup had spoken of looked like" (*RTP* 1302; II, 749). This isn't the ideal milkmaid:

> No doubt nothing really linked Putbus's maid to Balbec; she was not like the peasant girl that, alone, on the Méséglise way, I often vainly sought with all my willpower. But I had long since stopped seeking from a woman, her mysterious square root, which an introduction would dispel. (*RTP* 1325; II, 781)

She doesn't symbolize a place. He only wants to profane her to test his intensive magnitudes, for, in these finite segments, infinite debt is suppressed. That's why even Saint-Loup betrays his wife: he "was unfaithful to her" (*RTP* 2116; III, 695). But, unlike the transgression of the sacred, dear to Georges Bataille, Proust's work ignores it. He only follows the sadistic laws Deleuze depicts: "To sequester, to see, to profane" (*PS* 171; 142). These three laws ignore the sacred.

With these laws, Deleuze and Guattari say, Proust becomes a spider spinning webs around his victims. The hero's letters, for example, entrap the beloved and seduce her without actually divulging *his* love. But, by writing so many letters, he fears that his feelings may show through and entrap him, that he'll forget what lies he told, and that she'll not respond to his manipulation. Deleuze and Guattari call these fears a "superficial" guilt:

> Guilt in Proust is only a superficial envelop... but beneath this playful guilt, there is deeper panic in the recumbent writer—fear that he's said too much, fear that the letter machine will turn against him and throw him back into what he was trying to get rid of, anguish that the many little messages or the dirty little letters will entrap him. The incredible blackmail letter to Albertine that he sends when he doesn't know that she is dead and that comes back to him in the form of a special delivery message from Gilberte, whom he confuses with Albertine, announcing her marriage. He too will emerge broken from all this.[40]

But this letter-machine cuts both ways: it can wound the beloved to elicit her pleas, or it can express his plea to her as a lost object, as a withdrawn idol. The latter would return him to a dreaded idealization, making Albertine a despot *to whom he must plead*. He avoids this by making her a science experiment and by gauging her pain. But if his beloved turns this around and *sees* him, then *he* becomes the experiment, the rat seeking the cheese in the maze. Thus, he must dehumanize her so that she *can't* see him, judge him, or seem desirable for him.

In the end, Deleuze's reading of Proust's immanent guilt evades the transcendent variety. His schizoid-aggressive joke takes into account Nietzsche's "death of God" and Artaud's "to have done with the judgment of God." Using it, Proust's readers test guilt's great aesthetic effects superficially. They find desire's anti-sacred immanence—a profane festival of pain that withers the depressive position away. Therefore, Proust is a barbarian at heart, a Visigoth of the intellect. His words his only weapons, he inflicts a cruel and humorous rhetoric, which uplifts because it returns his readers to the festival of pain and to the theater of the cruel. In this way, he brings out the schizoid position in us all.

Chapter 4

A World of Inhuman Pleasure

What would a world without Others be like? We cannot know until these three roadblocks are abolished: First, Sartre and Lacan highlight the Other's face, either as a gaze or as a split in the structural field, but nothing lurks behinds these masks. Second, Socratic dialogue seems to reveal truth, but offer only mediocrity. And, last of all, Klein makes all part objects into parental-objects. These things cut us off from the real and destroy our adequate ideas. But Deleuze breaks these limits. What happens then? The Other no longer relegates us to a past world, the face melts, the present grows richer, lack comes to an end, and, finally, the self fragments into a trans-positional "I feel." With this, sex becomes a molecular, inhuman world of pleasure.

Molecular Desire

In *Anti-Oedipus*, Deleuze and Guattari demystify a desire, infested with capitalism, which diverts our attention towards a luxurious penthouse above the smoke and ash of real industry. That is, symbolic exchange mystifies labor just as symbolic desire does desiring-production. That's why Lacan's theory of demand, of lack—in short, of alienated desire parallels Marx's alienated labor.

Money begets money. Marx challenges this claim, which focuses on the speculator, but ignores labor. Deleuze and Guattari say the same thing about alienated desire. Considering only what other people value, the speculator fetishizes, and—as if it were an immaculate conception—overlooks the unconscious factory that built it.

This is why, in an economy of lack, exchange remains symbolic. This leads Lacan to reason that desire is lack—an argument speciously reasoned. After all, do the starving dream only of diamonds or of gold? The phallus is this gold, an origin myth that circulates desire as the stock market does: liquid-assets + speculation = value.[1] A simple formula. But, in the end, the speculator's possessions possess him like a pearl of great price for which he forsakes everything. Like a work of art, however, its worth is only projected—Is it signed? Is the artist dead?—questions that go beyond art itself. Such are the joys of possession.

Like anyone who yields to advertising, the hero is drawn into such potential worlds: "I have always been more open to the possible world than to real contingency" (*RTP* 1620; III, 16). But this obscure object of desire co-opts his unconscious. This is how *brand names* reterritorialize desires away from the real (Lacan) toward the hyper-real (Baudrillard). Thus, imagination blurs vision. That's why I imagine that I could be as cool as James Dean if I were to buy a leather jacket—it's that easy to pretend! The possible world *is nothing more than such* speculation. Even Leibniz's God speculates, like a rich investor, about the "best possible" investment. Isn't this the Theodicy of Wall Street?

But this contingent world is a late development. At first, an infant feels desiring-production: *feels* hunger, *feels* itself feed, but overlooks forms. But, like a Tantalus, when it speaks, it *demands* symbolically. And the symbol gives rise to an object. In the *object stage*, the fluidity of flesh is forsaken to obtain a solid signifying body. A Faustian bargain indeed! Under these circumstances, Lacan, the Mephistophelean stock market guru, sells the hottest stock of all: the phallus.

This is why the image of Combray-in-a-teacup baffles the hero as does Albertine-enveloped-in-a-Balbec-beach. They both hide behind symbols. And such place names, enshrouded in history like a Veil of Isis, seem *more real* than they truly are: "how much more individual was the quality they assumed by being named" (*RTP* 310; I, 420–421). Names evoke fragments, trapped in non-communicating vessels—names that divide the land and, when naming historical figures, that distance the past. So, rather than finding his Combray-in-a-teacup in reality, he confuses it with a concept. He then makes a symbolic *demand*, which initiates an associative chain. But when this chain breaks, as if briefly becoming schizophrenic, he notices something realer than Combray: desiring-production. In his *disavowal*, he touches *the real*, a "non-linguistic" comprehension.[2]

This is Deleuze's "esoteric knowledge": a molecular unthought-thought. Prior to our mental images, the mind is mixed chemically with the nervous system—for only materialism can drown thought in intensity. What is the mind, then? It is only that narrow range of intensities that you perceive, beyond which, neither subjects nor objects ultimately exist. You *are* this range. Thus, the interior (mind) only learns something when it captures and synthesizes the forces around it. Learning *is* capture. Nowhere is this *capture* better seen than in Uexküll's tick example that Deleuze and Guattari cite:

> The unforgettable associated world of the Tick, defined by its gravitational energy of falling, its olfactory characteristic of perceiving sweat, and its active characteristic of latching on: the tick climbs a branch and drops onto a passing mammal it has recognized by smell, then latches onto its skin. (*TP* 67–68; 51)

The tick has three powers (to fall, to smell, and to cling), but no object-awareness, which entails mental synthesis. In fact, its undeveloped consciousness is like that of the child who sees that the emperor has no clothes.

Molecular part objects become whole only when the mind clothes them in symbols. Thus, an imperative to symbolize puts what you see into knowable forms in the same way that you impose a pattern on a colored field, or on an abstract painting. Thus, what you *see* conforms to what you *say*—the emperor's new clothes. The trick, therefore, is to know that your symbols lack reality.

Man and woman are symbolically, not molecularly, distinct. From these molecules, like Pygmalion, I can sculpt another sex. But I only create it abstractly. Against this, Deleuze gauges the sexes by their *physical powers*, not by their classification. He remains concrete. But he can only overcome such biosocial classes by pursuing an "infinite analysis" down to the *haecceity* that is becoming-women.[3] As a result, classes give way to intensities. Of course, this sexual dichotomy is still useful: for with a thousand lavatory doors for a thousand different sexes, who'd ever find the right toilet? But, bypassing this dichotomy toward the molecular, however, Deleuze dares his readers to perceive a woman as if they were ticks—that is, ticks who sense a passing animal with their sense-receptors. Thus, sexual difference can no longer be abstract.

In this way, Deleuze offers a choice between Lacan and Leibniz. Lacan would solidify the male-female dichotomy, while Leibniz would make each molecule a concept. Where Lacan would see only lack, Leibniz would see plenitude. Lacan only gives us fungible Others (a "mother" can symbolize a sister, a maid, or a whore because they all lack). But, to find true *difference*, philosophers need to think like Spinoza and to regard such lack as an inadequate idea. After all, the molecular doesn't lack. Lack is symbolic, not molecular. For Spinoza, substance is plenitude. But philosophers usually denote general types (animal, man, woman, or child), which name symbolic individuals and ensnare desire in Platonic forms: as such, they don't want real justice, they want ideal justice; they don't want a real mother, they want an ideal mother.[4] But Leibniz's *identity of indiscernibles* doesn't let us ignore the *difference* in every garden leaf. Perhaps that's why the hero seeks flowers when he gets sick of human desires: "instead of paying calls and listening to nonsense, to set off for the country to see the first hawthorn-trees bloom" (*RTP* 122; I, 158). He seeks a world of inhuman pleasure outside the all-too-human world of faces.

The Face

For Deleuze, the face expresses a despotic phantasm, not merely another's subjectivity. The face, empowered by an infantile association, is truly flimsy. It's easily broken. And, as we will see, when seen up close, it's deterritorialized.

But where is the Other at birth? Clearly, such embryonic senses cannot grasp the Other. After all, did you immediately say, after leaving the birth canal, "Hi Doctor Swartz, how's the wife and kids?" Obviously not! Therefore, some stage must come between part and whole objects. During this stage, according to René Spitz, the mother's face gets attached to the breast:

> He does not look at the breast when the mother approaches him, he looks at her face; he continues looking at her face while he has her nipple in his mouth and

is manipulating her breast. From the moment the mother comes into the room
to the end of nursing he stares at his mother's face.[5]

Partial feeding-sensations get affixed to the mother's face, the first whole object
to which the child feels indebted. Hereafter, all sensations will be linked with it.

By breaking this tactile-visual link, however, Deleuze and Guattari expose
the face to the light of day. They show how neither the face, nor the eyes express
the soul. So, why prize them? Why not make the nose the gateway to the soul?
After all, you can no more get to the soul through the eyes than you can through
the proboscis. Such analogies fail to explain the "other person."

This reverses everything. Rather than the other person's gaze giving rise to
subjugation, your sense of subjugation gives rise to the other person's gaze. That
is, we self-subjugate *even when we can be free.* Normally, the face seems to
emanate from "the eminent unity of the despot" (*AO* 243; 205). But *don't pull
back its curtain* or you might see this despotic mother's true life-giving flows.

Karl Wittfogal's *Oriental Despotism* portrays this liquid source. The despot
moves the river and irrigates the valley. This gift of life indebts all those in his
realm. He thereby attains the right to signify. His vassals are his mouthpiece. In
this way, his power is mystified. It springs from the ventriloquist's hand, not
from the populace. In it, you only hear the despot's echo, not the people's voice.

Once this power source is exposed, however, despotic signifiers languish.
Normally, they usurp flows, alienate desire, and implant themselves in language.
That is, they create an object and then lock it away. This makes us like beggars
in a goldmine, who must plead before the master rather than partake of what's at
hand. That is, we become like infants, who consider etiquette before suckling,
for our adult world, crushed under the primitive genealogy of the face, belongs
to the Other *to whom we must ask leave.* Such is the nature of the face.

But *demythologize* the face and you'll sound its prima-facial hollowness.
Nothing seen of the despot projected there, your awe would vanish. Deleuze and
Guattari show how you can do this. They surpass Sartre and Lacan, who reduce
the face to a subject or to a split structural field.[6] Instead, they show how you
can *either* form an alliance debt and support flows, *or* despotic debt and support
your own misery. But, if you choose the latter, this phantasm will haunt you.

The face is phantasmal in the way Lucretius depicts it. It appears in clouds,
in distant mountains, or in streams. Its mold is stamped upon everything. In our
delirium, we seem to see it everywhere, as any Rorschach test proves.[7] Why?
The infant blames the face for withholding the breast. And this feeling persists
in adults, who confuse other people with the face-as-life-giving-source. That is,
adults mistake it for a maternal vending machine that takes from them and gives
them nothing. This hands an enormous power over to it. But faces don't have
this power. *We only think that they do!* So what's the alternative? A naturalistic
method that leads us to ask: "How do you dismantle the face?" (*TP* 228; 186).

Swann's love, for instance, is an adventure of the face's assembly and dis-
assembly. He *first* recognizes Odette's face when he likens it to that of
Zipporah, a painted face torn from the pages of history. By idealizing its beauty,
he grows indifferent to Odette's inner life. He becomes Platonic.

This first stage gives way to a *second* one, when Swann's jealousy makes him imagine the faces of his rivals. Artistic beauty is replaced by faces-in-flight. So, like a love-struck Sherlock Holmes, he must deduce the identity of his foe. Under these circumstances, his Platonic idealism wilts.

This slow death leads him to a *third* phase in which he no longer loves Odette. Faces, now meaningless, pass away with his jealousy. And just as Prospero was empowered by his staff, Swann's idealization of the face *was* empowered by his memory. But now he forgets the past and breaks the staff of nostalgia. Faces lose power. And, in this emotional blackout, he no longer sees Odette's otherness. His world becomes impersonal.

An ideal distance—that's what permits faces to exist. Without it, Odette's fragmentary features, which move around like pieces on a Mr. Potato Head, would fail to assemble a face on their own. Only a pure, timeless past could ground them. That's why Proust says that Swann could only take "a general satisfaction in watching these individual traits expand their meaning when he saw them, uprooted and disembodied, in the resemblance between an old portrait and a modern original that it never meant to represent" (*RTP* 184; I, 243). Swann facializes her in-silhouette and thereby obscures her inconsistent features. After all, even a Picasso and a Mona Lisa would seem alike if seen from across a misty sauna. The beloved's face does so as well.

But, you may ask, "Isn't the face physical?" Not exactly. The flesh set aside, Deleuze claims that facial recognition entails synthesis, for a few lines sketched on a napkin can be "just a few lines" or can be a face. But when seen close up, such lines lose their humanity as the hero learns when he sees Rachel:

> Near her, one sees only a nebula, the freckles, the little pimples, but nothing else. From a distance all that disappears and, the cheeks effaced, reabsorbed, arise like a crescent moon, a nose so thin, so pure, that one had wished to be noticed by Rachel, to frequently see her, to keep near her, but only if one hadn't seen her differently and so close! (*RTP* 879; II, 177–178)

This *molecular* focus splits her face into so many lines since it "is naturally a lunar landscape, with its pores, planes, matts, bright colors, whiteness, and holes" (*TP* 233; 190). That's why, when he idealizes it, Swann must ignore her flaws to enter love's embrace. Leaving it again, by way of jealousy, they must return. Only by observing her for signs of betrayal does he see a *lying face*: "He had already seen this sorrow, but he knew not when. Suddenly, he recalled: it was when Odette had lied to Madame Verdurin the night after the dinner, which she avoided on a pretext of illness" (*RTP* 228; I, 306). To read her signs, he can neither distance himself, nor can he ignore details. To see lies, he must view her as closely as a psychiatrist seeking signs of madness; he must diagnose. Even a twitch of her lips or squint of her eyes betrays her. Indeed, what an *exact* science this must be! With such precision, how "confident" he must feel!

Now that his passion for truth glues his eyes to her face like a second skin, he can no longer love her. Instead, he seeks, *not* the truth of her soul, *but* the possible worlds where she makes love to others. As a result, her face crumbles.

Now as stable as Mount Rushmore after an earthquake, no cosmetics can repair it. Unable to withstand his scrutiny, her face disintegrates: "This entire mechanism of significance... prepares the way for the second, passional subjective, moment, during which Swann's jealousy, querulous delusion, and erotomania develop. Now Odette's face races down a line hurtling towards a single black hole, that of Swann's passion" (*TP* 227; 186). How little his life means compared to such a face! Luckily, it fades. Though onlookers still see it, for him, it's dead. It vanished with his sense of lack, for, though he had Odette physically, she still seemed distant. His madness put her in an unknowable world from which he could read her signs.[8] But *now* he is indifferent.

Clearly, these signs aren't cerebral. After all, does Swann really love Odette for her mind? It could be as empty as a rotten coconut and he wouldn't even notice. That's why he seeks truths that Odette *herself* does not know: namely, his possible rivals. But once this search exhausts him, and he no longer loves her, he marries her just to be done with her. This is the third moment Deleuze and Guattari depict: "Swann attends a reception where he sees the faces of the servants and the guests *disaggregate* into autonomous aesthetic traits" (*TP* 228; 186). His passion to know now abandoned, faces no longer signify:

> But even the ugliness of faces which he knew well, seemed new now that their traits—instead of this or that being who earlier had represented merely so many pleasures to pursue, boredoms to avoid, or courtesies to give—rested in their lines' autonomy, coordinated only by aesthetic co-ordinates. (*RTP* 262; I, 355)

In his final moments, he sees the world in all its nymphean beauty. Now he is free. In his exhausted state, his debts shrink and his awareness expands to such a degree that he can sense *petite perceptions*.[9] These world-structuring faces now gone, *the symbolic* and *the imaginary* go too, leaving behind only *the real*.

In time, fantasy melts, but reality endures. The Other's inner-workings divulged, the structural changes, which Sartre and Lacan dismiss, can now be made. Since her face doesn't mirror her soul, Swann cannot capture Odette's "consciousness," or desire her as a signifier of lack. Instead, he follows a passional line of flight into facial regions, and, ultimately, beyond them.

In the end, these three ways of relating to faces correspond, point for point, to the *Recherche's* three levels, the heterosexual, the homosexual, and the transsexual, which correspond, not to acts or to needs, but to three abstract machines: a) Through his *heterosexual* bond, Swann territorializes Odette's face using Zipporah's portrait as a map. Art, like love, defines territories. b) But when his love turns into jealousy, Swann probes her face for *signs of other men*. He *fixates on their desires* as possible worlds that exclude him—just as the hero is excluded when his parents "Ishmael" him from the dining hall. The face now symbolizes *hidden truths*, thereby provoking a bloodhoundish passion in him, which could be called "homosexual." c) But once Swann is exhausted, he sees her face's infinitesimal lines. His passion wanes. He descends to a Leibnizian *species infimae*—a transsexual, lowest species—and sinks to an otherless world.

The World Without Others

The Other cannot survive a *necessary* world, cannot survive a molecular realm with neither depth, nor history. Such a world would strip away all the phantasms that structure space and time. It would leave behind a vertiginous world, the kind seen in Deleuze's "Michel Tournier and the World without Others." In it, the Other endures several reductions, which expose the illusions that support it.

The world without others is like that of Spinoza, one in which "the category of the necessary has completely replaced that of the possible" (*LS* 372; 320). And, in a world without possibility, *you can neither dream, nor suffer from illusions*. Dismissing them, Spinoza's philosophy analyzes only real forces or "adequate ideas."[10] That is, to know things adequately is to know real causes—not to believe in *a ghost in the machine*, but to take apart its clockworks to *see inside it*. Failing this, inadequate ideas, about metaphysical entities, will drive you to despair, to phantasmal Others, and to the conceptual choices that lead to bad encounters. Such erroneous judgments, as social conventions, lead to stark presence/absence, true/false contrasts, and thereby ignore the molecular world in favor of a dialectic with imagined foes. But upon this path, lies futility.

To grasp this, think about the bitterness that arises when a *mere* plebe defies "authority" *just by asserting a different viewpoint*. Now ask yourself, "if I were born on a desert island and never met another living soul, would I even have had a word for 'false?'"[11] Not unless someone defied your views. If no one did, you'd only sense immediate objects, which have hardness, temperature, and brightness, but no value. But find this immediate world and you'll leave behind the Platonic cave in which Others have entrapped you. That is, you'll have forsaken *their* viewpoints and *their* phantasms. If this is true, then shouldn't the agora be called the original cave of shadows? If so, his interlocutors should exclaim, "Socrates, you've enslaved us to an alien way of thinking. Stop!" They do not do so, however, because they're driven to conform, to share a *common* view. And this trumps the desire to see the world as it is.

But, without another standpoint, your world would have all the depth of a movie screen. With only a single frame of reference, space and time would be "absolute," as Einstein suggested, because only two views, profile and front, can structure them. Such *other* views come from *possible* standpoints, where you imagine another *could* rest like a surveyor's pole. You need them. Unable to pluck out your eye, to see literally "eye to eye" with it, you must populate space with others who create a cross-section: a width for them is a depth for you.

But does this prove that others exist or does it merely project them to a new place? You have a choice. You can take the Other *on faith* or enter an asylum. But if you accept a quasi-sane Husserlian method, and *bracket the Other off*, you'll see the origins of this faith: a frame in which an *a priori* Other molds your vision. Not even Sartre's "gaze" could do this. Only the Other creates *place* by isolating you from *yours*. How? By making you imagine a new world.

These other places, these possible worlds in your visual field, are like a ring of eyes around a spatial-playing-field with prospectival grids. This is clear. If this *other place* were unknown, the earth would move with your visual field as if you were looking under a speeding car. In fact, spatial points only coexist because you *imagine* them even before actual people fill them. For instance, Albertine encloses a place because she views the hero's world with *different eyes* and with *different desires*. And without different places—no people.[12]

How alike these possible places are to rainbows! After all, they both engender necessary-*illusions*. With them, Deleuze leaps from Kant's *a priori* space-time into this deeper structure. True, Sartre had already mapped out the intersubjective field, but, by *assuming* that other people exist, which not even Descartes would do, he overlooks the elements of their genesis. By combining aspects from structuralism and from Spinoza, however, Deleuze questions this: the structuralist categories of the real and the imaginary and the Spinozist categories of adequate and inadequate ideas.[13]

Given these concrete analyses, the question about how Albertine *could have seen* the hero must come from an *inadequate* idea, for he doesn't actually hook her up to electrodes to measure her galvanic responses. He's no scientist. That's why she seems to retain the mystery of a *freshly created world* in which the primitive tribes still believe in a goddess who moves the skies and the waters. She is his goddess, whose *possible* viewpoint is like an island lost in space, utterly mythical, yet strangely persistent. But, in the end, these *possible segments* cannot limit the infinite immanence of space or of time.

Only physical, not imagined causes are adequate ideas. And if the "actual existing thing" is the only true *object* of thought, then our foes only populate our minds. That's why the fearful mistake false causes for real ones. But to return their minds to real causes, Deleuze writes, "is to separate desire from its *object*, from its detour through the body, in order to relate it to a pure *cause*" (*LS* 369; 317). To see the real, the superstitious must cut out the *phantasmal* tumor eating at their brains. They must flick off the lenses of the possible, which no optician would prescribe. As Spinoza's jealousy example shows, the imaginary Other poisons us. After all, can physics explain the unreal bonds between a man's spouse and his rival? If not, then inadequate ideas would cloud his mind. And such shadows lead to misery.[14] Note how the frenzied never react to real objects, for when a natural disaster kills, and no *soul* is seen in nature, they don't feel the same outrage as they would toward a bluebeard. Yes, science has expelled the ghost from nature's machine. But why can't it do so for human ghosts, for inadequate ideas? To banish them, philosophers of immanence demystify the negative by getting rid of the possible. They seem to say, "Focus only on nature's *necessity* and you'll forget the subject, the object, and the Other."

Though as soothing as seasickness, much that is rich and valuable in life enters through immanence. That's why Deleuze and Guattari praise Spinoza's infinite movements. That is, since "infinite substance is indivisible," he denies that thought and extension can have limits.[15] Of course, you can divide time and space by imagining *the possible*. But you can do two things to stop this: know the infinite real and enjoy adequate understanding; forget all too human symbolic conventions and overthrow non-contradiction (as does quantum physics). These two ways of thinking undercut your all too human categories.

To do this, you need only think about four things: a) that *your* eyes don't *actually* see finite bodies, b) that *your* mind pre-consciously divides them, c) that *you* start with an immanently infinite substance, which d) *you* then divide through conventional categories. In the end, by creating the necessary myths of finite space, mankind has cut itself off from an adequate idea of Being.

But given the chance to form adequate ideas, thinkers cringe since immanence induces a vertigo, "which so many philosophers try in vain to escape."[16] In effect, when this schizophrenic vertigo threatens them, they get philosophically addicted to Others. But weigh the merits of each. On one hand, transcendent philosophies uphold the Other as well as indebtedness, guilt, and jealousy. On the other, immanent philosophies inspire madness, a boundless sense of intensive magnitudes, but lack fixed outlines, definable individuals, or any glimmer of tranquility. Then again, they also inspire sublime joys linked to art and to dreams. But consider the scorn they face—it's as if a parent rebuked them from above—for, according to the resentful thinkers who oppose them, no happy child should go unpunished. This is why Nietzsche said the strong must be prophylactically protected from the weak. Namely, from the virus of epistemology: an abstract, finitely defined knowledge, which stays symbolic. Though they clarify our quotidian symbols, epistemologists avoid the dirty work of exploring the reality that they symbolize. On the other hand, philosophers of immanence tell us to seek the *real* where it is, at the price of epistemic certainty (since the true and the false belong to the possible). They give us the most useful, life-affirming advice since they portray our modes of being ontologically rather than telling us what to believe logically. In a move beyond the linguistic turn, these philosophers seek *becoming*. They prefer flows to terminology. As rigorous thinkers, they question the roots of knowledge. Since the real surpasses the finite, however, they can only grasp it *intuitively*, not clearly and distinctly. As we will now see, it can only be grasped through part objects.

The Part Object

Part objects, Deleuze says, can break the man/woman dichotomy because they work like the attributes of Spinoza's nature-God (expressing a whole without forming one), each part being a local subject on a subjectless island of feeling. Though these part objects are not localizable (like light), they're real, but "real" in the Spinozist or even the Lacanian sense. That's why, by adopting the "object *a*" as a desiring machine, Deleuze and Guattari make part objects into what Lacan calls an "*encounter with the real*."[17]

Consider Freud's "encounter with the real" in *The Interpretation of Dreams*. In it, a father dreams that his child, burning in the next room, cries, "can't you see that I am burning?" In fact, the man hears a knock that evokes this vision. But, to stay asleep, the man takes it into his dream symbolically. For Lacan, this knock is the real: "If the function of the dream is to prolong sleep, if the dream, after all, may come so near to the reality that causes it, can we not say that it might correspond to this reality without emerging from sleep?"[18] It's as if *the real* yells "wake up!" But the fleeing somnambulist, who sleepwalks among the trees, only dreams of the Parthenon's columns. Such sleepwalkers ultimately stumble. His mind is compelled to make dream imagery by a real impression.

How does *the real* incite thought? To see this, consider the "fort-da" game in Freud's *Beyond the Pleasure Principle*. For Lacan, this game *symbolizes* the mother's return and departure. That's why it has nothing to do with lack. The reel doesn't *replace* her. It only "works off" anxiety. Thus, only after this symbolic stage, will he feel lack because the mother will *already* be a symbol. But this game precedes symbolic lack. Before this, he seeks mastery, not a *lost object*. Klein, on the other hand, puts this game under an Oedipus complex.[19] The part object's *real* source ignored and replaced by symbolic wholes, she confuses the lightening-bolts with the gods who hurl them. That is, she reduces the *multiple* sexuality of part objects down to a man-woman dichotomy.

Deleuze and Guattari, however, redefine her terms. Unlike her part objects, *theirs* cut across the sexes like Proust's bumble-bee. The man-woman double bind rejected from the start, they favor desiring-machines over *having* or *lacking* sex organs, favor natural intensity over the pleasures of love making. That's why Lenz's stroll puts *real* intensity before the man-nature split: "There is no such thing as either man or nature now, only a process that produces" (*AO* 8; 2). Clearly, these part objects are more akin to the affections of Spinoza's substance than to the psychoanalytic readings of Lacan, Klein, and Freud. After all, the nature-man nexus, underneath qualities, is physical, not psychological.

For instance, the light hitting my eyes is intensity, not the colors yellow or blue, which my mind creates. Light waves are *only* sensed. Perceived colors, however, suppress them.[20] Just as Freud's *working off* changes physical intensity into mental symbols, these intensities are worked off in the form of qualities. Therefore, the real isn't "impossible" because no one can *sense* it, but because no one can *know* it directly. As an unconscious factory, it *produces* desire from this unknowable *outside*. Nevertheless, it's empirical: *living things only learn by real encounters*. For example, that subdermal empiricist, the tick, only knows the molecular. From a molar viewpoint, however, this seems impossible.[21]

Though seemingly impossible, this ontological unconscious exceeds the personal. After all, it *is* Spinoza's substance or Lacan's God: "the true formula of atheism is *God is unconscious*." Lacking structure or contents, Deleuze and Guattari's molecular unconscious, modally expressing *the* substance, is closer to Leibniz or to Spinoza. Spatial limits now overflowed, every corner of the universe now lit up, each part object fills the entire *spatium* like a drop of wine mixed with the ocean. Lacking part/whole boundaries, Spinoza's trans-infinite mixture can now explain how part objects *combine as fragmented*.[22]

Spinoza's "real distinctions" clarifies this odd part object: attributes are only *really distinct* if "the conception of the one does not involve the conception of the other."[23] Like marbles in a bowl, things limit each other. But *in* the real, modal-fragments fill the whole like an electrified lake (*facies totius universi*). *If visible outlines don't separate part objects*, however, what, then, is a *real* distinction? Spinoza answers that *attributes* are numerically infinite, but really distinct *because* they differ in nature while they occupy the same level of Being.

These *real distinctions* make part objects into quasi-attributes of a Spinozist body without organs:

> The ultimate elements... are attributable to God, because they do not depend on one another and do not tolerate any relation of opposition or contradiction among themselves. The absence of all direct links guarantees their common participation in the divine substance. Likewise for the partial objects and the body without organs: the body without organs is substance itself, and the partial objects, the ultimate attributes or elements of substance. (*AO* 369; 309)

This *is* Spinoza's internal difference, "defined precisely by the absence of a link" (*AO* 369;309), from which Deleuze and Guattari extract prepersonal singularities—*one of which cannot involve the others*. This is only one of two ways substance can be detected: by an infinite attribute or by a Leibnizian *haecceitas*.

To be sure, Leibniz distinguishes substances qualitatively, for if monads were without qualities, they "would be indistinguishable from another," but Spinoza would reply that substance "cannot exist as finite, for it would have to be limited by another substance of the same nature."[24] But can monads share a nature (or a quality) without limiting each other? Leibniz thinks so. Without these individuating elements, all monads would merge. After all, does Caesar's crossing the Rubicon (his *haecceitas*) actually make him *really distinct*? Not ontologically. This *logical* distinction is only conceptual. And since it violates Spinoza's real distinction rule, only *one* monad can truly exist because Caesar's concept includes that of the Rubicon—something impossible in Spinoza's system. So, if you must, praise Leibniz for splintering the universe, but know that only Spinoza's attributes can express all these fragments univocally.

In fact, this real Spinoza-Leibniz difference parallels non-human/human sexuality in Deleuze's work. To consider sex's metaphysical implications, apply these philosophical lessons to sexuality: A Leibnizian method, on one hand, would define sex conceptually (wholes defined by their parts or monads by their qualities). A Spinozist method, on the other hand, would define sex by itself and by its affects. Imagine sex as the "affections of substance" or, as Spinoza defines them, "that which is in something else and is conceived through something else."[25] Given this state of affairs, affects generate sexuality. This Spinozist theory *is* the new sexual revolution. While humans continue to define one sex by its opposite, a *real distinction*, on the other hand, gives rise to a non-human sex, a transsexual who "does not confine himself inside contradictions" (*AO* 91; 77).

Expressionism *moves* this transsexual revolution. Without it, Spinoza's substance-God would seem distant because infinite Being is only partly sensed. Expressionism overcomes this. That is, I only clearly see my region, my little place, by *thinking* and by *being*. But Spinoza's "common notions," by reviving the fragment, permit me to feel an attribute's common *affectability*. I sense a rock's heaviness, for example. I feel its burdensome *affect*. Then I see an ox carry a great load, and I sense the *common* heaviness they both express. Through this common notion, I obscurely sense something that fills the universe.

In this way, through common notions, you can be affected by the attributes of thought and extension. Metaphorically, an attribute is like an infinite stadium, the modes are like the players, and substance is like the space they inhabit. Note, for instance, how a colored mark divides your visual field as do *modes*, how visibility itself comprises the *attribute* they inhabit, and how Being (the very existence of everything) acts as the *substance* encompassing them: the attribute *pervades*, the mode *inhabits*, and the substance merely "*is*." But only the encounter, not Spinoza's logical deductions, can reveal this Being.

For Spinoza, the esoteric knowledge of Being comes to you "in act." Think how modes share an attribute (how the attributes form a sea, and how the modes sense it). This is how finite intellects grasp the infinite *in act*: "The finite intellect in act or the infinite intellect in act must comprehend the attributes of God and the affections of God, and nothing else."[26] But how can you grasp God *in act* or *in flagrante delecto*? Find an infinite fragment. Grasp the real in it as you would the sea's wetness in its every drop. Then, plunge into it. Only then will this "in act" become immediately, and sometimes painfully, apparent.

This is why, in *Proust and Signs*, Deleuze tell his readers to arrive at the whole, not via principles (a Spinozist deduction), but via machines (an encounter with part objects). With these machines, the hero not only dives into his encounters, but also drowns in a Spinozist substance. In its immanent production, this substance contains all its intensive magnitudes just as a rock does all its weight. They're inseparable. Like Kant's pure intuition, which, starts from zero "up to any required magnitude," you can only know attributes through your modal affects (intuitions = attributes *in act*). And each part object expresses Being immanently, for intellectually hierarchizing Being is like stacking water. It can't be done. Thus, expressionism explains Combray: the hero draws near it, not to see the whole universe in a grain of sand intellectually, but to engage real forces, for such finite grains entail an intellectual act of negation, which cannot *express* infinite Being.[27] And given Deleuze's devotion to this method, doesn't the reading of Proust that makes the tea and Combray episode merely subjective miss something? In essence, it *represents* two grains (the tea and Combray), while it neglects the "common notions" (their common intensities). The first is put under the self-identical "I think." The second is dispersed into Being.

If the tea and cake express a Spinozist body without organs, then Combray *is* a part object, for Proust makes "every finite thing," into "a being of sensation that is constantly preserved, but by vanishing on a plane of composition of Being: 'beings of flight.'"[28] This "plane of composition" *is* the infinite substance, the univocal Being, the pure intuition, or the degree = 0. In short, only by an intensive *being of sensation* do the *Recherche*'s parts resonate, for artworks compose themselves, as do non-human sexes: transversally. Neither subjective, nor objective, this strange part object "plenitude" is the *real*.

So, if the hero finds a perfect moment when he tastes the tea, it's because he no longer isolates moments intellectually. For Proust, intellectual memory never *truly* recovers the past: "What intellect restores to us under the name of the past, is not the past." The intellect covers over intensities, which stay trapped there, "unless we should happen on the object, recognize what lies within, call it by its name, and so set it free."[29] Thus, the mind disjoins not only times and places, but the sexes as well. This is the intellectual negation that Spinoza criticized—an imaginary lack, cutting you off, like the hero, from the exotic lands you desire.

Briefly ponder this fragmented gulag, which dulls your sense of life. Like Kafka's sentinel, it limits you. But then a moment comes, as it does for the hero, when limits fall away, and you find this *being of sensation* "in the little cup of tea, like those Japanese flowers which do not re-open as flowers until one drops them into water."[30] And, like these flowers, his senses will not reopen until he goes beyond the limits put upon different places, times, and sexes, or until he surpasses the Oedipal phantasms that serve this disjunctive logic: "you must desire the other sex, which you cannot know." Given this perverse logic, you can go to Balbec, but never absorb its place; you can reminisce about the past, but never occupy it; and, though you can eat the madeleine, you can never *be* it too, all because the mind grants more reality to the abstract than to the senses.

But this is reversible if you divide until every molecule (or monad) turns into a substance, or divide the sexes until they no longer oppose one another.[31] This overthrows the exclusive disjunctions, the molar division: "either man or woman." Multiply them, as Leibniz multiplies viewpoints on the universe and, like splinters of glass, your molar world will fracture. In fact, his appeal to the prime mover aside, Leibniz goes the furthest toward this type of fragmentation.

With these tools, you can create molecular worlds of intensity—can stop negation and can bring about real distinctions that determine what your body can withstand—a method closer to kinesthetic quantification ("either or, or, or...") than to Aristotelian taxonomy ("either-or"). Make disjunctions inclusive and their apparent distinctness will vanish.[32] Or make a Spinozist real distinction and their inclusive disjunctions will appear. Choose a Leibnizian voyage to the infinitesimal or a Spinozist voyage to the infinite. In the end, both destroy limits.

Once representation ends, only trans-positional subjects remain. Normally, society judges you by what you have: your sex by your organs, your wealth by your money, your intelligence by your education, and your age by your years. And all these exclusive disjunctions situate you based on your outer forms (organs), on your quantitative elements (money, years), or on your qualities (education). All these standards bar intensive *becomings*. Put simply, each disjunction rests upon the "I think" and upon the verb "to be" that names all that you lack. Descartes' "I think" stabilizes you. On the other hand, the "I feel" engenders inclusive disjunctions.[33] You can't say "I feel therefore I am" in the same way. Feelings lack stability. Each gives rise to a subjective island.

The weeping philosopher, for example, steeped in despair, feels that life will never get better, feels that his present state will continue forever. But then a ray of sunshine enters his life. And the state that once oppressed him ends. Now, his so-called "self" changes from moment to moment. He realizes that his supposed "core" is merely abstract. By delving into petite perceptions, this once sad philosopher now breaks into trans-positional, metastable states.[34]

But this trans-positional schizophrenic subject isn't mentally ill. Not at all! He merely yields to a *drive to add*. Deleuze finds this at work in the schizophrenic's table in Michaux's *The Major Ordeals of the Mind*: "As it stood, it was a table of additions, much like certain schizophrenics' drawings, described as 'over-stuffed,' and if finished it was so only in so far as there was no way of adding anything more to it, the table having become more and more an accumulation, less and less a table." If the schizophrenic produces for production's sake, Leibniz's philosophy also partakes of this schizophrenia, for, like this table, it fills the cosmos with an *infinite* number of *infinite* monads. This tendency toward the trans-infinite results from a schizophrenic encounter with the real, which "lives intensely within the thinker and forces him to think."[35]

Isn't Proust schizophrenic in this way? After all, his jealous hero forever expands details. That is, the jealous explosion of possible worlds only exists on this slippery surface. On it, the schizophrenic slips between variants, as if turned out on an overheated assembly line. Proust's novel explores these variants just as a Spinozist explores the passage from one degree of perfection to another.[36]

Spinoza adopts the "I feel" to find out what a body can do. For instance, I don't represent my heavy limbs or my weary torso. I sense them. "Knowing" entails representation, but feeling only entails a simple act of bodily abiding. After all, I sense myself directly. That's why Spinoza states: "nobody as yet has learned from experience what the body can and cannot do."[37] Spinoza calls for the radical self-experiment Deleuze and Guattari depict: "Drug users, masochists, schizophrenics, lovers—all BwO's pay homage to Spinoza" (*TP* 191; 154). In their line of flight, they escape desire-as-lack, exclusive disjunctions, and fly to a nomadic, yet painful, life of inhuman pleasure.

The hero finds this inhuman pleasure at Montjeuvain, when he sees Vinteuil's daughter feign to defile her dead father. If this horrifies her, however, then it's still too transgressive. Hence, she must approach it coldly, for her villainy is but a ruse to mask a more delicate soul: "it is in the skin of the wicked in which they implicate their partners, to have the momentary illusion of flight from their scrupulous, tender souls to a world of inhuman pleasure" (*RTP* 136; I, 179). As Georges Bataille learned, evil is an experiment. For Deleuze, however, it merely *profanes* Others (to keep them from seeing). By imposing this *inhuman pleasure* on them, by shocking them, they're made into spectacles, so that, *contra naturam*, intensive worlds, which Deleuze depicts as a "perpetual movement of raging molecules," can sprout up like so many flowers of evil.[38]

This pain becomes joyful, however, when mixed with self-overcoming. It rouses the death instinct, a trans-human drive, which, unlike the one Freud imagined, doesn't make us return to matter, but to the world Nietzsche depicted: "my *Dionysian* world of the eternally self-creating, the eternally self-destroying, this mystery world of the twofold voluptuous delight, my 'beyond good and evil,' without goal, unless the joy of the circle is itself a goal," a world without humans: "*this world is the will to power—and nothing besides!* And you yourselves are also this will to power—and nothing besides!"[39] This is the world of inhuman sexuality Deleuze and Proust describe.

Conclusion

The door on time's emotional aspects is now closed. Their intellectualized top-soil now exhumed, let's conclude by reexamining how Proust uses these aspects to vivify time. Clearly, these first chapters have emphasized Deleuze's theories and, perhaps, also embellished them. But how does this relate to Proust's work? Proust clearly uses emotion to create temporal effects. To see this, let's re-examine the four emotions, but this time contextualized with four scenarios.

Though the *Recherche* begins with a parental drama, in the end, it destroys the traditional family. In it, the reader finds a cold mother and an indifferent father. Punishing one day what he will allow on another, the hero's father, like the law, lacks clear principles. Take his position: You've broken a taboo. If you ate human flesh like Thyestes or unwittingly committed incest like Oedipus, what would happen to your selfhood? It would undeniably undergo a deep change, especially if this sin went unpunished. Like the hero, your self-defined limits gone, you'd feel an abyss open, for selfhood needs limits. And, like a hall of mirrors, you only reflect because other people limit you. But what happens when these limits become dubious? Or when the taboo the hero breaks fails to elicit a penalty? Faced with this situation, your selfhood would rest upon the far more fragile ground of self-judgment. In Proust's novel, when you see the self crack, you can sense this deeper time emerge.

In the middle of the *Recherche* the hero meets Charlus at home—expecting a friendly greeting, his accusation shocks him. "Tell me who it is that has treacherously maligned me," he asks Charlus, but he will not divulge his gossipy source: the law's secret. Consider how he feels: If you were anonymously accused of a vague crime, what would you do? The authorities would come to cart you off to jail. Rotting there, you'd imagine the happy people outside your prison walls. Would you despair? Consider how Swann reacts when he reads an unsigned letter telling him that Odette is a lesbian. His lack is to blame for the illusion that others possess a viewpoint that he lacks. This same illusion drives the hero to imagine that Albertine enjoys a greater pleasure than he does. This illusion not only splits moments, but unites pluperfect pasts through the lenses of nostalgia as well. In each case, you're trapped by your inner despot. Therefore, you must ask the prisoner's question: "How can I break out?"

When the hero suspects Albertine, his own appeal comes into question. But rivals from his own sex don't upset him as much as his lesbian rivals because the latter defy his phallic privilege—an ideal that is the measure of man and of woman. This common standard now gone, his mind clouds over since it lacks a rival image. Consider his jealousy of his own sex: If you've been judged an inauthentic man or woman—ugly, unlovable, lacking your sex's ideal traits (you don't measure up)—you cannot say "I'm the true lover." Given this dilemma, it's easy to see why the hero starts to ask, "What world does she view me from?" If your ideal were ruined, what would you do? Would you continue to try to be majoritarian, or would you undergo a minoritarian-becoming? The hero picks the latter, but only after Albertine dies, when he tries to become her.

In the *Recherche*, Swann obsesses over Odette's face. Note how this mania affects his romantic ideals, his nostalgic aesthetics, and his abstract reality. But as his jealousy takes hold, his paranoia defaces her. And this reorders the world. Now take Swann's place: You see faces everywhere, in abstract paintings, in clouds, and in tree trunks. Every time you see them, you doubt yourself, measure space sentimentally, and entrust the present world to the Other, effectively exiling yourself to a past world. This Other inserts a screen between you and your world. Indebted to faces, even to ones you don't recognize, you start to feel more and more mediocre. Your viewpoint narrows as faces start to enclose you. Given these dramatic events, you'd begin to question: "How can I reassert an innocent vision? Can I live without others?"

Though only four scenarios have been examined, there are surely more. Only this book's limits bind us to these four. But now it's time to leave time's emotional causes and to argue for its ontological effects, to leave time made perceptible and to argue for the heart's intermittencies, for a fragmented time.

PART TWO

The Intermittences of the Heart

Introduction

What happens to time when you envision past events? Doesn't it split into days, weeks, and years? These are the pure *results* of time in which gaps appear. But without them, I argue, time would neither move, nor have any perceptible force. This second part will explain why.

"The intermittences of the heart" (*RTP* 1323; II, 778) are temporal fragments. With these words, Proust opens a floodgate to paradox. Here, Being appears against the void. True, Proust explores time emotionally. But Deleuze, unsatisfied with this limit, builds upon his foundations. This part will survey the structural traits that Deleuze finds in Proust.

These traits will be studied in this chapter-number order: (5) *imaginary* lost objects, *real* incorporeal transformations, and *symbolic* places; (6) *virtual* complication and *actual* explication; (7) the transversal *floating signifier* and transference's *despotic signifier*; (8) the blockage of *symbolic* time's unconscious parallel series and the *imaginary* clearness of manifested time; (9) the passage from the *intensity* of problems to the *practice* of thought—from becoming's abyss to thought's structure. Each chapter explores a temporal function: distance, unfolding, creation, contradiction, and thought-production.

Temporal distance appears twice: first, as a lost object's sentimental distance; and second, as a temporal rift. The first: when he likens Odette's face to that of Zipporah, Swann idealizes her remoteness. The second: when Dreyfus is found innocent, everyone forgets his guilt. History changes in a logical abyss that rips the past from the present. Between these two types of distance lies the symbolic *place*. The hero only obsesses over place-names because the displaced lost object is a reaction against an incorporeal fragmentation. To illustrate: because the hero neglects Combray's essence when he actually inhabits Combray, he must step back from it to sense it as a place. Naming creates this distance. But, without forgetting, even this would be ineffective: the hero *must have changed* to have made Combray more real. The imaginary Combray idealized, and the real Combray forgotten, the symbolic Combray must become the place's local essence as it is *in itself*.

As if unfolded from a complicated knot, time binds every moment into an all-encompassing point from which bits of time unfold as signs. For instance, the little musical phrase, when first heard, is a strange flurry of sounds. But slowly, it's differentiated. As it unfolds, so too does the time of our lives. At first, it's virtual. But as the hero (or Swann) hears it again and again, it unfolds from the ontological depths to become a sign of his love.

But if time abided *in itself* for the hero, he'd be forced to inhabit an eternal present like that of a cow chewing grass. Instead, for him, time will be recreated in his unwritten novel. When he reflects on time, he reflects on art. This is no accident, for his artistic endeavors drive it. For instance, because his creative powers are subordinated to his idealized Odette, Swann could value art, but not create it. But, because the hero's love dies, he can make his romanticism an aesthetic vision, can thereby forsake the despotic gaze, and can fixate instead on his aesthetic blind spot. In it, he finds art's temporal force.

Opposed to itself, time does not, in fact, form a clear sequence. While dreaming of his dead grandmother, for example, the hero imagines that she still lives somewhere far off—for, until he unbuttoned his boots, he had lived as if she were still alive, had lived a different past than he recalls. This occurs because, in the unconscious, time holds not one, but multiple narrative threads. And, the *Recherche*'s time is multiple, for it reveals again and again its characters' vast powers to fool themselves. Imagined as they *would like to be*, they select among these threads, repressing some and imagining others. These *symbolic* inconsistencies are sensed obscurely, even while their *imaginary* personas are preserved. They destroy time's linear nature, and reveal, instead, a symbolic one: contradictory and multiple at heart.

Then there's the question: What makes us think and act? This is a *practical* problem. From time's flows and currents, a being seems to arise, to *actively* assert itself, and to own up to its course. In the *Recherche*, the hero *is this being* who senses all the hopes and failures, all the inspirations and frustrations, but lacks the power to act. But what changes him? In short, he feels the threefold *forces of nothingness*: first, mourning's force, purging past loves; second, the body's force, his inner obstacles—his signs and teachers—revealing his monadic region of Being; and, finally, the force of will (a reactive self-punishment turned active and monstrous), directing him to obsess over an aesthetic goal. This forced movement changes the hero from a *passive being*, who feels intensities, into an *active being*, who remakes the world.

With these five aspects, derived from the heart's intermittences, time is generated. Reminiscence and fragmentation generate distance. Complication and explication generate unfolding. Floating signifiers or aesthetic blind spots generate artistic creation. Symbolic memory generates contradiction. Death and nothingness generate action. By distancing, unfolding, creating, contradicting, and acting, a force is revealed, which this second part will explore.

Chapter 5

A Passionate Astronomy

Continuity prevails in Leibniz, who unites a world monadically, and in Bergson, whose duration is often mistaken for continuous becoming. But monadic unity is compossible, not incompossible; Bergsonian duration, seamless, not fragmented. Defying this, however, Deleuze inserts an Other that maps out time-space. In so doing, he surpasses the readings of Proust, such as Poulet's, that merely *take note of* the fragment. For Deleuze, Blanchot found the fragment, not Bergson. Through Proust's passionate telescope, fragmented time can now be viewed.

The Opened Monad

The hero may dream of Venice, but when he arrives, he doesn't find a new place since, as he says, "I carried in my body the same consciousness" (*RTP* 529; I, 716). This is a problem. If he is always *in* his place, how can he *know of* others?

For Leibniz, place is a clear zone, a monadic cinema, which only seems to move. But everything occurs *presently* from this listening-point, which senses past and future signals, but only receives the closest ones *clearly*.[1] Why is this a problem? Since it's a fixed-point on time's moving line, if it were flawed, no one would know if it were truly opened or closed. Clearly, Leibniz's *closed universe* (Self = Self) holds every feeling, thought, and vision within a kingdom-in-a-bubble. But *open universes* (Self = Other), which can be seen in James Joyce's or Lewis Carroll's portmanteau words, sabotage Leibniz's *individuating* strategy just by having "an infinity of possible interpretations" (*LS* 112; 343). This is *our* dilemma. That's why, when he says "Rilchiam," a befuddled Justice Shallow, who's closer to Joyce's *Finnegans Wake* than to God's *Pre-established Harmony*, uttered the password to an incompossible world.

Leibniz bars this opening with his *principle of indiscernibles* in which *no two things can share a concept*. If true, then when you move, you only change concepts, not your "place," since "that which has a place must express place in itself."[2] But isn't this also the Tweedledee-Tweedledum principle? After all, they only *express* different places because one has "DEE" on his collar and the

other "DUM." Without this difference, they'd occupy the same place! How
this Wonderland-concept be accepted if not by such principles?

If Leibniz comes "at a time just before the world loses its principles,"
Deleuze writes, then Proust's Liebnizianism comes *after*, for one could now ?
"Does everyone read from the same page?" Does it not seem that the hero
Albertine, unable to imagine each other, do not merely have different view:
the same universe, but different ones *from* different universes? Of cou
Ignoring this, however, Leibniz clings to this last suture—now cut by a p
modern vasectomy—by arguing for his single-universe theory:

> And just as the same town, when looked at from different sides, appears quite
> different and is, as it were, multiplied *in perspective*, so also it happens tha
> because of the infinite number of simple substances, it is as if there were a:
> many different universes, which are however but different perspectives of i
> single universe in accordance with the different points of view of each monad.[4]

By trying to fit every standpoint into one universe, Leibniz did his best tc
our crumbling world together with his *principle of continuity*. But he over
the impossible. Thus, he could only accept the possible, but not the unkno\
Proustian worlds. For instance, the pyramid in *The Theodicy* allows for difl
possible worlds, but not the unimaginable ones, which would crack its hiera
Proust's "viewpoints" lack such harmony—for, without principles, in his \
only machines transmit messages between the hero and his grandmother.[5]

Think of Proust's closed vessels (or monad-fragments) as something
forms around each event—each a shipwreck strewn on time's sandy shou
something that must find its *own* coherence. They don't add up, not bec
humans are finite, but because they change constantly. For him, each ?
spawns a new monad, a new perspective that briefly lives and dies like a
fly. And like these short-lived insects, this *instantaneous* monad only lives
each new viewpoint. Since it no longer revolves around a single *ego c*
Proust's *nomadic* monad traverses events with each emotional death. Bu
death isn't fatal, for when his ego dies, as it does after he breaks with Gil
he foresees its future rebirth: "It was a long, cruel suicide of my ego, who
Gilberte that I constantly sought to effect, with the prescience not only of \
was doing in the present, but of what would result someday" (*RTP* 484; I
From moment to moment, he doesn't feel, think, or act the same. Thus, no
by thinking "I think," *ergo sum*, can he synthesize these fragments.

In an open universe, synthesis occurs in time: in a free act, not in a
sentation. This is why Deleuze appeals to a free moment: "The voluntary
free because the free act is what expresses the entire soul at a given moment of
its duration."[7] Without a core subject, this "freedom" resembles that of a water-
mill—whose forces *freely* incline it. But if there's no core subject, what actually
synthesizes? In essence, by purging Kant's noumenal self, Deleuze makes each
instant an island, so that each decision must create its own synthesis.

Suddenly, the monad hits a certain amplitude, a branch-breaking crisis-
point. After it bursts and a decision is made, the voluntary act turns into a

conceptual predicate as if the monad's bookkeeper tallied up its expenses.[8] And a surface forms. Now, the free act's intensities turn into an extended conceptual point (a Kantian intensity = 0) on an abstract line. That's why, when I struggle with a problem, I live my acts uncertainly, without representing them. Only afterwards, in memory, do they seem linear. But what is this uncertainty? With his decision to stay home to write *or* to go out to drink, Deleuze illustrates it:

> I hesitate between staying home and working or going out to a nightclub: these are not two separable "objects," but two orientations, each of which carries a sum of possible or even hallucinatory perceptions (not only of drinking, but the noise and smoke of the bar; not only of working, but the hum of the word processor and the surrounding silence...). And if we return to motives in order to study them for a second time, they have not stayed the same. Like the weight on a scale, they have gone up or down.[9]

Now this philosopher hesitates *intensively*, but, when he will have recalled yesterday's acts, he'll see them as if they were *extended* on a photographic plate. Such memory doesn't resurrect the act's uncertainty. Deleuze and Guattari call this intensive-desire's rendition into the pluperfect-past, a "disjunctive inscription."[10] Now, Leibniz's concept changes: *your acts decide what's written on your monad, what's written on your monad does not decide your acts.* This is clearly different. While, for Leibniz, finitude (the state of hypothetical, not metaphysical necessity) explains autonomy, for Deleuze, however, connective production *is* freewill. If it didn't produce, ignorance would be liberty and Bouvard and Pécuchet would be the freest men alive.

So, while Leibniz takes the monad's unity for granted, Proust does not. When I have a memory, according to Leibniz's theory, I recall a lifeless image of a former-present. For Proust, however, I regress to the past and thereby revive all its uncertainty. And, as it reopens, I feel *a bloc of becoming*. I don't simply read memory's hieroglyphic traces like an archeologist, for there is no longer any handwriting on this monadic wall. Why? Because Proust, in effect, unlocks Leibniz's reading chamber, his little peepshow, and casts out its perverted library, thereby reviving doubt. In essence, Proust takes Leibniz's one-big-container and threshes it into little time-capsules that apperception cannot mend.

This leaves two options: I can reminisce nostalgically about an eternally frozen moment; or, I can reactivate an original context like a traumatized soldier does old battles. The first is depressive, the second is schizoid. The first prevails only because it's unpleasant to *constantly* relive the past. That's why the intellect isolates it. But sometimes emotions engulf the mind and revive the past. Freud, rediscovers this type of *passive* memory when he forgets the present:

> It happened to me during the agitation caused by a great anxiety that I forgot to make use of the telephone, which had been introduced into my house a short time before. The recent pathway succumbed in the affective state: *facilitation*—that is, what was *old-established*—gained the upper hand. This forgetting involves the disappearance of the power of selection, of efficiency and of logic in the passage of thought, very much as happens in dreams.[11]

His anxiety reactivates old-established pathways: this is involuntary memory. Passion can dredge up the past by a simple formula: emotion + past = involuntary memory. When the hero compares steeples, for example, he reopens uncertainty and unlocks the *vas deferens* of the past. Then, time's "punctual organization" turns into *a bloc of becoming*.[12] But to appreciate this *intensive* time, we need to examine the possible worlds from which it springs.

Proust's Possible Worlds

Proust certainly read Leibniz, for he makes his hero imagine other lands as Leibniz did possible worlds.[13] But he refers to Leibniz indirectly as a philosophy book: "You remember the philosophy book we read together at Balbec, the richness of possible worlds compared to the real world" (*RTP* 834; II 115). Unlike the Panglossian Leibniz, however, Proust favors the richness of possible worlds to the real one. Not satisfied with the poor hand dealt him, he laments the loss of possibilities. He wants *all* the cards. Moreover, unlike Leibniz, Proust's possible worlds belong to Others. That's why the hero asks how he *might* appear in Albertine's world: "Within what universe did she represent me?" (*RTP* 626; I, 851). This defies Leibniz's stitching God, who sews order into differing views.

A different perspective isn't an *opposed viewpoint*, but a mental succubae folded within the monad's shadows, something that *belongs to* Others, but not to another person's mind. Proust's novel mirrors this. In fact, it's Albertine's face that *expresses* a possible world just by being outside the list of things that the hero's monad possesses.[14] Of course, Deleuze parts company with Leibniz, whose monads have nothing to do with possible worlds (since they belong to the primordial story of divine selection). For him, possible worlds come from the dual monadic nature, its "outside," not from cosmology.

What is this dual nature? For Leibniz, monads are either spiritual or physical. But the spiritual one only *hallucinates* when it represents the physical ones. For Deleuze, this is unacceptable. According to him, you encounter the Other *in* material monads, not perceptually, but unconsciously. Once again, Deleuze speculates since, although Leibniz permits an outside, he bars any contact with it. Against this, Deleuze asserts his molecular philosophy by way of this analogy: *A man, drawing a parallel with his own flesh, infers that the Other's flesh must be another person's clear zone. Being obscure for him, he assumes that it is clear for another.*[15] The hero does this when he stumbles upon a flesh that senses him externally and that alienates him from his own body.

But the monad's *dark corners* are not another person's gaze. Radicalizing the Other in a two-fold way, Deleuze rejects the existential theory and reads otherness into the *Monadology* instead. He thereby creates an Other without an interior (like the soulless animals of Descartes). This makes sense, for, if I were to logically follow Leibniz to the letter, I must believe that every molecule is a soul or another possible world that sees me. Or, if I gave credence to a vulgarized Catholicism ("every sperm is sacred"), I might show concern for potential lives. If I followed this logic, even the molecule "looks" at me—for my molecules *each enjoy a separate viewpoint*.[16] And yet, I never wonder how my finger sees me since, in the end, what I imagine creates the Other, not what I see.

If my mind were infinite, however, the possible would vanish and I'd ignore the virtual. Fortunately, it isn't. That's why, with my vague concepts, I can imagine several possible Adams, several conceptual variants, as does the sleeping Theodorus: "Dreaming, he found himself transported into an unknown country" where Jupiter goes to review his worlds, "to enjoy the pleasure of recapitulating things and of renewing his own choice."[17] But unlike Jupiter, the hero belittles *this* world and, instead, obsesses over Albertine's, which, like a complex equation, eludes him only because he cannot fully know himself.

A short man, for example, ignorant of his size, imagines a shorter one to feel tall. This is the problem of relativity. For Leibniz, God's book of truth would end this problem. Read this book and all doubt ends (the philosopher's secret dream). But postmodern thinkers have *even* begun to doubt that this book exists. Perhaps it has gone out of print. Or perhaps, by clinging to his *faith* in it, Leibniz avoids the alternative: a relative universe where the Other rules his concept. His choice is clear: to be enslaved to a divine predestination, *or* to an uncertain world like the hero. Either way, the Other threatens him. Thus, the hero doesn't fear Albertine's viewpoint because her gaze makes him feel unsure; he feels unsure because he imagines her viewpoint. Thus, cause and effect trade places: *his* uncertain nature empowers his inner Other. As a result, God's death and the book of truth's loss cause the mind to dream of other possible worlds.

Even Sartre, in his early work, depicts this *magical* world: A face behind a window reveals something unseen within the seen. This foreshadows two possible acts: "the window as '*object which must first be broken*,' the ten yards as '*distance which must first be covered*,' must be annihilated." Note how the possibilities the face expresses structure this world, everything in it is imbued with a new significance. Unlike his later gaze theory, this early one results from *possible acts*, not from reflective shame. In this example, uncertainty predates other people: a face-event is the *effect* of possibilities implicated *within* the face, not behind it. This is the face as an event. In short, this horrified expression expresses *the world's* horrible state (the world-becoming-horrible), not a personal horror. Since it fills this world, the spectator only participates *in* this horror-quality.[18] Ultimately, the horror-event is internalized and is called "mine." Nevertheless, the encounter is its true source.

For Deleuze, the event causes the face to appear; the face doesn't cause the event. Why is this important? Since the event precedes all things, Kant's synthesizing apperception cannot go unchallenged. He assumes that, although I seem to turn into a different person in time, it's always me who changes. His is an all too "common" sense embedded in language. He subjects the event to the "I think," while Deleuze insists that any "I" must result from an event. In short, Kant's silly little syllogism cannot explain the original mitosis that splits the "I think" from its conjoined twin: the "Other thinks."

This Other cuts my thought off from itself in time. That is, this partitioning-face cuts me off from my world and the objects I see off from my mind.[19] If this logic holds, then mental representation isn't the synthetic principle Kant thinks it is. The *encounter* will not permit it. The face, however, by disrupting my non-represented time-structure, defies Kant's notion of time-consciousness, for a face can always usher an unthought-of possibility into the world.

Consider this. When the structure-Other wanes, so too does the alien view that sees what I don't. In this case, the world ends at my horizon, for only an *adjacent* one can limit my own. This parallels Spinoza's first argument in *The Ethics*: one substance "would have to be limited by another substance." To put it another way, without debate, I could universalize my views because no apple of discord disturbs my solitary nuptials. But introduce debate into my world and it fractures as it does for the blind men feeling an elephant: one, feeling its leg, insists it's like a tree trunk; one, feeling its ear, insists it's as flat as a leaf; and another, feeling its tail, insists it's like a snake. Kill the other two and one of these blind philosophers can claim universal truth, for the wise fool only has doubts when he imagines other views. Hence, *the world is flat* when nobody injects a depth or a profile that cuts me off from the immanence of space.[20]

The Other also temporalizes life. In Sartre's example, before the face emerges, the world is grasped directly. But, when a new possible perspective is found, this immediate world turns into a *past world*. Now, past and present split apart. And, in this hall of mirrors, one time-block moves another as Others force me to reflect on my past—a situation that causes anger, anxiety, and sadness.[21] But realizing this is the first step to overcoming it.

Forced to reflect on his past, the hero grows as indecisive as Hamlet, not because he loves to think, but because Others have destabilized him, have alienated him into a past world. So, what can he do? Since he can no longer act, he must profane the Other in one of three ways: a) through art (perspectives mixed within metaphor); b) through violence (the Other's vision expelled); or, c) through the laws of love that Deleuze depicts: "sequestering the beloved," "seeing the beloved when she can no longer see you," and "making her see the partitioned scenes of which she is... the horrified spectator" (*PS* 171; 142). The world now restored to the present, to a state before the structure-Other distorted it, these laws allow the hero to digest Albertine and to defecate her from his heart. *Love is a matter of digestion.* By imprisoning her, he restores a necessary world. Asleep, she becomes "just a body," a sleeping beauty: she snores, drools, and twitches. And such an "angel" couldn't possibly have a human viewpoint!

During these calm intervals, the hero annuls her viewpoint and enters her time-frame, for her immobile corpulence no longer excludes him. If this is true, then a simple sleeping-pill cures alienation. It restores all the power she had sapped from him. Her otherness now gone, the world is made complete—a state Deleuze calls "otherwise Other"—a perverse eunuchoid state in which the hero denies sexual difference. Without her unknown worlds, she becomes his mirror, his double. He thereby neuters Albertine. Her sex is returned to its basis. Otherness gone, he sees the world as it is: free from her viewpoint.[22]

What is this otherless world? It's the Combray vision, a total observer's *natural* vision, which annuls relative positions. Like Husserl, Deleuze brackets the transcendent Other. In this reduction, Combray opens up into an essential difference that "does not exist 'on the surface of the earth', but only at a particular depth" (*DR* 160; 122). After all, the earth's surface belongs to the structure-Other (relative positions), unlike the Combray vision (an absolute position), for its subterranean "clearness" lacks all visible landmarks.

But so long as Others exile you to the past, you can never truly have this vision. Overcome this, however, and mediocrity ends. In this respect, Proust follows Spinoza: freedom is impossible until the possible *itself* is abolished. Both demystify sentiments that make you spatiotemporally remote.

Sentimental Distance

Do fragments need a substratum? This question, along with Proust's many-colored self, defies Kant's so-called "necessary" representation.[23] But how necessary is it? Uncertain memories, like that of the "three trees," are islands on this abyss. They drain Kantian time of unity as one critic of Proust notes.

In *Proustian Space*, Georges Poulet replaces Kant's substratum with places.[24] Combray, Paris, Venice, and Balbec cohere as if capsulated, unlike nameless, abiding space. But, then again, without space, places would be like uprooted islands, like horizon-lines of a mental spotlight. Beyond this, space is an infinite Cimmerian desert. But does it really underlie a place?

How strange this blind, but universal, cartography seems to me when I see the world at hand and imagine space's edgeless globe! Does it not, in fact, rely on an unquestioned cosmology, one that doesn't end at the Pillars of Hercules? Perhaps. But Kant seems right to the modern city-dweller for whom a space is a chessboard. Without it, we'd wander aimlessly like pawns. But must this board continue into the void? Conceptually, it lacks bounds. But, practically, the horizon limits it, for a simple phenomenological reduction makes infinite space merely "possible," as if some divine razor circumcised the *actual* world. [25]

Poetically we dwell within Proustian historical mythologies, etymologies, and sentimental maps, unlike the anonymous, unquantifiable space around them. Take two places, Paris and New York, for example: a travel time quantifies their distance. But envision *all* the places between them and you'll fail, for you and I may imagine the two cities as maps, but we can't envisage the interstitial void. That is, you gauge these spaces with your heart, not with a ruler. That's why Poulet claims this distance "has nothing to do with quantity."[26] Though felt constantly, Proustian topologies, viewpoints, or poetic zones cannot be quantified since each has a different mood. Thus, a desert city and a metropolis will differ spatially. Hence, qualitative distances replace quantifiable ones.

For Poulet, countable distance is only a "space without force, without efficacy, without power of fullness of coordination and unification." It's unsynthesizable. That's why he writes, "there is never a question of space; there is only the question of places, and the distance that exists between places."[27] Unlike a Kantian *a priori* intuition, which unites, this anonymous distance divides. After all, for what reason should New York be separate from Paris? None. Space is an irrational desert, a void, which defies thought as it cuts one oasis from another. And, just as places fragment empty space, moments fragment empty time.

How un-Kantian seems this fragmented space and time! Clearly, Kant has a good reason to favor space and time: cities come and go, but space persists. Places break up abstract space like marble blocks. That's why, for Poulet, discontinuity "came to disturb an order undeniably initial and promising to be eternal."[28] But Proust's places seem eternal despite their eventual ruin. Thus, the eternal-temporary dichotomy no longer holds. But why?

A depressive position eternalizes places—forming tragic distances between which a vessel floats from Iseult to Tristram. Poulet says that they're "inscribed on infinite vastness, of the great principle of separation that affects and afflicts men. One is here. The loved one is there. Between these points there is no bridge, no communication."[29] The message never arrives since, between them, the white flag blackens. But, in this expanse, places attain a mythical shape. But it's Sartre, not Poulet, who first saw this *hodological* distance in Proust's work:

> This is because a being is not *situated* in relation to locations by means of de-grees of longitude and latitude. He is situated in a human space—between "the Guermantes way" and "Swann's way," and it is the immediate presence of Swann and of the Duchesse de Guermantes which allows the unfolding of the "hodological" space in which he is situated. Now this presence has a location in transcendence; it is the presence-to-me in the transcendence of my cousin in Morocco which allows me to unfold between him and me this road which situ-ates-me-in-the-world and which can be called the road to Morocco.[30]

Note how this differs from Kantian space. Only a lost object can make an uncountable *human* space livable. While in New York, for example, I see buildings tower and streets crowd up with people. In the midst of this throng, I can't see it as a *place*. To imagine it, I must draw a mental street map, but with personal landmarks. My mind summons it by way of a sentimental distance just as Sartre's mind does for his cousin on the road to Morocco.

Deleuze rarely criticizes, but he criticizes Poulet for ignoring temporal fragments. He does so because Poulet only takes note of them, or treats them too lightly, and ignores their true basis—space's coherence is questioned, while time is ignored. Since Bergson had grown so popular, Poulet felt the need to attack the Bergsonian image of Proust and to replace it with a Leibnizian one.[31] Thus, he serves them to us *à la poulette*. But he doesn't serve them well by assuming they're incompatible just because one speaks of space and the other of time. For him, Leibniz is a codeword for fragmentation. But he argues for Leibniz's space and against Bergson's spatialized time by allusion. Because Sartre already made his point in *Being and Nothingness*, however, Poulet's study seems redundant. He hasn't really explored the fragment further than did Sartre.

The Fragment

The fragment—that unexplainable puzzle-piece shut out of your self-narrative—upsets orderly, seamless time, by changing you on that old Damascus road.

Propelled into an uncertain future, your present is toppled. Encounter it and the world changes as the past, like a broken branch, falls away. Time—no longer coherent—now splits into closed vessels.

Leibniz and Bergson move too quickly to question this fragment. For them, if it surfaces at all, it instantly returns to the depths. Is it too difficult? As a singularity drowned in generalization, it is *indeed* a thorny problem. For instance, Aristotle asked: When does a heap become a heap? How many grains must one add? Or a hair-splitting question: When is a man bald? How many hairs must one pluck? But his question deems them to be merely parts: Do they form a whole? And when? But the question is already framed too abstractly.

For Deleuze, however, Blanchot, more than any other, questions this since, for him, the fragment expresses the *whips and scorns of time* overshadowing a seemingly seamless life.[32] But it can't be ignored. Repress it and it returns. Instead, it must be worked-through. And that's where its true limits lie: not in the fragments you see, but in the ones you feel.

Consider, for example, how the fragment floats between two wholes: a finger either refers to a lost whole (the hand) or to a plentiful state to come (theological resurrection).[33] But aren't these wholes just infantile fantasies? Note how the dejected feel depressed when they lose paradise and how the religious strive to restore a heavenly union. Both, however, fail *to affirm* the fragment on Deleuze's terms. Thus, *their oneness is reactionary.* After all, *if* they were to awake from this dream, their disjointed lives would seem all the more traumatic. Perhaps that's why this nostalgia is so tightly clung to. When elderly people remember me as an infant, for example, I refuse to see myself as *that* infant. Indignity soon follows. But do they really want to humiliate me? No. These doddering old fools merely grow nostalgic since their teeth rot, their skin wrinkles, and their bones clack. Why should they *not* romanticize youth to keep me as young as they imagine themselves to be?

Like them, Kant rejects fragments with his trinity: God, self, and the world. With them, he dialectically negates chaos, but gives no clear focus. Besides, why should he? He has logic on his side. But *logos* only seems to solidify, when, in fact, as Blanchot writes, it only knows philosophy's empty seriousness, but "knows nothing of chance, play or laughter." Think how Enlightenment philosophers forgot how to laugh. Diderot, for example, forgets this when he protests that the standard dictionary, not written by experts, allows "false, incomplete, absurd, or even ridiculous definitions to creep in." By fixating on expertise, he undervalues absurdity—unlike the ribald Rabelais, who extols it. But humor has its own logic. Recall what happens when the hero forgets this: by trying to hold Albertine's hand, he seeks unity. And those who take such aims too seriously, may, like the hero, miss the playful fragments in their path. That's why Proust embraces chance, play, and laughter in his novel. Even at its end, its fragments can't be redeemed. Not even involuntary memory can do this, for the heart's intermittences don't add up.[34]

When I read Proust, I realize that life, like the novel, lacks a thesis. And despite all efforts to narrate it, I can't possibly arrange all its events—a bitter pill, not easily swallowed. But once done, time no longer seems whole. I then realize that *logos* inspired me to justify everything—the impossible dream of total synthesis. But not everything finds its place on my personal timeline since fragments can always assert themselves, like the "three trees" memory did for the hero, and revolt against the whole. So, I affirm chance. Yet I still repress fragments occasionally, as a dreamer does on awakening, since they don't quite fit into my waking life. Thus, I'm now able to realize that they've spurred this becoming, for, without this illogical remainder, nothing can disrupt the perfectly balanced symbols of my dream-life.

Nevertheless, the dewy-eyed thinker assumes that Kantian intuition can unfold *becoming*, but it does not; assumes Bergson's duration can unfold it, but it does not. Or at least a vulgarized Bergsonism fails to question it by treating it as a mere interval when, in fact, such metaphors of flowing time actually hide deeper fragments. Only fragments have force, not duration. So, when Blanchot seeks them, he turns to Nietzsche, not to Bergson, who overlooks them.[35]

To see what I mean, consider this scenario: An accuser shouts, "You're the murderer!" Only a good alibi can prove you innocent. But the accuser brings in more proof. So you revise. In this courtroom drama, you constantly shift your identity. Though *this isn't becoming*, it certainly can make you aware of it—as if, briefly confused, you sense an inner stirring, for the accused only feels time's force *between* these new bits of evidence. But think. Doesn't the accused's revision *itself* merely make time *seem* linear? Or do fragments *force* the accused to think, to revise, and, ultimately, to become? Under these circumstances, logic cleaves to continuity, while fragments *activate* becoming.

In countless conversations, I've heard egomaniacs portray their life as some sort of a heroic struggle. But under their nutty surfaces, I feel as if their cookie-cutter stories would crumble under the least pressure. They remind me of the lawyer who brags that he can *even* get an innocent man convicted by making the judge *rule out* any evidence that would prove his innocence. This is what the ego's perfect lies do. And yet the trial would only continue if new data, which the ego-lawyer tries to repress, enters the judge's hands.

Since the fragment can't be justified, on the Freudian couch, all analyses are interminable, for any final judgment, would literally *end the world*. That's why Joseph K's pleas never stop: "No doubt it was a task that meant almost interminable labor." This would *indeed* be an infinite task, "because to meet an unknown accusation, not to mention other possible charges arising out of it, the whole of one's life would have to be recalled to mind, down to the smallest actions and accidents, clearly formulated and examined from every angle."[36] His *logos*-driven mind tries to reintegrate his entire life. *But why bother?* This question preoccupies Deleuze as well as the author of *The Trial*. The fragment seems to clamor, "You cannot satisfy everyone's accusations." Every possible world splits him in the end. So when Joseph K envisions all the *possible worlds* that defy him, he can no longer represent himself with the Kantian "I think."

But consider how such *self-representations* would stagnate without an Other, internal or external, who asks "who are you?" After all, without prying eyes, no man would avow his hidden fragments. So perhaps, like Odysseus, he should answer, "My name is No-man!" For the future belongs to the "Man without Name" (*DR* 379; 296) because the fragment doesn't need a name, but *he* needs a name to be fragmented. Thus, the superego, by trying to name him, to accuse him, and to force him to revise, defies the ego's illusions.

In the end, this anonymous Other (a structure-Other) demands that the Man without Name prove himself *to be just*. But how does he react? By being named, his intersubjective landscape is reorganized—something even Sartre's gaze couldn't do, for the Other doesn't make you self-aware, it merely questions your existence. Anyone could be the Man without Name. Anyone could be this dying and renewing viewpoint. I *could* be him. But my memory forces me to say "it's *me* who changes!" And, like Odysseus reclaiming his rightful home, I feel that I must declare this to my rivals. But think. When the superego pronounces you guilty, doesn't it name you? Doesn't it also make you question your identity?

The Man without Name, as your unconscious, prompts this *naming*. He's behind this psychoanalytic obsession. With it, the *named* ego hopes to be cured by synthesizing the hitherto *unnamed*.[37] But the *cogito* (the "I think" that comes with images in time) represses the Man without Name with an immaculate sublimation. But why value the unseen ego, like Kant, over the fragments that bear it? Imagine this self-serving ego, if you will, as an eternally youthful Dorian Gray, who consigns all change to his alter-ego. In this way, don't such threats *drive him to create* a scapegoat-canvass? Without fragments, he wouldn't form this alter-ego: his outside, his hidden portrait.

Now that we've seen how the fragment defies active syntheses, it's clear that neither Leibniz, nor Bergson could fully realize its power. The time has come for a passive synthesis. Now that Leibniz's monadic universe has passed away with the age of reason, this old apperception has given way to the unconscious, which is an "outside," not only *molecularly*, but also sensorially; not only a mental leap *into* the outside that topples mental habit, but a new freedom to explore difference, or what Blanchot calls the "intimacy of force."[38]

The world is now an open work that defies synthesis. Arriving passively, by involuntary memory, synthesis now sidesteps the ego—arriving by an intimacy of force, hitting you when you awake with a new identity, it starts in the past's shifting layer, makes its way through the nervous system, where it's finally trapped in a subjective matrix. This has a literary parallel. *Finnegans Wake*'s epiphanies, or Gestalten patterns without a preset harmony, are unlike those of the monad. Instead, as its etymological roots are mixed, it snares us in allusions.[39] Under these circumstances, what happens to interpretation?

Though it expresses becoming's innocence, the open work is condemned by the interpreter's superego, perhaps because its synthesis is demonically passive. Such often cited (but rarely read) works are about as accepted as "the curse" nowadays, since their bloody flows undermine the linguistic order while the work's openness protests the simulacrum's innocence. But the paranoid interpreter's ire isn't as strong as experimenter's joy. In his foolscap, the playful sage laughs with infinite jest and with excellent fancy, but is no less noble than these

Alexandrian interpreters in the end: "Alas, poor Yorick!" This metaphorical jester, while carrying you on his back, trains your mind to play conceptually and to value paradox over solutions; and process over results. But why should quick-answers bury such a lively and experimental jester? Interpreters, who fixate on answers, tame the text, and submit it to the whip of a justified end—thus, they ignore its expressive power. As such, they don't lament this jester's death.

Interpreters ignore the fragment. They see it as a change. From Swann's love for Odette, to Saint-Loup's love for Rachel, to the hero's love for Gilberte and for Albertine, they see only succession, not fragmentation. Though the Guermantes way and the Méséglise way divisions are seen, they say "so what?" By simply ignoring them, however, don't they reduce the different to the identical? By ignoring difference, don't they favor an easy simplicity? And such smug critics don't debate complex theories; they deride them. Swann declines from a vibrant Peter Pan to a broken old Methuselah; Saint-Loup converts from a Jekyll-like womanizer to a homosexual Hyde. This isn't character growth; it's forced movement. For example, Proustian aristocrats show loyalty to France when they ban Dreyfusards and invite only generals. The Dreyfus case splits them: "Everything Jewish… went down, and many obscure nationalists replaced it" (*RTP* 412; I, 557). Their change forgotten and their history rewritten, they're certain that they *always* knew he was innocent: "Dreyfusism was now integrated in a series of common respectable things" (*RTP* 2154; III, 747). The past subjected to the present, they don't evolve—they deny. With such deceptive egos, how could they ever have resisted this dull image of continuity?

Let's be honest about this self-deception: time doesn't flow like a river; it cracks like an iceberg. The hero crosses a Rubicon every time his so-called fixed identity changes. And, by the novel's end, marked by scandal, society no longer welcomes Charlus (though it knew he was scandalous when it *did* accept him). But if these transformations don't surprise you, perhaps they haven't been grasped. Find them and you'll feel time's force.

Incorporeal Transformations

Rather than petrifying them under Medusa's eyes, Proust drowns his characters in Protean waters, ebbing with the waves of fashion, invading societies, frag-menting and partitioning them from epoch to epoch, until, one day, they no longer obey the same laws: "from one moment to the next, they evolve, crystallize, or give way to other signs." (*PS* 12; 5). After the First World War, for example, society changes: "for one of the most fashionable ideas was that the pre-war days were separated from the war by something as profound, of a seemingly long duration, as a geological period" (*RTP* 2155; III, 748). These truths without substance, persons without foundation, and signs without meaning defy philosophical dogmas.

But our task as readers, Deleuze writes, "is to understand why someone is 'received' in a certain world, why someone ceases to be so" (*PS* 12; 5). Charlus falls from favor, the Verdurins climb to high society, and Swann sinks into the shadows. To map these changes, Deleuze applies a structural analysis, setting up a statistical distribution, "within which 'the worlds' are as separated as infinitely distant stars" (*PS* 151; 124–125). Using a possible world as a resonator, he serializes *change*. But signs shift so much in the novel that everything collapses into "the great mixture of the end" where the hero reaches a "threshold of proximity at which everything disintegrates" (*PS* 151; 125). Now, the depressive law scatters possible worlds, which the schizoid forces have broken. Indeed, the schizoid, the great leveler, decomposes society with its destructive humor.

Code-confusion drives much of the *Recherche's* humor.[40] When Cottard, impressed by Swann, praises him after he is disfavored, he's rebuked: "Heaven save us from him; he's so deathly, a stupid, poorly raised boor" (*RTP* 234; I, 315). Straying from their sign-system, he fails to move with the group. Its shifting hierarchies splinter him. Of course, his body persists, but personas are social; they come from worldly signs, not from physical beings.

In Proust's novel, a chasm splits the hero's private being, which he finds in the flowers, from his public persona. This florid region goes beyond symbols. His personal inner sense inhabits this floral, yet ill-defined, *being of sensation*. As the narrator, he's unique because the reader sympathizes with him: other characters are known by worldly signs; he's known internally.

Harold Rosenberg makes this distinction between the personal and the abstract persona in *The Tradition of the New*. For him, the first is felt privately:

> The single being may be compared with other organisms which it resembles, it may be... subsumed under a type; but its individuality can only be 'felt.' To the human person himself his own coherence is... "an organic coherence intuitively based on the real world of sensation."[41]

Beyond his social persona, the hero finds this "organic coherence," Rosenberg's "felt personality," or Deleuze's "anonymous bloc of becoming" directly, for, without a judiciable social position, readers can only consider his sentiments.[42] Therefore, social guilt doesn't penetrate him, for if he were to assume a public role completely, he'd be alienated from his inner sense.

Under these circumstances, speech acts set up superficial identities, but, underneath, the body's destructive mixtures go on churning. Therefore, you can imitate Marilyn Monroe as an icon, but you live her fits, depression, and overdose organically. Though idealists imitate the good, badness infects them. In an anorexic society, for example, each new waif entering the scene alters the cosmopolitan categorical imperative. But, while despotic centers shift, each pretender-to-the-throne hesitates. Like Cottard, chastised for praising the disfavored Swann, every pretender knows when he or she symbolically deviates.

Have these despots no feelings? They ignore it with their scathing wit, the vicious attacks that they palm off as emotionally detached humor. As symbolic tokens, they're alienated from their inner-selves—having, for so many years, prostrated themselves, they're slaves to fashion. Acting only from pure duty, feeling is nothing to them. Their symbolic economy gives their social personas a universal exchange value—each one a token pegged by a binary opposition.

But is this all they are, a structure? In Proust's novel, one group falls and another one supplants it. And feelings never rise above Madam Verdurin's alleged reaction to the musician's death: "one might have concluded that it would be insane to regret the death of a friend of thirty years" (*RTP* 1434; II, 930). In this cold, empty world, emotion becomes a coded display, easily faked. But, at the end of the day, these frigid people aren't really monsters. By studying the effects of worldly signs, Proust finds that we're all symbolically superficial.

In some ways, the social world and the monad are alike: without contact, each monad merely reads through the other's signs. In this symbolic world, you're either innocent or guilty, either included or excluded. Harsh stage critics assess your every act, falsify you as a human being, and judge you in effigy. So, when Saint-Loup falls in love with Rachel, his family ignores *his* feelings: "make him understand the pain he is causing his poor mother and all of us by dragging our name in the dirt" (*RTP* 959; II, 287). Perhaps, this is why Deleuze scorns *the politics of identity* and the inhuman judgment that comes with it.

This is why Dreyfus's myth *stays the same* while he changes on Devil's Island. Symbols, or the "sayable" (*lekta*), cannot be touched, tasted, smelled, seen, or heard. Thus, becoming doesn't apply to them. The physical world *becomes*, but a word records it in *eternity*. So, when his symbol fades, so too does the pretext for his sentence. He dies symbolically after a new inquest proves him innocent (but not before he had served a long sentence).

Suddenly, Dreyfusards and Anti-Dreyfusards no longer differ: "It was no longer 'shocking.' That was it. No one remembered that it had once been thought so" (*RTP* 2154; III, 747). Society changes abruptly, like Lot's salty wife, without evolving or maturing. Not that his true nature is finally revealed. His sign merely shifts. Freed from the island, his symbol-as-a-traitor fades like a Cheshire cat. Found innocent, a criminal like Dreyfus "having been converted in an instant into the hypothetical and undefined figure of an innocent man, would no longer exist under the eye of the court."[43] Like him, every man, woman, and child changes with fortune's blind justice.

Nevertheless, justice is memory's moral base, without which no one would reminisce. That's why, Leibniz writes that souls must "preserve some sort of memory or consciousness or the power to know what they are, upon which depends all their morality, penalties and chastisements. Consequently, they must be exempt from those transformations of the universe which would render them unrecognizable to themselves and, morally speaking, would make another person of them."[44] After all, you can't rightly be judged if you can't recall. That's why everyone must have a memory. And perhaps that's why you never see scatterbrained goldfish in paintings of the last judgment.

Without this active synthesis, individuals would multiply, divide, and sub-tract everything from the past. To stop this, however, Leibniz closes the monad, writes all your faults and all your virtues in it, thereby leaving no doubt. But Proust opens the law to change and destroys its moral underpinnings, for his characters span as many subjects as they do roles. Think about it: fragmentation is like an amnesiac enacting all the roles of *War and Peace* in turn. To avoid this, Leibniz stresses memory's continuity, for only memory can stitch your life together. Memory, in Leibniz's words, is "a kind of consecutiveness which copies reason but must be distinguished from it." But memory is also like a dictator, who executes dissidents, who relentlessly negates those fragments that defy a symbolic plot just as a screenwriter crosses out every counter-dramatic scene. Thus, Rosenberg writes that symbols order memories "into a scheme that pivots on a single fact central to the individual's existence."[45]

This selective amnesia lurks in the *cogito's* plot. Artificially unifying our self-image, it decides our fate. As a painful scenario rehearsed to contest future blame, this primal paranoia drives active synthesis. But can everything be anticipated? When we try to, we reason ourselves into irrationality. This plot *is* the narrative defense Leibniz calls "practical remembrance."[46] Under it, the fearful await judgment in an "indefinite postponement," the kind Joseph K endures. This is why Leibniz thinks that moral laws would fade without memory, and memory would fade without moral laws. Do philosophers forget this? The Kantian "I think," therefore, wouldn't synthesize without this moral basis. Even atheists, who feel free from superstition, are subject to this judgment as long as they have memories. At the end of the day, such a Calvinist position makes all human struggles in vain. But why should you live if every repetition, every struggle, in the end, comes down to a predestined judgment? This is why I argue that Proust, by returning the fragment to memory, demystifies eternal judgment, and drives his unholy wedge into this divine crack.

And that's why, in the end, the *Recherche* isn't really unified. One snazzy dinner party after another, one lover's quarrel after another, each an island on a temporal sea, but the readers never truly see under its murky waters. What happens between them? Proust links them, but he doesn't organize them around a paranoid unity. Instead, time's force *envelops these events*, slits their chains, and grants them a strange plasticity. But I know that, for some, Rome could be burning and they would still fiddle with memory to make it seem consistent. But such an effort is not only Nero-nic, it's moronic. Against this, the *Recherche* creates paradoxes, narrative shifts, that fracture: Swann witnesses Odette's letter to Forcheville, the hero witnesses Charlus seduce Jupien and hears Albertine's involuntary utterance. Indeed, don't these moments split the story into a before and an after? After all, the world shifts with them. And if change truly affirms life, as Deleuze says, why not call Heraclitus "the laughing philosopher?" After all, for many, fatalism is more dismal than uncertainty. In the end, who could despair knowing that a new world will emerge with each new crisis point?

Often arriving in still moments, these crisis points are enfolded in pure events.[47] But such events, unlike daily occurrences, are expressed by verbs like "to run," "to hop," and "to swim." Since these points no longer represent anything, they're unconscious dramas—one univocal event that embraces all real ones. This alone makes them "pure." As a result, different beings no longer need *analogy* to synthesize them. Instead, the hero gets caught up in them until he sees forgetting-within-memory in a hyper-real Combray.

This suggests a simple lesson: Repress, and memory fragments, resonates, and recombines into phantasms. But reduce Combray to reverie, and you'll miss these deeper implications. And yet, this dull theory of reverie prevails. Against this, however, I maintain that involuntary memory is *certainly not* a daydream, and *certainly not* somewhere-over-the-rainbow—it's here-and-now in a "screen memory" that tries to lay a bandage across our past. Despite all its efforts, this screening-bandage cannot finally heal time's scars. By defying this process, the fragment complicates the past and thwarts memory's coherence.

Therefore, no more smooth plot transitions! No more unified self! Hitherto, plot has created the self abstractly. Though self-knowledge sets you apart from garden slugs, plots can persuade you that your story represents you better than your body does. On the other hand, once these stories break, you can be thrust outside time, as Proust shows, since narrative paradox can't be chronicled.

With this extra-temporal incongruity, the hero inhabits a temporal outside, in different places and with different eyes: "for if we went to Mars or to Venus while keeping the same senses, they would clothe everything in the same aspect as those of the Earth" (*RTP* 1797; III, 259–260). The imperative to be oneself now defied, like a metaphysically fragmented Magellan, he must survey unknown worlds. And though they leave a breadcrumb trail, such fragments don't ever lead back to a "true self." They do, however, nourish involuntary memory, for, in this fragmenting, the hero feels a spatiotemporal force far *beyond* the distance of which Sartre and Poulet speak. He feels incompossibility. That is, unlike Leibniz, Proust finds an incompossible world, where Caesar can *and* cannot cross the Rubicon. Flouting the plot, these worlds form a differential unconscious. And, through his telescope, he sees Saturdays that will never arrive, ancient landscapes that he'll never know, and worlds that he'll only be able to imagine. With his passionate telescope, he *affirms* distance.[48]

The incompossible worlds now disjointed by crisis points, voluntary memory can be sustained on the level of local solutions and the involuntary on the level of problems.[49] Hence, I only walk down memory lane to work-through the vagueness that pure events initiate. And, when I feel a sudden change (a crisis point), I look to memory to *deny* it. Now, the involuntary sets up a problematic pure event, the paradoxical moment that voluntary memory tries to ignore. The first spawns *unknown worlds*; and the second, my world.

With these unknowns, I build temporal resonators imbued with emotion. And, to see from one level to another, I turn to the astronomy Proust depicted:

> How many patient, but not at all serene, observations must one amass of the seemingly irregular movements of these unknown worlds before attaining certainty that one isn't led astray by coincidence, that one's foresights are not mistaken, before deducing certain laws, acquired through cruel experience, of that passionate astronomy! (*RTP* 653–654; I, 890)

This astronomy brings irregularity into the hero's world, the normally excluded fragments of Albertine's lesbian desires, of an inhuman pleasure. It absorbs all his energy just to see them with the aid of his passionate telescope.

Chapter 6

The Birth of the World

By making the "I think" a symbolic synthesizer, Kant puts time under psychological representation. But is there an ontological option? With the three hypotheses of Plato's *Parmenides*, Deleuze builds his own theories of complication, explication, and unlimited postponement. But two problems arise. First, negative theology, by adopting the "One is above Being" hypothesis, makes the One transcendent. To restore its immanence, Deleuze must make it an unlimited postponement in which the One is futuristic, not otherworldly. Second, he must rid complication of its theological overtones to return the "One is equal to Being" to the unconscious. With this, he shows how an *essence* not only draws moments together, but apart again in the world's continual rebirth.

The One

Deleuze's expressionism, which defies negative theology's emanative cause, comes from Plato's *Parmenides*. But Deleuze turns its vertical tower into a horizontal position, making it an immanent plane on which Spinoza is "the Christ of philosophers" since he "inspires the fewest illusions, bad feelings, and erroneous perceptions."[1] But perhaps, for Deleuze, Proust is a Spinoza made literary since, like that of Spinoza, Proust's work "brings with it fragments that can no longer be restored... that do not belong to a preceding totality, that do not emanate from the same lost unity" (*PS* 136–137; 113). This Proustian immanence isn't a lost oneness, but a line of flight.

How can this be explained? Perhaps this struggle—amid the One fleeing-into-the-heights and the One bathing-within-all-beings—also begins with Plato. And yet, they differ. While a lost-One (psychological memory) blurs moments, a univocal One (Spinozist common notions) links them without *resemblance*. All in all, this modern debate is but a footnote to these hypotheses: One is above Being, One is equal to Being, and One is under Being.

The first hypothesis engenders many errors, illusions, and bad feelings. In it, the fleeing-One, as an emanative cause, abandons mortals to an underworld since it is "superior not only to its effect, but superior also to what it gives the effect." Its hierarchical difference, though leading up to mount Olympus, puts you on life's lower rungs as it threatens to cast you into a Tartarean abyss of mediocrity. But Deleuze and Guattari cut this hierarchy into immanent, horizontal segments. They topple the One's vertical, transcendent, ithyphallic tower, and *level it* since, for them, "it is always in the office next door, or behind the door, on to infinity." The transcendent-One becomes an *immanent* motor, a lure drawing us *out of* our mediocrity. In effect, they put the transcendent *into* immanence since the first *serves* the second. Thus, they don't oppose each other by *kind*. Instead, they differ in use: the transcendent use—a crushing fatalism; the immanent use—a liberating line of flight in an *unlimited postponement.*[2]

The second hypothesis affects complication. Being, which inhabits the One, complicates all beings just as a dream does—by condensing them into a single figure—or, just as Boethius' wheel unfolds all things on its outer rim. But draw near its hub and time slows until it folds everything into an instant (as do dreams). In this way, Boethius squares God's omnipotence with our freedom—whereas, if he clung to Aristotle's "first cause," we'd be forever fettered to it. But if his chain were exchanged for a Stoic *immanent cause*, causes would no longer *follow* each other. They'd *coexist*. Thus, Being holds them all in an immanent complexity, in the primal struggle that spawns the visible world.

This complicated cause is a bodily time, an instant, which can be seen in such abrupt changes as death or pregnancy—these are the limits that temporal wayfarers cross, ones that forever change them from Saul to Paul on that old Damascus road. But such limits also bring about the terrible freedom that Sartre depicts. After all, who knows when something may pop, or when your body may forever be changed as a result of a chemical reaction? Those who feel that time is *continuous*, however, neglect this. They fail to see that this instant alone exists. And, by expressing itself, it expresses everything. That's why a Stoic diviner finds fate in a falcon's entrails, which hold "a sequence of causes… an inescapable ordering and interconnection." This *wound up cord* of fate awaits unwinding—just as every genetic event does an environmental trigger. But do not think of these Stoic causes as Newtonian billiard balls, "causes are not *of* each other, but there are causes *to* each other." They're molecular, genetic, or bacterial—a sub-dermal, virtual cause that breaks with if/then logic. They enshroud time, which only occurs in the *Parmenides* thesis "Being equals the One" or in the Deleuzian thesis that all causes are univocal.[3]

The third hypothesis affects explication, or Aion in which "a future and past divide the present… and subdivide it ad infinitum into past and future" (*LS* 192–193; 164). As it splits into relations, the One sinks into becoming. Normally, I count time by my steps. But when relative terms lose fixity and *themselves* become ideal, time goes mad. For Plato, this is a paradox in which time goes "from past to future, it will never overstep the present… leaving the present behind and reaching out to the future, and so passing between the two."[4]

This paradoxical time expresses such relative terms as hotter or colder, shorter or taller, and darker or lighter. That's why, I go beyond all the milestones by which I could gauge my progress. For example, I grow older as the years pass, but the young man that *I was* grows younger relative to the man *who grows older*. Thus, eighteen seems younger to forty, then to fifty, and then to sixty. One point recedes while the other proceeds. Similarly, when something grows "hotter," I cannot say when it reaches this *relative* state, for "hotter" always refers to a receding, nonexistent point. *Hence, it's below Being.* Growing "hotter," all its past temperatures seem "colder."

As mental paradoxes, relative terms belong to the logic of meaning, not to the bio-logic of bodies. In bodies, causes mix perfectly. But, on the surface, with its sayable things (*lekta*), the stitches fixing them to the world are cut. Now they unfurl into simulacra. Thus, when I say something is "hotter," without naming a temperature, I detach it from fixed points. By occupying time without counting, and by passing these relative terms, I *become* in this intensive flux.

In the end, when bodies and words diverge, they *turn away from* Being. Normally, words can name non-existent things, or spatiotemporal relations. But, while *bodies* retain their mixtures (the One is Being), *thought* turns away from them (the One is under Being). Thus, by speaking, humans sense *a lack*, a future and a past, in the stark contrasts brought about by language. Now, the One turns into a *lost Oneness* as well as *One to restore*. These are the time of signs.

The Time of Signs

The Stoic theory of divination affects Deleuze's view of natural signs, but not of linguistic ones. After all, diviners feel an animal's entrails. As such, they read their *fates* from their forces as if from a hieroglyphic text. This leads Cicero to wonder "if there were some human being who could see with his mind the connection of all causes, he would certainly never be deceived," but the gods reserve this power so that "man must be left to gain his foreknowledge from various signs which announce what is to come."[5] Because the depths are cut off (since a somatic language doesn't translate directly into a cerebral one), the ontologically isolated must learn by explicating its signs like a foreign language.

Signs are explicated from complicated folds just as a genetic code is on the Elephant-Man's face. These non-signifying signs rise to a molar level where they grow into a tumor, or, on the earth's body, into an eruption.[6] Thus, how we *represent* causes and how they *naturally* occur differ. Deleuze and Guattari depict these two orders, calling the first (the Stoic mixture), "a connective synthesis of production," which you feel, and the second (the incorporeal), "a disjunctive synthesis of recording," which you think. That is, connective-production mixes with Being. This is a cause. But the disjunctive recording *falls below* Being, into the linguistic code of recorded history. This is an effect.

Unlike the usual cause and effect (one billiard ball hitting another), for the Stoics, the two balls *together* cause each other to move: the first ball's rolling *causes* it to hit the second; the second ball's being hit is also the *cause* of the first ball's hitting it just by being there. The two are bound up in a common fate. But fate isn't a chain. Only the mind draws events out into a linear cause and effect. Before that, signs lack order or actuality and are thus problems.

The forces of time arise from these signs: you find problems, read their signs, and, eventually, wonder what they portend. Thus, learning to swim occurs *between two substances* that struggle chemically like an acid and a base. Though the swimmer *knows* it linearly, its physical causes are more like a bursting dam insofar as a cause *is* a crisis-point, which *always* occurs in the moment-of-contact—a moment when the water's signs vie with the swimmer's limbs. The brain only imagines the results. Hence, learning is *physical*, not mental. Without a mind-body link, the mind cannot affect learning. That's why Cicero says that the gods "give us no routes to scientific knowledge of sign-inference."[7] You must learn to interpret signs *while* the body learns. You must *learn to learn*.

Deleuze sees learning at work in Proust. He writes, "to be sensitive to signs... is doubtless a gift" (*PS* 37;26). And his hero shares this gift with ancient diviners, a gift Deleuze depicts as "the relation between the pure event (not yet actualized) and the depth of bodies, the corporeal actions and passions whence it results" (*LS* 168; 143). Seeing beyond the epidermal surface into the sub-dermal depths, these diviners *feel* signs by grasping at entrails to touch the truth. In short, for them, "it is always a question of cutting into the thickness, of carving out surfaces, of orienting them" (*LS* 168; 143). Similarly, the hero seeks nature's complicated depths, sensing them painfully as if by so many cuts and wounds of time. Like Cassandra, he must ignore surfaces to read what's in the depths.

But no one can truly encounter outward things, whole persons, or formed things, for this gift of divination "risks remaining buried in us if we do not make the necessary encounters," which would "remain ineffective if we failed to overcome certain stock notions," and "to attribute to the object the signs it bears" (*PS* 37; 26–27). Forsaking Descartes' clear and distinct ideas, the mind must first encounter blurred images, unclear speeches, phantasms, and, ultimately, paradoxes. Since Charlus envelops many personas, the hero must forever wonder *who he really is*. He is a paradox: a virile man at one moment, a woman the next; a criminal at one moment, a nobleman the next. Charlus *is* a complicated state.[8] Thus, the hero learns about him as swimmers learn: by an encounter. Thus, what he thinks *about* Charlus is less vital than his influence: "an unconscious reminiscence of lying scenes enacted by M. de Charlus" (*RTP* 1868; III, 360). Eventually, through this power, he detects such aspects as if they sprang from a *complicated* genetic seed awaiting time's waters to nourish it.

Explication and Complication

An anonymous Other opens up other possible worlds, but *hides*, like a Polonius, behind our mental tapestries. It unfolds new worlds to us from the beyond, for time's tightly-wound spool can't be seen from the surface.

Consider Boethius' *wheel metaphor* in which God views time in eternity, but, on the wheel's outer rim, time seems to move. Draw near its center and you cast off the bonds of fate.[9] But Deleuze changes this "divine present." He keeps its strophe-like implicating viewpoint and its rival explicating-antistrophe, but discards the theological, and leaves behind two motions that mirror a nocturnal and diurnal flux. That's why, when the hero thinks, it's as if he were emerging from a dream: at first, his thoughts mingle. As they untangle, he awakens. But sleep's *complicating movement* drives his mind by drawing near the ontological axis. Without it, fragments would never resonate, and seemingly ordinary events wouldn't be synthesized. On one hand, this enveloping viewpoint resembles Spinoza's thought-extension parallel; this is thought's *ontological* basis. On the other hand, for Deleuze, thought only arises from obscure causes. Draw close to them and moments blend as the whole mixes with Being. And, as old thoughts fall away, the thinker reemerges with bloodshot eyes. Enter this Dionysian fold and worlds rise and fall, but each time with different subjects and objects.

Clearly, we're no longer talking about Boethius' "eternal viewpoint," but about Deleuze's *becoming* in which Elstir draws out ever-new angles by setting up a "resonance" among them (*PS* 200; 167). In this complicated act, he draws near Being's simple state, not to assume its viewpoint, let alone to envelop time as a whole, but to seize its fragments, mixing them to save them from change in the way that dreams slow time—by melding them into a pre-individual state—in short, by climbing the ladder and, from *that* viewpoint, re-throwing the dice.

By definition, "complication" mixes modes immanently because Being inhabits them as wetness does water. That's why Boethius' "expressionism," doesn't split the One from Being or fate from providence: "For providence embraces all things [*complectitur*], however diverse and however infinite; but fate arranges individual things... so that this whole temporal unfolding [*explicatio*]... is providence, but the same uniting of things, when arranged and unfolded in time [*explicate temporibus*], is called fate."[10] Providence and fate belong to the same flux, to the same immanent-cause.

Time grows from nature, but not on a preset path—not as a Russian nesting-doll grows, but as *epigenesis* unfolds the differentiated: losing its identity from one level to the next. Now, philosophy must follow science and make time *genetic* because, today, not only does nature spawn time from a seed, but every seed holds, ready to burst forth, a temporal flower. And the world's unfolded and explicated flower still holds traces of a complicated ontological bud.

Deleuze sees this epigenetic Other, not in Sartre's "other person," for the gazing person is only an object, but in the *a priori* Other embodied in Proust's anonymous letter: "One day he received an anonymous letter that said Odette was several men's mistress" (*RTP* 285; I, 387). In an early essay, he depicts this:

> A lover receives an anonymous letter about his beloved that reveals horrible things to him. The important word is "anonymous." (1) The anonymous letter reveals to me a possible external world in which the beloved appears as beloved only *through me*, and no longer as lovable but on the contrary as reprehensible. (2) The letter is written by a "friend," or rather it is given as an offer of friendship... (3) The letter is written by the a priori other, and not by any particular Other. It is anonymous, that is, its author is without determination, name, or individuality.[11]

By cutting Swann off from his beloved, this letter subjectivizes him because, in possible worlds, he can leave her. The letter also seems to offer friendship—"I'm telling you this for your own good." But its anonymity obscures its source and makes him suffer. It offers a gift, but it gives only horror. Now, like an ancient diviner, Swann must seek signs on Odette's face. But he looks in the wrong place: he sees her *as if* she really could envelop time as a whole. The hero, on the other hand, seeks time in a complex image.

The Complex Image

A complex image, or memory's immemorial *non-perspective*, predates the structure-Other that Sartre and Freud only partially grasp. In *The Psychology of the Imagination*, Sartre cuts unstable mental images off from stable visual ones. Many assume that memories are only pale photos of the past. But when recalled, they lack visual solidity since they retain a bit of their *complicated* nature. But such complex images usually go unseen, but when Sartre asks his readers to count the Pantheon's columns mentally, they become readily apparent:

> "Many persons," writes Alain, "Report having an image in their memory of the Pantheon and being able to evoke it quite readily. I ask them to please count the columns that support the façade; and they not only fail to do so but even to try it. However, this is the easiest thing to do the moment they have the real Pantheon before their eyes. What then do they see when they imagine the Pantheon?"... The Pantheon could not appear to the imaginative consciousness in the same manner as it does to a perceptual consciousness.... the imaginative consciousness presents the object to itself as entirely undifferentiated.[12]

As Sartre points out, an explicated monument would have pillars that differ. But this explication starts in a non-extended *spatium*, not in the mind.

Mental images are in flux. If I ask myself how high the Pantheon is in my mind's eye, I cannot answer. If I ask what's next to it, I cannot imagine this "next to" without remaking the entire scene. And yet, it seems to subsist in a solitary universe bordered by a Stygian void. It lacks contrast. And, without contrasting points, I cannot answer the question, "Where are you standing in relation to the Pantheon?" To imagine myself looking at it, I must alter its image to include myself in it as if it were a tourist photo. But when I really see it, I find *real perspectives*. So, because my imagination lacks such angles, my image of it is *a non-perspective*. For instance, I *cannot* ask, "How high am I in relation to the image?" After all, the image, with its *intensive* and *complicated* parts, lacks extension. Why? The answer is simple. Without another person to oppose my mental image—someone who may see it from a different angle—I could never perceive it more than two dimensionally. It lacks depth. And, though I can spin it mentally, I can never see it spatially, for a structure-Other sets up space.[13]

For Sartre, the Other affects your self-image. Only taken another step, by way of Freud, it can be made to affect spatiotemporal vision as well. Thus, the mind's fluid forms aren't *re*presentations, but pure preconscious *presentations*. In Freud's terms, they have "perceptual-identity," which gives you *mental* aims, but no "thought-identity," which then drives you to seek that aim physically.

Therefore, the non-extended Pantheon image helps me see the real one, but not by a mental-visual likeness. After all, the imagined Pantheon lacks viewing angles. And, if it had them, I couldn't compare it to the real one. That is, while I see the real Pantheon from different angles, in different lighting, in rain, and in sunshine, my imaginary one lacks climactic variants or shades of light. Thus, it has more potential to have an *identity* by being vague than any real one could.

Usually, Platonic ideals allow us to weigh images. But now, *resonance* unfolds them from obscurity. This changes everything. The real Pantheon differs from *itself* spatiotemporally, depending on the viewer. But if I actually had definite Pantheon-photos in my mind, and if I *then* saw the *real* one from a new angle, I would not, in fact, recognize it. The Platonic idea is thus refuted.

This also solves an Artificial Intelligence problem: how can any machine recognize an object given visual distortions? If the abstract image came from what *you once saw*, then it would exist with perspectives—something a machine can see. Since it lacks them, mental images couldn't have started there. Moreover, a simple question defies the *blank slate theory*: "Can photo-memories ever equal the Pantheon image?" An empiricist must reduce *the imagined* Pantheon down to *the seen* one. But Deleuze cannot *fully* ascribe to this view either. Lacking *relative conditions*—no one could ever have seen it. Thus, when Proust says that Combray rises up *as it never was*, we must take him seriously.

Using Freud's terms, an essence is a "perceptual-identity" (an imagination-fueled projection) that thought-identity then seeks externally.[14] In other words, perceptual-identity makes you imagine a pleasing virtual object that "secondary process" links to a thought-identity (Freud's term for recognition). How does this happen? Intensity splits inner and outer worlds—hence, *complicated* mental images are more intense than *explicated* visual ones. This is why you can question what you see while you're awake, but, as soon as you doze off, you blindly accept your dream. Its "intensity" is a degree of belief, not of clarity. When you awake, you flee from its hypnotic images, which *then* grow more real. In effect, your mind condenses this gaseous abstraction into visual water and then freezes it into the ice of a solid figure. With each step, it loses intensity and gains focus. This leads to the idea that real objects (thought-identity) are of a present ("the attention to life"), and that mental images (perceptual-identity) are of *a pure past* (the jumbled base of Bergson's cone).

But, if memory-images reproduced the past like photos, they'd lack the "non-perspective" Freud and Proust give them. By calling memory "reproduction," philosophers assert clarity. But this new theory admits difficulties that *common sense* neglects, for, in it, memory-images are "real without being present, ideal without being abstract" (*PS* 76; 61). Logically, therefore, the two times, past and present, would resonate, not by judgment, but by an essence that links their differences. For example, the hero could not match two events if Combray lacked "perceptual-identities." And that's why real memory-traces can't explain Combray's ideal, but not abstract, image.

Combray is a "local" schema, a "topology," not an *individual* town because, for Proust, it is "more different from anything that the towns of Normandy or Tuscany could be in reality" (*RTP* 312; I, 420). This local essence, is "the differential truth" of a place or of a time, not an individualization (*PS* 77; 61). In this way, it skirts the particular-general dichotomy, for essences aren't archetypes *or* particulars. In fact, Deleuze abandons such dead-end dichotomies.

Of course, linking "perceptual-identity" with internal difference may or may not be entirely valid; however, they both mix places and moments and thereby synthesize them *a*-temporally or *semi*-consciously. In the end, this theoretical link proves that the forces of time *do more work* and *have more sway over* your senses than any abstract chronology ever could. But Deleuze pushes Freud's insight further by reducing every involuntary memory and every resonance to three terms: the two *real* ones (past and present) and a third one (essence) that mixes the first two. Thus, Combray's *internal difference* makes actual terms resonate.[15] Without it, past and present would languish, separate and alone.

Despite their superficial likeness to Plato's ideal forms, Deleuze's essences cannot have logical identity. Thus, if Proust's readers see the word "essence" and think "Plato," they'd miss its *true* undertones. While Platonic forms typify such self-identical terms as "the just" that's *nothing but justice* or "the Good" that's *nothing but goodness*, the essences that Proust depicts, on the contrary, are implicated: Gilberte that *mixes* with Albertine, that *mixes* with Odette, that *mixes* with the portrait of Zipporah. Even the Pantheon's schema, as we've seen, lacks Platonic identity: I can neither count its columns, nor give them sizes, nor places in space and time. Even if I imagined them one by one, my heart would mix them. And I'd be forced to hold them all together in one image. Hence, this image is "erotic," as Deleuze writes, not intellectual or voluntary (*DR* 115; 85). As such, it shares almost no traits with Platonic essence.

Resonance and Memory

For Deleuze, the *Recherche* isn't about memory, "not recollection, memory, even involuntary memory" (*PS* 9; 3). If Proust studies distorted memory, he doesn't do so for its own sake, but to find something else. The *Recherche* is a "search for truth" (*PS* 9; 3), one drawn from the world—from occupying time.

Deleuze looks for ontological, not for mental associations, because the bond between events has more to do with *time* than it does with memory. That's why Proust writes: "Nothing more than a moment of the past? Much more, perhaps; something that, common to the past and to the present simultaneously, is much more essential than either of the two" (*RTP* 2266; III, 905). Not even Deleuze seeks it in the imagined past, for essences are so much more than this.

In an essence, two events resonate as if outside time. Therefore, the Kantian synthesis (the "I think") cannot grasp its extra-temporal being: "a being that only appeared when, through one of these identities between the present and the past, it could be found in the only medium in which it could live and enjoy the essence of things; that is to say, outside time" (*RTP* 2266; III, 904). The subject can't bear this extra-temporal state, which, in turn, can't bear the subject since every involuntary memory moves it. Its active synthesis is thereby displaced, for it *puts a passive synthesis in charge* so that time gathers itself, not via the apperceptive self, but via the erotic realm of essences.

An essence is a "region of Being," an objective viewpoint (*PS* 56; 43), not a simple disclosure *to* the mind. Just as the Parthenon's complex image goes beyond normal images, Proust's Combray, as an *in-itself*, goes beyond typical thoughts, for when I simply imagine foreign places, I don't feel transported as the hero does. Clearly, Proustian experiences are more than *mere* flights of fancy. But how do they differ from simple mental associations?

To understand this essence, consider how representations and Ideas differ: "With representation, concepts are like possibilities, but the subject of representation still determines the object as really conforming to the concept, as an essence. That is why representation as a whole is the element of knowledge which is realized by the recollection of the thought object and its recognition by a thinking subject" (*DR* 247; 191). By *re*presenting pasts, Platonic reminiscence evokes a *hypothetical*, subjective link. And since it is merely potential, this link must be tested. That's why representations, unlike real beings, lack *necessity*.

Only *minds* can err. Nature only acts. And all its acts *must* be alike (*a rock falling is always a rock falling*), unlike mental images (*do I see Peter or Paul?*). This inverts the Cartesian view: not the inner, but the outer world is clear because the outer one fixes the image, while the inner one shifts. That's why the hero never knows if he *really* sees the same thing he saw yesterday. Granted that it seems the same, and that it probably *is* the same, but he has changed and, thus, he must encounter it differently. So, he needs to grasp *reality's steady rock* rather than a mental image to save his world. Deleuze, Bergson, and Freud, to a degree, take this position. But only Deleuze's "Idea" takes essence seriously.

Since they mix different scenes, Deleuze's Idea-essences can't be Platonic *forms* or *mere appearances*.[16] They have an "unconscious nature," which "is incomprehensible only from the point of view of a common sense" (*DR* 249; 192). The hero runs up against these discords when waking still dizzy from a dream. His faculties fight like warring armies and, as if driven involuntarily, he is made to think the "unthinkable" (*DR* 249; 192). In short, he finds the *real*. But this "real," like invisible Epicurean atoms, only emerges in the fog of thought.

The Pantheon, for example, seems simple. But when I imagine its parts, I can't tell them apart. That's why Combray lacks the space that streets or buildings have. The mind now inundated, the entire city can't be seen. I can only sketch its *Idea*. And Deleuze pits this *Idea* against Kantian schemata—a process whereby "my imagination can delineate the figure of a four-footed animal in a general manner, without limitation to any single determinate figure."[17] Unlike, Plato's ideas, those of Kant form images. But Deleuze still seeks *real* genesis.

When I draw lines, do I *really* have *a priori* concepts? Or do I form them slowly? Kantian conditioning would cut my concepts off from my senses since I need not actually draw lines to know Ideas. But, by making concepts and intuitions internal, Deleuze defeats Kantian dualism: "the shortest may be understood as an Idea which overcomes the duality... interiorizes the difference between straight and curved, and expresses this internal difference in the form of a reciprocal determination" (*DR* 226; 174). When I draw lines, I eventually draw the shortest. Then the line is straight. I don't impose a concept *on* the world. It *develops* within the world. Thus, *a straight line implies all the curved ones that determine it.*[18]

Of course, we grasp the concept *now*, but humanity didn't always do so. Innateness only suggests a potential that experiment actualizes. That's why I can imagine my cave-dwelling ancestors accidentally finding the straight line—perhaps, the same way they did fire. I still undergo this each time I see a line. That is, I sense these variants dimly just as the hero does a Combray that mixes with other cities, real or imagined—indefinite zones that implicate other places, as the Pantheon's image does all *its* possible views—indefinite columns of indefinite sizes that make differences internal. These are complicated characters.

Being *complicated*, Charlus is a zone of indeterminacy: the hero finds a criminal, then a nobleman, then an old man, which he must link together. But Platonic essences would bar such change. Charlus would need ideal forms for an old and for a young Charlus *in turn*. Though the hero's mind fixes these images like photos, how could he grasp the protean Charlus without a *differential* essence to track him *across time*? Would such essences be eternal or temporal? Since differential ideas lack identity, they can't be eternal. Removed from time, they retain a virtual portion within time's partly unwound spool—thus, temporal (since they link events) and eternal (since they reserve them). This is the virtual.

Ultimately, Freud fails to see this extra-dimensional *third term* that links *recalled* and *perceived* images. But he does see that *difference* triggers memory: "the non-coinciding portions 'arouse interest' and can give occasion for activity of thought... which is thus moved by differences and not by similarities, or it... exhibits an equally aimless *activity of judging.*"[19] Alas, he answers a complex problem predictably since, despite finding difference in memory, he picks active *judgment* over passive difference. He thereby leaves the ego in charge.

But why leave such a fallible faculty in charge? Perhaps he does so because judging seems to link events. Without it, he argues, the mind would search aimlessly. That's why memory reduces difference to identity and the table before you to a past table. *But this is too reductive.* Only a third term, an internal difference, affirms that the two real tables really differ. The *act of judging* now abandoned, two events, restored to a passive source, can *now* resonate.

Internal Variations

The virtual is simple: an essence is virtual when it is formed by many overlapping clear elements. Like Leibniz's monad, it mixes the clear and the obscure, but Deleuze's clear-but-obscure *virtual* belongs to essences, not to monadic apperception. Like Whitehead's eternal object, this obscure essence piles up images until they form the indefinite object that Richard Rorty depicts:

> Whitehead, abandoning the identification of actuality with definiteness, solves the problem by letting in *all* forms of definiteness at once, and by making the criterion of degree of actuality consist in the extent and complexity of the choice among those forms.... "Pure potentiality" is to be found not in the *absence* of definiteness, but in piling definiteness on definiteness until no guidelines for decision between these alternative definitenesses remain.[20]

Clearly, an eternal object's complex "definite forms" and Plato's ideal forms differ, for *the event itself*, not the intellect, differentiates them. That is, one event prehends another until the *virtual* eternal object is actualized.[21]

The eternal object is neither seen, nor heard—sometimes assuming a vague shape such as a pyramid, sometimes a vague substance such as gold or marble, but it never turns into a fixed shape or quality because it links variants the way that Leibniz does many intermediate species—*as if*, between a monkey and a man, there were an infinite chain of slightly more evolved specimens.[22] Deleuze uses something like this *species infimae* in his theory of memory.

Whitehead's eternal object and Deleuze's pure event use a *third term* that does not mix the other two. Portraying this, in *The Concept of Nature*, Whitehead writes: "Two events have junction when there is a third event such that (i) it overlaps both events and (ii) it has no part which is separated from both the given events." The eternal object *is* the third term. Whitehead's Great Pyramid clarifies this further: "For example, the event which is the life of nature within the Great Pyramid yesterday and to-day is divisible into two parts, namely the Great Pyramid yesterday and the Great Pyramid to-day. But the recognizable object which is also called the Great Pyramid is the same object to-day as it was yesterday." While the actual pyramid changes, the eternal object "Pyramid" stays the same, but only by *internalizing all its differences*. It stays above the fray, occasionally inserted *between* a series of actual pyramids, though never incarnated *in* any one of them. This method solves the difference-identity paradox and, therefore, makes these eternal objects "virtual."[23]

The Birth of the World

A concert is being performed tonight "and the notes of the scale are eternal objects, pure Virtualities that are actualized in the origins, but also pure Possibilities that are attained in vibrations or flux."[24] But its notes aren't played on a keyboard. That's why "Swann thought of musical *motifs* as actual ideas, of another world, of another order, veiled ideas, unknown, mentally impenetrable" (*RTP* 280; I, 379–380). The *motif* stirs such ideas from the lamp of imagination.

By seeking its mystery in its notes, however, Swann fails to grasp the motif's essence: "Vinteuil returned to the same phrase, diversifying it, amusing himself by changing its rhythm, by making it reappear in its original form, those calculated resemblances, the work of his intellect, necessarily superficial, never could be as striking as the disguised, involuntary resemblances, which erupted in different colors, between the two masterpieces" (*RTP* 1795; III, 257–258). For Proust, intellectual and emotional variants differ. Only the latter are made *internal*. So, by recalling *the* musical phrase, Swann actually mixes all the concerts into a stream of sound. Their differences vivify it more than memory ever could. Each time it differs from itself, yet stays the same.

Since difference never ends identity, the world begins anew. But the heart, not the intellect, detects these variants. This essence appears at the beginning— as if the phrase were a universe, which, with each encounter, begins anew, with new elements. Each time Swann hears the little phrase, he is filled with joy, for each splits his life into *a before* and *an after*—a knife clipping time's thread, shuffling people and places within it. Plato's essence could never do this, for only what *differs from itself* can make time's uncoiling rope differ.[25]

This enveloping point is an "immaterial site," unlike the material one where it is found (*PS* 133; 110). Art makes the mind mix normally diverse qualities. It makes the mind overlook spatiotemporal distance. In it, dreams fill reality. And, just as dreams lack discrete places or times, when the mind comes across an artwork or a musical phrase, it also fails to discern them. Depicting this moment when isolated qualities give birth to their own world by mixing, Proust writes:

> At first the solitary piano cried out, like an abandoned bird in its countryside; the violin heard, it replied as if from a neighboring tree. It was like the beginning of the world, as if there had been only the two of them on earth, or rather in this world closed off from the rest, made by the logic of a creator, and where there would never be more than these two: this sonata. (*RTP* 282; I, 382)

An implicated world includes the bird and the tree. These are, in Whitehead's terms, "prehensions that are prehending one another."[26] The virtual sonata links the piano and the violin with the tree and the bird, spawning a new countryside on a new earth. While Swann grasps the sonata and the countryside in their virtuality, he *also* grasps the violin-bird and the piano-tree in their actuality. Notes could never stir such emotion without the virtual landscape around them.

Swann climbs from an emotion to a virtual state, from a psychological to an ontological state. In effect, the phrase fills the world with his mood. But then *a state of the soul* passes it: "Was it a bird, was it the incomplete soul... whose cry the piano heard and repeated so tenderly?" (*RTP* 282; I, 382). This creates new links: "it existed buried in his mind on the same level as certain other notions without equivalent, like those of light, of sound, of perspective, of physical pleasure, which are rich possessions with which our inner realm is diversified and adorned" (*RTP* 282; I, 381). But then, by a coup, art rises above it, making him doubt: "Perhaps it is non-being that is the true state, and all our dream of life is inexistent" (*RTP* 282; I, 381). Proust's characters flee from the sounds, to the self, to the soul, to the mind, but also beyond these, to an essence. That is, they start with an explicated note and end with a pure viewpoint.

For Deleuze, whose transcendental viewpoint *is* immanence *itself*, this Proustian journey is totally unlike Plato's move from appearance to objective forms.[27] Plato's forms are *transcendent* since they interrupt becoming, unlike the *immanent, transcendental* viewpoint that renews our world.

This chapter has revealed time and thought's ontological aspects. It opposed Kant and Freud, for whom judgment synthesizes time. Free from such *faulty* bases, essence injects the real into time, spawning it again with each unfolding.

Chapter 7

Between the Two Routes, Transversals Established Themselves

How can the world be recreated? How can vision be unblocked? This calls for a transversal—a vision beyond the artist. The transversal is in the mania Swann feels when he views Odette's possible worlds. It's what Elstir's paintings produce when he mixes the land and the sea. It's what the viewer sees in the painting, or rather, what the painting makes the viewer see. For this, a blind spot is needed. Only then, can we know how Guattari's transversal defies creativity-killing transference. Then, and only then, will we know the full meaning of "style." And then, hopefully, the two ways will meet in this transversal realm, not only in Proust's novel, but in our lives as well.

The Blind Spot

Transversals resonate, Deleuze writes, in a "questioning 'blind spot' from which the work develops like a problem by making divergent series resonate" (*DR* 257; 199). But how can we identify it? It has three guises:

First, across *an abyss*, words and images only seem to clarify each other. Hence, the phrase: "Do you *see* what I *mean*?" But *can* I really see *meaning* like "I see nobody on the road?" To these words, the *Looking Glass* King says "I only wish *I* had such eyes.... To be able to see Nobody! And at that distance too!" Foucault mirrors Carroll's paradox: No matter how detailed his portrayal, he can never make *Las Meninas* visible verbally. Because *speaking isn't seeing*, his words enrich, but cannot replace it. The blind spot, where words and things meet, never runs dry. If it could, you *really* would see "nobody" on the road.[1]

Second, like this word-image abyss, a Kantian noumenal-self seems to un-fold empirical selves like a floating signifier. That is, the floating "I" comes with empirical selves *and* with words (represented selves), but never mixes them. As a result, it no longer synthesizes time. Instead, it floats between parallel series, synthesized passively. Of course, this defies Descartes' "*cogito ergo sum.*" Though he could think that "everything was false, it was necessary that I, who thought thus, be something." But, as we've seen, this "I" lacks quality *in itself.*

That's why psychoanalysis stays idle and physics advances. To this paradox, there are three replies: a) Since Kant's synthesizing, but unseen "I think" is outside what it represents, it yields to the "barber of the regiment" paradox. Though Kant calls it self-identical (self = self), he ends up creating an Other, who haunts the I, for this noumenal puppeteer's strings can never be seen; only its puppets. Perhaps, Kant claims that *it exists* to save ethics, our transcendent master. b) Leibniz's monads lack a noumenal self. His infinite analytics only have clear regions, not representations. Thus, like Heidegger's *Dasein*, his monads are *already* outside. But Leibniz also gets caught in a loop since God becomes *his* "barber of the regiment." Seeing all the monad's corners that humans can't, *He* is barred from the set of all monads. He can't be *in* any of them. c) In the end, as we shall see, only an open work defuses this paradox by making the self shine against a non-self's hidden, transversal backdrop.[2]

Third, the steeple envelops Combray, which the enigma of Elstir's optical illusions break up. In the end, these blind spots objectivize them: unlike a single-point one, the superior viewpoint of Combray's church absorbs the landscape like a vacuum. It's infinite. But its essence, whose timeless complexity envelops this perspective among others, isn't infinite because it's total; it only seems total because it's indefinite. Thus, it exceeds any view *upon it*, for, as Deleuze writes, it's the viewpoint of "Combray *as it is in itself*" (*DR* 160; 122). That's why a painting like Velázquez's *Las Meninas* doesn't need viewers.[3] For Foucault, its unseen perspective isn't that of the painter, but that of King Philip IV. The first person turns into a third person—replacing the self-who-sees with the self-seen—for the King and the viewer share a view. Of course, a painting cannot literally see itself, but its laws impose their alien angles on us. Thus, you vanish in its vanishing point. And if it represents at all, it does for an I that *is* an Other.

Peter faces a painting, for example. When he moves, the picture doesn't change. But when Peter circles Paul, Peter's standpoint shifts: the one he gave to Paul relativizes his. As a structure-Other, he gives Peter's landscapes angles. Now space is structured. Only the schema-Paul creates an alien view, Peter's eyes only gather light, but don't make a standpoint; each place *already* has one.

In Elstir's studio, the hero learns that art can express the unseen—like those of an Escher drawing. Though non-artists may think that they see the world that their paintings portray, actually, by developing their craft, artists only draw near it slowly, for no one truly sees land becoming sea as they do in Elstir's painting.

Thus, when I see such paintings, a forced perspective trains my eyes. I learn by paradox, as Alice does in Wonderland: she can travel faster and faster while standing still, and she can dry herself by telling dry stories. At no time is the world's implicit structure clearer than when such ambiguities test it. That's why Elstir's painting contains them:

> For example, one of those "magnificent" photographs will illustrate a law of perspective, will show some cathedral usually seen in the town center, taken instead from a viewpoint from which it will seem thirty times higher than the houses and seem to shoot from the river bank, from which it is actually distant. Now Elstir tries to expose, not things as they are, but the optical illusions that

our naïve vision creates; having brought these laws of perspective to light, we are all the more struck because art first disclosed them. (*RTP* 659; I, 897)

As if under a phenomenological whip, these never-lived perspectives defy me. Like subliminal swamis, they train me to see. But this is only the first step.

In the second step, vision goes beyond its fixed, represented viewpoint and draws, instead, toward a multiple one, which is not unlike Leibniz's multiple viewing angles on a town from which I may draw my own. In fact, landscapes build their own laws. Lines, vanishing points, high angle shots, each handles them *their own way*. Though strange to say that a town has its own standpoints, since we think that we create them, the lines of a town do not naturally merge. That's why Leibniz's *Monadology* inserts viewing angles into the world as does the painter, Robert Delaunay, with his Parisian landscapes. Such vision extends to a kind of essential viewpoint in which Combray becomes a problem *in-itself.*

If each point in a town *is* its own viewpoint, do I cross these points when I pass through it? Even if I carry the same eyes with me, they don't create viewing points. *Space does.* And, when I move, roads, rivers, and steeples are synthesized. Of course, this isn't the case in the *Looking Glass* universe, where "it takes all the running *you* can do, to just keep in the same place." But this exception proves the rule. Without multiple views *within the landscape*, I could run and run, but never move. By this rule, the steeple unfolds Combray's viewpoint, not to unify, but to split it according to its own laws:

A river that passes under the city's bridges was taken from a viewpoint that made it seem utterly dislocated, spread out here like a lake, narrowed there like a thread, broken elsewhere by a hill... and this broken city's rhythm was assaulted by rigid, vertical steeples that did not rise, but rather, plumbed like a plumb-line marking the cadence like a triumphal march, seeming to suspend beneath them, all the confused mass of houses in fog, along the banks of the disconnected and crumpled river. (RTP 659–660; I, 898)

Though swirling around the steeple as if in a Van Gogh painting, such fragments don't add up. Instead, they divide into *multiple series*. Thus, the city piles up in a mass of houses. And the river, like a severed wire, splits apart. Since it escapes me, however, I can never grasp such a city, even with a thousand eyes, for the blind spot works beneath my universe. It's too complex. That's why Combray snares the hero in a Gordian knot as it transversally links spatiotemporal points. But this extra dimensional plane will go unseen until he overcomes transference.

Transversals and Transference

The transversal is opposed to therapeutic transference. Against the latter's group mind, Guattari backs a random, leaderless type of group. I will now show how, by weakening subjugation, he exceeds the "unrevealed" and "internalization."

Sartre tries to go beyond the self. His non-positional "consciousness *of* the world" undoes the reflective-awareness that another's gaze sets up. That is, a standpoint only becomes yours when someone opposes it. You're guilty—for

Sartre, that's enough to create your inner world. But this assumes you are only the Other's object—a proposal that Kafka's priest refutes: "The Court wants nothing from you. It receives you when you come and it dismisses you when you go." The Other-as-court doesn't demand guilt. You could just as easily reply to this mad court that demands "sentence first—verdict afterwards," with Alice's words: "Who cares for you? You're nothing but a pack of cards!" Since the Other is just a pack of cards, something more than a gaze is needed.[4]

Nietzsche goes further. For him, you're self-aware when your instincts turn inwards. Only then do you inhabit yourself. Thus, you must subjectivise yourself even when unseen, or when the structure-Other makes your viewpoint one-among-many. You must then become mediocre. Without this, not even the gaze could internalize you.[5] Sartre, however, assumes humans feel shame when seen, but he fails to see how this came to be—or he shows only its obvious effects, not its causes—unlike Nietzsche, who sees how bad conscience objectifies the "Ugliest Man" *even when no one sees his acts*. But the transversal reverses this.

Deleuze uses Guattari's transversal to go beyond transference, which, for Guattari, is "a way of interiorizing bourgeois repression by the repetitive, archaic and artificial re-emergence of the phenomena of caste, with all the spellbinding and reactionary group phantasies they bring in their train."[6] Like dogs to a sled, it ties us to its group superego. It internalizes us just as Nietzsche says it does. How can it be overcome? Not by protest, for that, as Job found, supports the despot and proves parental mastery.

As the source of repression, Nietzsche's "internalization" mirrors Freud's father-sublimation. That is, once internalized, a group develops "the mutual tie... based upon an important emotional common quality... this common quality lies in the nature of the tie with the leader." Under repression, Freud finds a sexual wish that "remolds the ego in one of its important features—in its sexual character—upon the model of what has hitherto been the object."[7] And the more aloof this phantasm, the more devoted such voluntary-slaves become. Churches, armies, and universities have ones. Conservative groups mimic *parental-authority* to serve those who try to be "the good child." Progressive groups mimic *teacher-authority* to serve those who try to be "the smartest kid in class." These slaves protect their chains by electing a leader to fulfill their needs.

Though this may seem like democratic progress, for Guattari, it is a regression that emerges "when fascist, dictatorial regimes or regimes of personal, presidential power give rise to imaginary phenomena of collective pseudo-phallicization that end in a ridiculous totemization by popular vote of a leader."[8] This phantasm is the group's *a priori* Other—each member, cut off from others, is internalized. And, like a child seeking lost parents, each will seek idols in every person she meets. But transference inflicts this *imperial viewpoint*, not the gaze. Though the Other abases life, once seen, it can be fought.

As a first step, each person must look inward to find signs of paranoia: A paranoid creature plans dialogue and imagines likely encounters—a sense of expectancy supporting servility. But when instincts are thwarted, repression only fuels internalization. Thus, while chance affirms, anticipation denies the future.

So, to free the subjugated egos, Guattari's institutional therapeutics must take the superego apart, must weaken castration: "its object is to try to change the data accepted by the super-ego into a new kind of acceptance of 'initiative', rendering pointless the blind social demand for a particular kind of castrating procedure to the exclusion of anything else."[9] This externalized-ego deprives viewpoints, even Sartre's non-reflective ones, of their bad conscious. Its forces now made external, the castration complex, which normally cuts subjects off from objects, unravels. This is the transversal's psychological aspect.

But the transversal also has an ontological aspect: the fleshy fold that antedates thinking subjects. That is, the pure sensibility of signs, which Merleau-Ponty depicts, predates the inner-outer divide. The transversal self-feeling-flesh, which is not of specific bodies, manifests itself in three ways: the theatrical, the cinematic, and the museum-effect.[10]

First, in theaters, each spectator sees the stage from different angles. Leibniz differentiates monads using this model—a sphere with infinite equidistant points around a central one—each a monadic view on this world. But, by submitting the monad to the same preset stock, Leibniz overlooks its anti-Copernican potential: if they could only swerve from their orbits, their difference would be truly different. *Second*, in films, all see the same screen as if, like the Gray Women, they shared a single eye (an anonymous view into which each one falls). In this cyclopean vision, each shot is frozen on a moving frame. This single screen replaces that of the Leibnizian preset harmony. (Am I thereby freed from the monad? Or am I enslaved to an Orwellian group mind?) While an avant-garde film expands my views, a propagandist one narrows them. But, because it only swaps subjective for an objective one, even this example fails to reach *the visible*, fails to defeat the inside. *Third*, when I leave a museum, after having seen some odd things, my visual field shifts, as if their images have marked my eyes: Turner's landscape alters how I see the sky; Van Gogh, how I see textures; and Rothko, my whole visual field. Their disharmony expands my harmonies. They merge with the artwork's style and, in this way, *visibility itself is remolded*. In effect, it reshuffles my deck, dealing out new visual cards, thereby re-coding my old eyes. Absorbed in an impersonal aesthetic force, I now open up to the outside. This, at last, *is* Deleuze's transversal milieu.[11]

Neither subjective, nor objective, this view from nowhere, which makes our ego ebb and makes nature's beauty flow, begins in resonating qualities—in a "pathic moment" that Deleuze credits to Merleau-Ponty, who sees "Cézanne as the painter par excellence," because he analyses "sensation, or rather, 'sense experience,'... insofar as each quality constitutes a field that stands on its own without ceasing to interfere with the others (the "pathic" moment)." This painting's quality enters my vision as if it slipped rose-colored contact lenses onto my eyes: "as a spectator, I experience the sensation only by entering the painting, by reaching the unity of the sensing and the sensed." That's why, by fusing seascapes and landscapes, Elstir's optical illusions stun the hero to such an extent that his perceptual doors open to *vision*, which dead metaphors normally close. Proustian metaphor, however, topples ones that analogize. Only such complex lines exhume eyes to retrain them—an apprenticeship, therefore.[12]

But this apprenticeship is no mere thought experiment, for thought yields the hypothetical while sensation arises *in the world*. It's physical, not mental. That's why Deleuze says sensation "has no faces at all... it is Being-in-the-World, as the phenomenologists say: at one and the same time I *become* in the sensation and something *happens* through the other, one in the other."[13] Merleau-Ponty speaks of these resonances in *Phenomenology of Perception* when he cites Cézanne's effort to paint Balzac's tablecloth:

> In his *Peau de Chagrin* Balzac describes a 'white tablecloth, like a covering of snow newly fallen, from which rose symmetrically the plates and napkins crowned with light-coloured rolls'. 'Throughout my youth, Cézanne said, 'I wanted to paint that table-cloth like freshly fallen snow.... I know now that one must try to paint only: "the plates and napkins rose symmetrically," and "the light-coloured rolls." If I paint: "crowned", I'm finished, you see. And if I really balance and shade my napkins and rolls as they really are, you may be sure that the crowning, the snow and all the rest of it will be there.'[14]

In this synesthesia, which links the snow-white cloth to his nerves, inner and outer worlds meet, for a transversal resonates between Balzac and Cézanne. A *point of capture* nets the verbal and the pictorial though they are very different kinds of fish. In the world's deep aesthetic sea, it spans words and images.

Just as Cézanne tries to express Balzac's verbal depiction, Proust explores other authors' styles via pastiche. Paved with a qualitative element, his work spans those of other writers as a path does two towns. Thus, original authors don't imitate; they transform: Balzac's tablecloth *enters* the painting. But unlike transference, these transversals bypass the artist's idolizing tendencies, now replaced with unconscious, random affects—by cutting interpretation off from authority or from the artist's transference. That's why Guattari writes "the interpretation may well be given by the idiot of the ward if he is able to make his voice heard at the right time, the time when a particular signifier becomes active at the level of the structure as a whole, for instance in organizing a game of hop-scotch." Cézanne finds Balzac's tablecloth *at the right time*—a chance meeting that calls for resonance-sympathy, which only order-words can block.[15]

In the end, this transversal is more radical than any left or right wing shame, for shame upholds all reactionary leanings but one: the shame *of* human shame. This alone fights repression. Though shame seems good when you see rudeness, kindness done in shame, not in joy, would be false. And, if shamelessness taints us, this is no reason to back shame. Under the transversal, however, repressive forces no longer bring shame. And, by entering worlds of pure seeing, I avoid those in which I *see* and ones in which I'm *seen*. Intersubjective phenomenology surpassed, the phantasmal master ousted, the slave's shameful rituals can now end: "Unlike what happens in individual analysis, there is no longer any imaginary reference to the master/slave relationship, and it therefore seems to me to represent a possible way of overcoming the castration complex."[16] In short, castration thwarts Being-in-the-World by making us reflect. As such, it only grows the more introverted we become. Shame blocks the transversal.

That's why Deleuze and Guattari seek shorter routes to desire. In *A Thousand Plateaus*, they portray this as a plane of consistency on which three illusions alienate desire. Alas, the open side goes unseen. To the west, for them, lies "a plane of consistency... where desire was lurking, west was the shortest route east, as well as to the other directions, rediscovered or deterritorialized" (*TP* 191; 154). Thus, the alienated think that desire must be lack when they find that *something* on the Sheep Shop's shelves and think that, with a metaphysical stool, they could reach it. But they're blocked. To destroy this illusion, Deleuze tells his readers that desire not only crosses an erotic sea, but the oceanic plateau, which artists float freely upon once obstacles to creativity are defeated.

Obstacles to Creation

To escape writer's block, true artists follow a vision, not their patrons' whims. That's why Deleuze says they don't speak to a public, they "give rise to" *a people* (*PS* 202; 169). Hence, Proust lacked a readership before he published his tome, but he got one because it altered the reader's vision, a vision that he only writes to capture. Perhaps that's why Kafka plans to burn his novel: to make it an act of world-creating, not of communicating. Yet we enjoy its novelty.

Nevertheless, with so many brave new worlds to choose from, many seek the most prejudice-affirming novel. They only seek themselves. But to truly write *for* such people, "write *for* the illiterate—to speak for the aphasic, to think for the acephalous," the writer must become naïve like Elstir, must write *in the reader's place*, not to envision a reply, but to remake *the place of reading.*[17]

But this making of a new people, Proust writes, calls for suffering: "imagination and thought can be admirable machines themselves, but they can be inert. Suffering is what drives them" (*RTP* 2295; III, 946).[18] Ideas without suffering leave about as much of an impression as pens without ink. Normally, it bolsters our inner world. But unlike the literary-romantic kind, this mind-expanding suffering provokes de-individuation, a mind-nature nexus that defies "the seen."

Transference darkens the world *because* it picks at our narcissistic wounds—the scar that marks a lost paradise. If adult life seems mediocre, it's because, unlike infants, adults feel shame—one to which the servile react by bowing to the powerful. Envying their strength, they study them closely. Fascism gets them hot. Thus, the shame-transference Freud depicts is volatile:

> The early efflorescence of infantile sexual life... comes to an end in the most distressing circumstances.... Loss of love and failure leave behind them a permanent injury to self-regard in the form of a narcissistic scar, which... contributes... to the 'sense of inferiority' which is so common in neurotics.[19]

In this scar, the *a priori* Other grows. And the sun that feeds it *is the demand for love*. It doesn't matter who validates this scar since the Other is general. Even in solitude, it makes life a plea to unseen gods. Such is the true nature of shame.

Sartre's portrayal of shame falls short of this. Stressing freedom, he denies narcissistic scars and compulsions—shame's roots. He misses the point. Like injuries the weather enflames, such scars reoccur. Here, Sartre is of no use. His sketch is *too human*. But, as we shall see, no one has a human nature naturally.

Freud's transference goes deeper than Sartre's gaze theory since it creates an inner world in which "patients repeat all of these unwanted situations and painful emotions... and revive them with the greatest ingenuity." Thus, with the neurotic *bond of lack*, the Other is bolstered. The rude can *lack* respect and, in envy, can *lack* the object. The Other is its true source. So, the narcissistic scar isn't an original loss, but a growing rapport with an inner despot. Seemingly old scars can be cast off at any time, but the hero would also have to give up his self and this complaint: "I can't accomplish anything; I can't succeed in anything." Fate neuroses, self-punishment, *bad conscience*, and the Freudian "unconscious need to be punished" all save a self that thwarts creative vision.[20]

Admittedly, a fictitious self affords you some rights, but it also calls for support: a judge, a cop, and a soldier. Submit and they'll grant you sovereignty. Or so you think. But their orders, above all else, "put you in your place"—under a brute. Even if unnoticed, this *bad conscience* still affects you. To feel it, Freud says, you merely have to repeat painful scenarios:

> The subject becomes involved in the misery of an unhappy marriage, or loses all his money, or develops a dangerous organic disease. In such instances one form of suffering has been replaced by another... all that mattered was that it should be possible to maintain a certain amount of suffering.[21]

Suffering is the rain of pain feeding an inner life—the self-surveying of Kant's "I think." Perhaps he didn't see how his law sets up apperception. But, as Freud shows, representation without taxing restraint is impossible. He revives *bad conscience* when he notes how neurotics repeat a trauma to save their egos. The pleasure-principle can't explain this, for even egomania is only a compensation for self-hatred. Even here, the ego sees itself by upholding old taboos. No gaze need sustain pain, for, even alone, the ego is of a subjugated group.

This subjugated group isn't a minority, but the oppressed majority—the self-oppressed adult-white-male-city-dweller—an ideal making *even* those who resemble it an "inferior" race, for none can live up to it. By it, we are judged. And, as self-surveying grows, so too does a need to be punished. But when this suffering-strategy fails—the sense-expanding transversal replaces the ego. Like Miller's "drunk on a glass of water," it opens the senses you have, not those you don't. Since transference blocks it, Guattari must find ways to unblock it:

First, he topples the order-giving hierarchy: "Transversality in the group is a dimension opposite and complementary to the structures that generate pyramidal heirarchization and sterile ways of transmitting messages." Once this is expelled, language becomes musical. It no longer makes you shout like a cop. It makes you sing like a singer, who never sings about the majority, about *the* man, except disparagingly. Though despots use music to inspire loyalty, this only usurps its power. Second, the transversal isn't dialectical since it bars "all possibility of the dialectical enrichment that arises from the group's otherness." The master/slave ends, for artists ignore others. Third, transversals expel the need to belong: "at each phase of its symbolic history, the group has its own demand to make on the individual subjects, involving a relative abandonment of their instinctual urgings to 'be part of a group.'" If they conform, artists would lapse into clichés. This would kill their muse. So, rather than feeling lonely, artists create a "new earth." That's why, even Kafka, who spent nights alone writing, shares in a world of his own making. Even great philosophers don't write for the present, but for a future filled with their ideas. Indeed, those who expect an instant effect are often frustrated. And those who *do* have one almost never last. Hence, each artist remakes the world to defy the present.[22]

This world doesn't begin in lack, as Freud thinks. Since art is mental, he thinks that it bolsters an ego. But it doesn't. If it did, all portraits would be self-portraits; all books, autobiographies; and all philosophies, opinions. But Proust's painters fixate on colors; his writers, style; his philosophers ("the Norwegian philosopher"), ideas. For Freud, however, artists fool themselves by becoming "the hero, the king, the creator, or the favorite he desired to be, without... making real alterations in the external world."[23] He is wrong. Making art a panacea, he mends an ego with a reader's respect. But this fails.

This idealized autobiography couldn't be further from Proust, whose novel favors expression over content. Indeed, he never idealizes his hero. But Freud, for whom everything has to *mean* something personal, could never see this. Favoring the human, he supports the plot. But style goes beyond it. (While people create stories, only forgotten affects create a style.) Style isn't a writing method; it's a "nonstyle" (*PS* 201; 166). Style doesn't need you; it only needs an open mind. (That's why Beckett has more vision the less he attends to content.) Above all, the writer's ego is *never* a style. Hence, Proust says that Elstir gave his life "to the task of better discerning those lines, of reproducing them more faithfully. What such an ideal inspired in Elstir was a cult so grave and exacting that it never let him be content" (*RTP* 668; I, 909). He doesn't have vision. It has him. As Proust defines it, style infects us all, it "inhabits at each instant all men as well as the artist... the writer's style and the painter's color is not a technique but a vision" (*RTP* 2285; III, 931). Thus, artists, who share vision, ignore order-words, like those of a shampoo ad, and pursue an *as yet* uncoded vision instead.

Like Mona Lisa's smile, this vision *draws the Proustian artist in*. Of course, he can try other methods, mediums, or even change artistic schools, but his mania pursues its phrases, yellow patches, and recurring sensations. Art is repetition. Consider how Vinteuil's sonata and his septet meet in this vision:

> I realized that, in the septet's core, different elements were presented one by one to combine at the end, and even, his sonata, as I was later to learn, his other works, had been no more than timid essays, exquisite but very frail, beside the complete, triumphal masterpiece now revealed. (*RTP* 1792; III, 253)

A masterpiece has an extended family in which each member shares certain traits. And, these artistic themes recur like a mutating genetic code. As its spectators, we question what it *makes us* see, not what *we* see in it. That's why, with each encounter with the little phrase, Swann's vision expands like time ripples radiating from an artistic water-drop. In this drop, the two ways meet.

The Two Ways Meet

The two ways communicate transversally and, therefore, indirectly. That's why Proust's writer, Bergotte, with his own vision, knows nothing of other writers: "If Bergotte slandered him, it was less, I thought, due to the jealousy of his success than to the ignorance of his work. He read nearly nothing" (*RTP* 1000; II, 339). And, without direct influences, Balzac's snowy tablecloth and Cézanne's paintings transversally unfold one within the other. In his fragment, Cézanne finds a universe. And, once found, there's little need to notice others.

So, when artists struggle with an ideal that beckons them to the future, they produce chance parallels. This is true creativity. Thus, imitation is regression; creation, progression. This is Vinteuil and Wagner's secret legacy:

> While playing that passage, and though Vinteuil aspired to express in it a dream utterly foreign to Wagner, I could not stop myself murmuring *"Tristian!"* with the smile of an old family friend that finds the grandfather's traits in the grandson's intonation and gesture. (*RTP* 1721–1722; III, 155)

Vinteuil and Wagner ignore each other, but they mix in a resonance, just as the two ways do at the novel's end in Swann's granddaughter: "numerous for me were the roads which led to Mlle de Saint-Loup and which radiated around her" (*RTP* 2387; III, 1085). Transversals establish themselves in this family trait—for this hereditary trace, not preformation, is social epigenesis.

These two ways meet in Madam de Saint-Loup, who's a symbol for all that lead him from Balbec back to Combray:

> Between the two routes transversals established themselves. For this real Balbec where I had known Saint-Loup, was largely caused by Swann having told me about the churches... and by Robert de Saint-Loup, the Guermantes' nephew, I returned to Combray, to the Guermantes way. (*RTP* 2387; III, 1085)

The two ways meet by chance: Swann depicts a Persian church, which leads to Combray and to Guermantes way. Saint-Loup as a Guermantes and Swann's daughter unite in this face just as Wagner-Vinteuil do in a fragment. And the hero is the family friend who sees transversal links in Swann's granddaughter. He finds the style of both families in her. And, like Elstir's seascapes and landscapes, it mixes two visions. She sets up transversals among the two worlds.

Transference's shackles now broken, the transversal renews vision. Guattari has questioned the superego; and Deleuze has shown how, for Proust, creativity isn't personal. It is style, a resonating influence that cuts across not only artists, but *a people to come* as well. This wouldn't be possible unless vision had a blind spot. This is how, between two routes, transversals establish themselves.

Chapter 8

As if There Were in Time, Different and Parallel Series

What is a memory one cannot recall? This question splits Proust from Bergson. The first seeks the past in dreams; the second, in recall. Both seek it in the virtual. But what is the virtual? As we will see in this chapter, it's the obscurity of the clear, the repressed past that shifts time, the lost dimension that pulls repetition to the present, the ontological unconscious just beyond the threshold, and the intensity that forms a world. All this leads me to ask: "Is Bergson's virtual more like Plato's reminiscence, which revives ideas, than it is like Leibniz's possible worlds, which vie to be actual?" Here, I argue for a virtual, multiple past, which swaps present-past equality for different and parallel series.

The Three Blockages

In *Difference and Repetition*, Deleuze names three blockages: the discreet, the alienated, and the repressed. Each is a blind spot, an alluring, hidden core that rouses a wonder-born-of-ignorance: ignorance of the nominal (since words are concepts), of the natural (since stones lack memory), and of the unconscious (since it's locked away). How can these possibly be clear and distinct? When these blind spots multiply time, time *itself* becomes a force. To mend its cracks, storylines must be re-sown. But the mind wavers when a foreign word suggests many etymologies, or when a natural thing recurs: one leaf looks like any other, as does every snowflake, even if they naturally differ. And this is where true difference and repetition lies: in the discrete, the alienated, and the repressed.

The discrete nature of things haunts the ancient Greeks. That's why Socrates asks "is fishing an art of acquisition or of production?" Two things compel him. First, his dialectic distills thought's baser metals from its gold. This *metallurgical method* separates discrete substances that participate in gold *to a degree*. A bed painting participates in bed-like things, a real bed to a greater degree, the ideal bed, the *greatest*. But such hierarchies demean what differs. Though they divide by degrees, does this really make the divided discrete?

Consider Aristotle's reaction. Though trained in Platonism, he broke with it. Deeply empirical in his zoological studies, he asks: How to classify discretely?

Note how he divides: some animals have wings, others don't; some have reason, others don't; some walk on four feet, others, two. And if you're lucky, you'll be a wingless, rational, biped that cares about categories. At least this is better than being a thinking substance, which could have almost any shape! But classes, unlike Plato's divisions, don't rely on participation. Instead, he sets up a *taxonomical method* to divide *unique* substances, but this ends equivocally. After all, do things fit into classes just because you've named them?

Several problems block discreteness, however. Though I easily grasp broad ideas such as "rational animal" or "human," it's not easy to apply them, for life defies order. Though the logical link "rational and animal" defines humans, when applied, however, they become "something other," for humans seldom seem rational and they often deny their animal natures (*DR* 21; 12). The smartest ape and the most debased human defy this. When I consider them discretely, my concepts shift. This simple fact saps my power to name every beast in Eden *distinctly*. Why? Though I *know* what a human *is*, when I try to grasp an individual, I'm blocked. That's why I can identify my friend abstractly. But *can I*, under a microscope, identify him through all his parasites? He is more complex than my concept of him just as life is more complex than a screenplay.

"How to define things?" This discrete-nature problem vexed thinkers from Plato to the middle ages. It's still vital today, though harder, since, in our will to truth, we've shifted the question from "*what* differs in nature?" to "*how much* difference can we detect?" So, rather than the general/particular Greek classes, a clear/obscure Cartesian dilemma now upsets reason. Concepts now alienated, the mind must face its own limits. Now, Descartes' *cartographical method*, his coordinate system, replaces Aristotle's taxonomical one. Before, things were qualities. Now, they're measured since his "clarity and distinctness" parallels his geometry. For him, you're cut off from your ideas because you judge them too hastily. But measure corrects this. For him, alienation is *only* a demon soon expelled by reason. But this optimism will be his undoing.

While, for Descartes, clear ideas are innate, for Leibniz, you only grasp them *after* you've discerned them. But, without diversity, mental images only *seem* clearer to a thinking substance. For this, Leibniz attacks him: "It is not enough in order to understand what the me is that I am sensible of.... I must also conceive distinctly of all that which distinguishes me from other possible spirits and of this latter I have only a confused experience."[1] Defined relationally, the clear and distinct remains uncertain. Instead, each thing has a concept as every snowflake does its own shape. So, if I *seem* to find a likeness, it's only because I fail to see the difference at the base of my knowledge. I only seem to see a clear island on an abyss. Thus, clear and distinct ideas are only a go-between, which belongs neither to mind, nor to nature. This is a blockage since concepts (such as "human") *isolate* me from nature (*DR* 22; 12). In effect, concepts aren't actual, and actual concepts (in infinite analysis) never penetrate the mind's threshold.

Today, such limits haunt philosophy. After Kant, even reason is internally limited. If it weren't, *could* you know, like God, nature's frozen totality? Indeed, *would* not such a total awareness be any different from nature *herself*? This

Leibnizian dream, fueled by a Cartesian drug, proves unrealistic, for, without obscurity to keep us thinking, the mind would have all the creative power of a solar calculator. But, by inverting the mind-nature nexus, Leibniz makes the mind only an obscured view of nature, for human nature comes from the blindness to the dog, the monkey, and the jackass in our humanity. Such names isolate us. Abstraction is nearsightedness; a problem, not a solution. That's why, when you recall, you must *forget the actual*. Thus, you need virtual obscurity.

But this limit only affects the conscious mind. In the dark corners of the monadic-unconscious, however, the concept is *actuality* lived as "extension=1" (*DR* 22; 11). Individuals are found in the space they occupy. What does this mean? It means that I'm not a finite mind (Descartes), but a monad sensing the whole *virtually*. Thus, I live more than I represent mentally. My eyes see more than my mind reflects. Being is an iceberg of which the mind is but the tip.

From nature's position, every detail is actual—as if, from within, all rocks, trees, and hills fully discern themselves. But, without virtuality, nature can never be self-aware, for it has *actual* being-ness since it endures in-itself, but not for-itself. This means that a descent into the actual kills awareness, for the blocks that cut me off from nature's details also bring about a sense of self. Thus, I'm not alienated. I *am* alienation! So, if I knew myself in my body, I would be *that* and nothing more. In fact, I imagine myself *only in ignorance*, the self being a mere image, and the image being nothing more than a reaction to repression.

Only in my inactuality do I *grasp ideas*. It's as if I'm trying to return to nature, but, unable to reach it, I fill it in with dreams. My mind's lenses *intentionally* blurred, I am twice exiled: first, from nature since I rise above the actual; second, from concepts since the chains of the actual keep me from pulling concepts down to it. That's why I neither feel at home in my animal, nor my rational nature. Indeed, what kind of rational animal am I then?

This is why Deleuze picks a third term, the virtual object, to fill in the aerial regions between celestial ideas and an earthly state. Thus, I live in limbo. This dream-state-that-is-life, therefore, floats between the words that I say and the things that I see without being at home in either. For the first time, I feel a finitude—not of intelligence, but of a repetition that allows *nature* to repeat and that adds memory to time. Thus, if I see the sun rise, the clouds pour rain, and the seas tremble each day, they'll attain a *sense* outside what their names denote. I live them virtually. But if every actual object seemed distinct *in nature*, and everybody seemed unique, then two days would have nothing in common.

Perhaps no one has made repetition a principle more than Kant. Besides his clock-like walks and his sock-tugging habit, his extra-conceptual time is also repetitive. For instance, why does a donkey pick one equidistant bale over another? No reason. It is simply set out in time. Then, can Kant's walks be any more rational than Buridan's ass? This way, Kant discloses time's irrationality, but then he buries it under a new hyper-rationality. Deepening our isolation, he sets up an *I think*. In this theater, time and space are a stage; intuitions, actors; and the *I think*, a spectator. The stage is now set for our modern unconscious.

This theatrical milieu is extra-conceptual, an esoteric knowledge outside of thought, where repetition reigns. These repetitions *are* the empirical or larval selves that the "I think" can never completely see. If it could, repetition would stop and the conscious/unconscious barrier, through which time unfolds, would vanish. But what, then, would be left for the future? That is, if you saw everything from a god's-eye-view, time would stop, the repressed would return, and repetition compulsions, now reduced to the identical, would stop. But this *absolute* would terrify. Though many would welcome such a final synthesis, it would literally end time. But the *cogito* needs time to act! And only conceptual blocks can set up this essential delay that occurs between time and thought.[2]

To become an outside, the Kantian *cogito* must be its own unconscious, its own doppelganger. This isn't at all what Kant intends. But, by repressing, Deleuze says, an aborted *cogito* spawns images at thought's edges (as do phantasms). By calling them the objects of "primary repression," Freud draws near to the virtual (*DR* 29; 18). Thus, the unconscious *is* multiplicity. Unable to rise to the mind, its thing-structure blocks the word-structures with which I think. Hence, it's timeless—or, at least, that's Freud's story—for it doesn't begin in a trauma. Instead, such an event is the phantasm that gives rise to the mind. Neither real, nor dreams, the virtual goes beyond general concepts and singular things. Indeed, philosophy doesn't usually allow it in so-called "serious" thought, for it evades categories. That's why it's repressed.

Perhaps unconscious repression, as a third blockage, starts with Leibniz—not a private unconscious, but the one he made for his neurotic God who represses the less perfect. *Is this not* what Freud's patients do? Of course, God picks the best rationally. But, as His lawyer, Leibniz is biased. He defends Him against irrationality or, worse, malice, skillfully arguing for divine freedom, while actually promoting necessity. But he only pulls off this shysterism by repressing *the worse*. Thus non-conceptual repression begins on a celestial scale.

Non-conceptual repetition, unlike recurring events, injects the repeated with singularity. That's why marathons aren't run by equal steps, but by more difficult ones. Words also stand on a general/singular border. Though discrete, in parallel structure, words don't retain their sense. Likewise, a concept can't be actualized without changing. When I write, a word becomes a particular, inscribed with all the sense that repetition at an exact place and time gives it. Does this not annul Leibniz's identity of indiscernibles? Words, as a set, must repeat as a recast die does its numbered points. How unlike discrete extension! Each thing has but one space and time conceptually—like Caesar crossing the Rubicon—it only occurs once. That's why nature can't repeat.[3] And yet it does.

Thus, I can tell Romulus and Remus apart because, though they persist conceptually, they differ spatially. This paradox inspires Kant to make space-time non-conceptual. Now, repetition begins. Before him, thinkers posited that, if something has a place, it does so for a sufficient reason. But there is a "paradox of doubles or twins" (*DR* 22; 13). As an existential difference, true repetitions recur in these "repetitive milieux," not in our inert fantasies (*DR* 23; 13).

By seeing all the possible worlds and by choosing the best, however, a Leibnizian God would miss nature's obscure beauty and time's repetitive power since each instant would be distinct. With nothing unexpected, drama would bore Him, for no sign could foreshadow the end. Then again, my lived-world reveals virtual objects that repeat, that do nothing but repeat, that logic cannot grasp, not because I have a finite mind, but because virtual objects have a repetitive force.[4] And this force of time is the wellspring of freedom.

The repressed isn't to be overcome, for it is vital to the act of repeating. Through it, memories emerge like worlds vying to be actualized—like the mixed elements in Elstir's paintings, which "dissolve that collection of impressions called vision" (*RTP* 1070; II, 435). Repetition starts in a resonance that bathes the whole scene. Neurotics, for example, repeat when, like Oedipus, they deny the events that recur. These events lack the process Freud calls "working through." It takes time to recognize the new, to *work through* it. For example, a formerly unseen insult rouses delayed anger; a child's game repeats in this delay. But Caesar's crossing the Rubicon can't repeat. Unable to live this memory *process*, his monad couldn't be self-aware. The mind needs time-as-an-ontological-unconscious to work through the past. But there's nothing to expel. Born of problems, repetition is neither real, nor conceptual; neither singular, nor general, but symbolic.[5] The mask never reveals an origin. That's why the hero doesn't repeat a love for his mother, but a mask of Swann's love for Odette.

All in all, these blockages, or conceptual limits, emerge somewhat in the way that an actor repeats lines with different inflections. Each repetition tests limits. But when thinkers make the repeated eternal, they miss something vital. Time goes beyond *abstract concepts* that define, *discrete extensions* that limit, or *conscious representations* that you visualize. But these limits are not due to weakness, but to an unconscious power, which injects resonances into time. Thus, they spark self-awareness. Recognition delayed, the drama grows into a series of missed clues, portending a moment of recognition.[6] Thus, memory is partial, not because ignorance must be overcome, but because a displaced remainder forms *new* differences. It's a puzzle piece that fits everywhere and nowhere. And the more you try to place it, the more you repeat. That's why the truth Hamlet seeks is manifested in so many soliloquies, for memory works by slowly fixing images and by testing alternatives. This repeated terror *is* freedom.

Repetition, as a conceptual-remainder, however, subsists in every clear thought, for every obscure zone is expressed *in* every clear one. Traditionally, the clear and the obscure are kept apart. But if you reconsider this tradition, you will see how they were severed and how they eventually come back together.

The Clarity of the Obscure

The history of clear ideas starts with Socrates. Acquainted with the sophists and their dull ideas, he goes to Delphi (or so the story goes) to ask who's truly wise. The oracle says "you are" because he knows that he knows nothing clearly. From this moment, thought changes: the path to clarity starts with a lack of it. So what does Socrates do? As a fan of the Olympic games, he uses its methods:

he tests ideas in the Agora. But he doesn't stop there. Since he assumes that ideas pre-exist the contest, he believes that, when you think, you merely recall what you forgot. Beyond all logic, his "certainty" rests on an unstable premise. For this same reason, Descartes errs when he assumes ideas must be innate. Yes, they must be, but *only if* you assume his first principles. Clearly, then, this "clarity" is a canard, for, in it, only an otherworldly realm, or Nietzsche's "necessary fable," justifies knowledge. But like all fables, it has an origin.

First, Plato fosters preexisting ideas—like the one Socrates' slave boy recalls: the briefly obscure puzzle made clear by *remembering*, not by *working through*. Going from the real to the possible, from the singular to the general, his memory lacks a virtual plane. He stops at a word-thing association, at a psychological recognition, therefore. Second, for Bergson, memory is like the "focusing of a camera" unfolding the past bit by bit.[7] But, if *focusing* is read as a Cartesian "clarifying of ideas," then obscurity would be brief—or Platonically, as a filing cabinet, then memory would be sought like a file. Third, in Leibniz's hands, Plato's preexisting ideas crumble. As a founder of differential calculus, obscurity fascinates him, for, in higher math, problems call for a step by step analysis. By making every idea *clear insofar as it is obscure*, he puts his math into his theory of knowledge. That's why he proves to the court's ladies that no two leaves are alike. Only in the mind do mental images seem obscure.

So, because my eyes fail me, I don't clearly *and* distinctly grasp an *individual* concept. The choice is: I can imagine clearly by *dimly* seeing many similar leaves or I can *unclearly* view a single one (without a microscope) and grasp it distinctly. But, as a Heisenberg would say, "I can't do both." This obscure-clarity, I believe, is the first expression of the concept of the virtual. It's that which lies just beyond my grasp, but still affects me. It's like the wave's sound, made up of many waves, which my ears register clearly, but my mind knows obscurely. This is why what I know and what I encounter differ. And, it's *on this unconscious plane* that the virtual dwells. Though Leibniz saw it first, Deleuze purges his clear-obscure *mixture* of the divine and makes it a differential unconscious, a war that sets up real accords (unlike the mind-body ones)—ones that actualize the virtual by going from a murky base to a relatively clear surface. And the deeper this base is probed, the more memory expands.

The virtual is neither *general*, nor *particular*—which are mere categories. The *particular* is seen; the *general* is abstracted. But the virtual is ontological and, thus, predates the mind.[8] Memory starts in Being, not in brains, for as Bergson found, pure memory *is* incorporeal. Now blurred, a mental fog forms in Being. Thus, the virtual is total, not by being whole, but by being fragmented.

Unlike the Freudian one, Bergson's "ontological unconscious" parallels Leibniz's possible worlds since, as Deleuze writes, "recollections try to become embodied, they exert pressure to be admitted so that a full-scale repression originating in the present and an 'attention to life' are necessary to ward off useless or dangerous recollections."[9] These rival memories must be clogged, kept at bay, otherwise they would distract us. To stop this, the mind needs an *attention to life*. But this is only the last stage—a superficial one, blind to its own roots—one that uses a general-particular dichotomy. This categorical crust hides a mantel of ontological lava, which mental focus has cooled and separated.

To grasp this underlying realm, consider an analogy. Leibniz's petite perceptions are like a television screen's many dots *insofar as they're immersed in a horizon-limiting fog of bad reception*—they must be fixed and set apart on the clear-obscure threshold, which the mind lowers when it finds new patterns. Thus, the obscure can be made clear, but never entirely. Its borders shift. That's why Deleuze asks if one can take the phrase "confused *in so far as it is clear...* to mean simply that a clear idea is confused because it is not yet clear enough in all its parts" (*DR* 275; 213). Clearly not! The clear is already naturally confused.

The clear-obscure can be read two ways: *First*, it could be said that ideas are obscure because monads are finite relative to God. In this version, the clear and the obscure stay distinct. But a *second* reading would remove God. This would make a monad infinite *and* finite: infinite because it knows the whole obscurely and finite because it views its own region clearly. Deleuze calls the second "expressionism." The first is closer to Descartes. In the second, each leaf keeps its traits, though all of them seem unclear *to my eyes*. But the leaf's general idea seems distinct *to me*, though I've abstracted it from many. Thus, it's distinct or obscure depending on my approach as it is in Leibniz's example:

> Consider Leibniz's famous passages on the murmuring of the sea. Here too, two interpretations are possible. Either we say that the apperception of the whole noise is clear but confused (not distinct) because the component little perceptions are themselves not clear but obscure; or we say that the little perceptions are themselves distinct and obscure (not clear): distinct because they grasp differential relations and singularities; obscure because they are not yet 'distinguished', not yet differenciated. (*DR* 275–276; 213)

This clear-obscure border replaces the real-possible one. Under it, in a differential unconscious, *distinct* petite perceptions still affect the mind like needles. Each one *clearly* hits a nerve, but the mind *confuses* them in a vague pain—grasping it, not *distinctly*, but *obscurely* like a wave. Since these intensities *are* virtual (from a conscious view), the "actual" actually has *less reality* than the virtual, for that which is actualized is but a pale shadow of a virtual multiplicity.[10] The actual-virtual border now clear, let's apply it to Bergson.

Though it began with Leibniz, "the virtual" wasn't named until Bergson used its principles for memory. With this, the ontological unconscious becomes a past *dimension*, not an archive for events. Seeing how matter and memory differ, Bergson reasoned that memory-images belong to an unconscious, but fully real, spiritual realm, not to a brain. This is easy. The real challenge is to explain how a virtual-past is actualized. Does this occur more like Leibniz's clear-obscure ideas, as I say, or more like Platonic reminiscence?

Bergson's actualization, at first, invites analogy with the slave boy's *temporary* obscure problem. But, lacking a virtual plane, he moves *too quickly* from the real to the possible. He merely names things—a psychological act. For Bergson, on the other hand, memory's "focusing camera" delves into the obscure depths and unfolds *what does not preexist.* This Leibnizian method doesn't start with real events. Instead, an act of recall brings about its *own* events. Bergson's camera, like Leibniz's ocean-sound, *generates* images, but not arbitrarily. It's like a Rorschach test, not like a photo. But it's never fully focused, for if the past could be as clear as the present, they would seem exactly alike. Clearly, Leibniz prevails over Plato since memory never fully actualizes the past. Obscurity persists. Thus, *it does not work like Platonic reminiscence.*

At the end of the day, no one can summon the whole mammoth of memory from the deep. You recall the past *as obscure,* you represent it *as lost,* and actualize it *as virtual.* Even when you revive it, you retain a virtual reserve. This means that *in* every recalled past lurks ones *you cannot recall*—as if, in time, there existed parallel memories vying like athletes. In fact, to light up this obscure zone, you must leap out of the clear one and grasp the ungraspable, as Bergson's camera focuses, to grasp the obscure past with your ever-expanding psychological memory. Or, in the other way, the memory-camera can shrink your sensitivity until it is vague. Just as monadic-souls expand and contract *with* their clear zones, so too does memory. That is, the known universe varies in this vast cosmic remembrance.[11] But recalling is nothing without forgetting. As we will now see, a baseless abyss, not a foundational subject, drives memory.

Essential Forgetting

Nietzsche belittles the self, perhaps because the idea of a Schopenhauerian "impersonal will" swayed him. Or perhaps he simply noted how memory, as a judgment, makes two moments seem equal; though they aren't. This is why forgetting is a problem: How do we select memory and how do we falsify it?

Deleuze sets empirical and transcendental forgetting apart. The empirical type makes us forget *something,* but the transcendental type saves the forgotten *within* memory. This type is needed to break the past-present equality. That is, when you *recognize,* you posit two equal events as you would when exchanging money. But *forget* and parity vanishes.[12] In fact, this illusion is due, in no small part, to memory's falsifying power. Usually, the past is assumed to be solid. But, what if, in fact, recall only makes it seem so? What if, before recalling, many virtual memories vied like screaming voices? In this case, every actualization would limit its rivals. Wouldn't this make the actualized seem realer? Such concerns force Bergson to make a "judgment of equality" into a "practical selection" based on needs. This answers: If no two memories are *naturally* alike, then why pick one over another? After all, levels mix in a single cone, which the attention to life splits apart—drawing out some aspects, repressing others.

For Proust, however, *this selection fails* and the levels mingle. Now, dreams and reality fuse. If saved in all its details, as Bergson says, then an abrupt failure to select would unleash the *whole* past *at once.* When this occurs, you cannot imagine it clearly. So you symbolize. Combray *is* that symbol, which masks all those opposed details—Proust's answer to: "What is a past one does not recall?"

This is nothing less than repression. Recent memories supplant repressed ones as if they were stomped under the intellect while the mind climbs ever higher.[13] But the repressed returns. Like a refrain, the symbol recurs in the novel. Just as the *already-seen* Combray returns as the *never-seen*. And this screen memory sparks such questions as: "When was it?" and "Where was it?" In fact, it stirs the mind to such an extent that when you try to place it, it flees:

> The 'never-seen' which characterizes an always displaced and disguised object is immersed in the 'already-seen' of the pure past in general, from which that object is extracted. We do not know *when* or *where* we have seen it... it is only the strange which is familiar... only difference which is repeated (*DR* 145; 109).

In this odd mitosis and zygosis, the familiar *implicates* strange, floating-qualities blowing in the wind of time. The pure past, like this wind, has its hot and cold fronts, its tornadic memories that form the Bergsonian cone "where all events of our past life are set out in their smallest details."[14] And because the whole can't be actualized at once, a screen must repress it. But, unlike Freud's repression, this one comes from contrary memories, not from trauma—or rather, this clash of memories is *itself* traumatic. Deleuze calls this conflict "Thanatos."

In the dead grandmother memory, for instance, unlike the earlier involuntary one, dissonant images intrude. This ungrounded ground—a contradiction of survival and nothingness—breaks up time, now felt as a force. That is, when events are no longer equal in memory, the timeline fades and the self, which upheld it, is questioned.[15] Could this self not also be a fiction of memory? Or, to put it another way, is the self the repressor and the selector of memories, or is it *itself* the result of repression and selection? If the second were true, *repression* would be the true reason for synthesis, for it is an "attention to life," not the self. This force, however, cannot endure the death instinct's counterforce. In the dead grandmother memory, involuntary resonance breaks under a forced movement, under an abyss that normally drives us to select, even if it goes unnoticed.

Freud discovered this memory-factory when he invented his talking cure with Anna O. While speaking, she would associate and, in time, would form new pasts to ease her symptoms. Whatever the cause, it worked. But, Freud, as a theoretician, couldn't rest content with this. So he theorized that she must have been traumatized. Hence, for him, repression and recall work together.

For our aims, it doesn't matter if the repressed memory is real, only that it works. In fact, this virtual memory parallels Freud's "primal repression": it never enters the mind, it lures you to the pure past (forcing you to reminisce), and it defies you as a *not-self* (an *a priori* Other). But it would be wrong to say that primal repression represses *something* since infantile sexuality, not trauma, drives it. As such, it sinks into a virtual realm. In this way, Freud's amnesia theory needs coexistent series, or memories one doesn't recall. In fact, infantile amnesia *withholds* them without abolishing them.[16] Isn't this what Bergson's cone does? If so, the cone wouldn't exist without an initial repression.

In essence, when I repress, I die to myself and arise from the ashes, but with a new standpoint. Neither memory, nor the self can grasp the epoch that Freud portrays as prehistoric: "infantile amnesia... turns everyone's childhood into something like a *prehistoric* epoch.... The gaps in our knowledge which have arisen in this way cannot be bridged by a single observer." Like a flower beneath a boot, the present epoch represses the former one. But like the flower, this memory flourishes again as a *screen memory* that saves all indifferent and ordinary memories, which "owe their preservation not to their own content but to an associative relation between their content and another which is repressed.'" Using Lacan's terms, the repressed signified lures conscious signifiers just as a magnet does metal. That's why, when I speak, my words draw on unconscious allusions. Hence, the repressed is implied in every word, act, or mental image.[17] *Is this not the shadow of the attention to life?*

This process parallels that of possible worlds. When it *rises above* a repressed incompossible, a compossible world becomes actual. But the coherent world is caught up in an incoherent one. And because it draws from *excluded variants*, this unconscious works as a Freudian screen or as a Proustian essence. As a graveyard memorial, the repressed and the forgotten drive memory—while one is resurrected, others enter an unconscious crypt. This forgetting is essential.

Nowhere is this essential forgetting more clear than in Proust's dead grandmother episode in which a pain blocks involuntary memory. Or rather, memories clash, for they no longer cut one path across time's desert. With many to select from, it's "as if there were in time different and parallel series" (*RTP* 1327; II, 784), as if two rivers split in his dream (a dead-alive grandmother). It's as if the mind, like a machine gone haywire, loses its selective power and, no longer seeking a single past, makes you seek a more general one instead.[18]

But, on this point, Proust and Bergson part ways—Proust to dreams; Bergson to clear recall. Deleuze writes that, for Bergson, the dream is "a corruption of pure memory.... While Proust's problem is, indeed: how to save for ourselves the past as it is preserved in itself" (*PS* 74; 59). Proust seeks fracture points. Not seeking selection, like Bergson, Proust seeks memory's power *to blur* to find time in a pure state where series coexist. Each battles while pushing through the mind—as if fleeing a building—some memories burn.

Memories, like possible worlds, form a hierarchy according to Proust—and the most coherent rise to the top and enter the world; the least sink to its base:

> In any case, if they stay within us, it's mostly in an unknown domain where they are useless to us, and where even the most ordinary are repressed by memories of a different order, which bars all simultaneous occurrence of them in consciousness. But if the context of sensations in which they are preserved is recaptured, they achieve the same power to purge all that is incompatible with them by imposing only the ego that lived them. (*RTP* 1327; II, 784)

If the whole can't be restored, what does this portend? Perhaps that recall *itself* blocks memory, not its *failure*. But, then again, what *is* an unrecalled memory? All the coexistent series would exceed its limits. Beyond it, the virtual resides.

So we've seen that, to become conscious, memory must replace the infinite movements at memory's base (the repressed series) with finite ones. Leibniz's God followed this same move from the unlimited to the limited (order out of chaos). And, in this chaos, lies the past's multiple and parallel series.

Chapter 9

The Strange Contradiction of Survival and Nothingness

By pitting nothingness against memory's survival, Deleuze not only makes the death instinct produce, he also makes thought resist entropy, for to think is to defy intentions gone awry. Though such imperfect mixtures frustrate, the death instinct affirms them. And, through apprenticeship, the hero equals such events.

Resonance and Forced Movement

In *Proust and Signs*, Deleuze depicts the *Recherche's* three orders (*PS* 189; 157). The *first* is the part object (the closed vessel), which I described earlier. The *second* is memory's resonance or Eros (closed vessels opening), which seems to negate temporal distance as do people who buy their middle-aged grandchildren toys. And death is the *third* (that breaks the second's link). In this case, an *I dream* attends symbols (no longer an *I think* attending representations) as it does for a sleepwalking Man of la Mancha, who symbolizes battles on a counter-timeline. The present rewritten, he changes their sense as do Freudian slips of the tongue. His ego selects symbols, under which lurk a death instinct.

When the hero's grandmother dies, so too does her view. But, if he grows too close to her, he'll become nostalgic. So he *disavows her*. But, as a scythe to his heartstrings, death serves psycho-physical growth, not "inanimate matter." If it seems like an end, then he knows it *inadequately*. Instead, for Deleuze, it's more like a problem, which is "acted without being represented" (*DR* 150; 114).

For instance, in the body, our cells outlive our death. And under every chess-game played geometrically lies a much more chaotic one in which all the pawns are molecules and none end in checkmate. Cells play on in their monadic existence. For a rational animal, this can only seem like universal ruin, while, for the Panglossian virus, this is *indeed* the best of all possible worlds!

In *Difference and Repetition*, Deleuze singles out death as a unique event. Why? Unlike ones to which the "I think" can be present, this event always eludes me. What happens? With death, the *first order* (the part object) climbs to the *third one* (the surface). In short, the idea that my body will decay after I'm gone makes me think. This *reactionary* ideal, Deleuze says, is thought's source, which "must be interpreted as expressing the passage from one surface to another" (*LS* 242; 208). Thus, thinking begins when I deny that my social persona will end. That's why I don't fret about the time before my birth, only *after* my death. Clearly, this is an unsolvable problem.

But what is this problem? For thought, it's stupidity or that which defies all intentions. If my body and the sense that I intend *for* it were the same, then I would, like Humpty Dumpty, merely have to see its shape to know its meaning. But when they clash, the mind is structured. In frustration, my body drives my mind to "sublimate"—a surface that over-codes the body—a process whereby destructive energies, like digestion, turn into a type of mental negation.[1]

Every instinct makes us seek mastery. And the stronger the mastery, the more loss is denied and sublimated. That's why strong mental activity can stop any vicious repetition (and why the neurotic kind always stops thought). Examples abound. Note how Schreber's memoir parallels his father's childcare manuals. The latter inflicts body mastery; the former, a mad cosmology. Thus, pain feeds thought. That is, to the extent that childhood narcissism is wounded, to that degree *also* thought will be extended.[2] In short, it reacts by denying.

Now problems forsake their empirical natures (how to feed, to reproduce, and to acquire wealth); they're solved physically. On the other hand, pure events arise from problems such as "life and death" or "the difference between the sexes" (*DR* 141; 107), which no force can resolve. But death is stronger. After all, would Proust finish his book without it? Even his hero feared, not oblivion, but the death of his novel: the event that was to outlive him. Indeed, his sublimation is strong enough to subdue his survival instincts. Thus, his forced movement produces ideally, not empirically.[3]

When this forced movement denies the depths, it mirrors its acts incorpo-really as *pure results*.[4] Physically, particles collide; superficially, events are recorded. Disavowed, their unintended results, which the body creates by acting, defy the representations that repress gaffs, wrong turns, and disasters (like the grandmother's death in the *Recherche*). And what does this do? It splits you more than any mind-body dualism ever could. Perhaps it would resemble the Spinozist extension-thought parallel. But, for Deleuze, extension and thought differ because what you *intend* returns *as something alien*—a split along the lines of molecules and pure events, not along what *you* feel and what *you* think.

As a result, the Kantian "I think" no longer synthesizes, it merely picks a direction: "I like what I get" or "I get what I like." It only seems to be in control. Therefore, if the part objects are the event's laborers, then the surface is an ontological human resources department that *misrepresents* their acts. Hence, Kantian synthesis is now inverted: this non-productive record splits you, projecting never-lived shadows that read like a second-hand account.

For example, Pierre Klossowski describes a photo in which Roberte "whose skirt is starting to burn and who leaps away from the fireplace and into the arms of this gentleman who has rushed up to her rescue and is snatching off her burning clothes."[5] This austere woman exposes her other nature by involuntarily setting herself afire. This is truly revealing. This solecism exposes her rejected double: a "pure spirit" that thinks within her, which a photo records.

This double can bring joy or sadness. You can affirm or deny it. That is, you can take a perverse interest in catching yourself *in flagrante delicto*—or, in Falstaff's words, "Well, I am your theme: you have the start of me; I am dejected.... Ignorance itself is a plummet o'er me: use me as you will." Like a good fool, he enjoys even his own downfall. Though historic agents act, historians record what actors themselves couldn't know. The only way they *could* do so is by humor (Falstaff) or by projecting it into a distant past (Proust).

Deleuze portrays this distant-past point as being "as if geological periods had intervened" (*PS* 190; 158–159). In this gap, heroes are born. But if they were here today, such Cro-Magnons would seem no more than overgrown children. So, how are they born? With its resonances and forced movements, time makes them poetic: an event *affirmed as lost*. Thus, memory's other side, a non-productive producer, takes over when you no longer select. As if in a midsummer night's dream, disavowed bits that span the horizon now mingle: "Like horse, hound, hog, bear, fire, at every turn." They return as symbols.

To grasp memory's other side, consider what Bergson does: when memory spans the cone's base in *Matter and Memory*, you start to dream.[6] Deleuze ties this process to Proust. The hero mixes his childhood with history: the Princesse de Guermantes mixes not only his magic lantern and her "way," but her family's vast history as well. The world now cast aside, there's no more "attention to life," no more practical problems (food or shelter), but only theoretical ones (birth and death, good and evil). Such large questions are pondered when mental focus dilates. Admittedly, philosophy calls for focus, but it only comes after terms are defined. But I couldn't do this if my act's results were not, at first, disavowed. This is vital. If they weren't, personal problems would devour me. Thus, I need to ponder them *sub specie aeternitatis*. Doesn't this make Spinoza's "third kind of knowledge" an annex of psychological denegation?

If this focus is an "attention to life," then perhaps its counter-movement is an "attention to death." Why not? After all, in it, I judge the world with eternal eyes, as if indifferently from the grave. Philosophers have long advocated this. But, for Deleuze, only the death instinct makes time timeless, as do heroic acts. For instance, Brutus betraying Caesar, Judas betraying Jesus, and *even* Sam betraying green eggs and ham, all symbolize the event of betrayal.

This is why *resonance* creates a lost dimension: Combray, Balbec, childhood, and lost loves. They're all symbols born of phantasms. That's why the heartbreak of death can lie dormant while it unconsciously fuels repetitions. But which is dormant, the image or the trauma? It's the *force* that is *repressed*. The image stays inert, on the surface, where event's splendor dries up all tears.

In *forced movement*, symbols play a lesser role. They're only projected: eighteenth century castles seem lost, as does Swann's love for Odette when it's gone. In forced movement, events seem realer. But Eros serves another end: a never-lived past.[7] The first symbolizes time; the second, a force. The first symbolizes survival; the second denies. With this, nothingness can now produce *because* it defies memory. The hero discovers this when he unbuttons his boots.

The Work of Mourning

Chapter two of *Guermantes Way*, right after his grandmother dies, begins: "I had just been reborn." Behold, the stone has been rolled away from his emotional tomb, but he was never truly dead. He merely emerged from a prolonged stage of mourning. In it, there's a delay between her death and his loss. Without it, they would merge. So, he must live them together, frozen before her death.

In "Mourning and Melancholia," Freud calls mourning a slowly fading *identification with lost objects*. The hero mourns this way as he kills the selves that loved Albertine. Though painful, he embraces heartache in hopes of a cure:

> At each instant, there was some of these innumerable and humble egos that comprise us, still unaware of Albertine's departure and who must be told; it's necessary—which was crueler than if they had been strangers and didn't share my suffering—to announce the pain to all these beings, to all these "egos" that didn't know yet; it's necessary that each hear for the first time the words: "Albertine asked for her bags"—those coffin-shaped bags that I saw loaded at Balbec next to those of my mother—"Albertine is gone." (*RTP* 1927; III, 437)

In this emotional liposuction, other-love *parallels* self-love because the self must be destroyed to destroy the Other, for the dead only inhabit the heart, and from the heart they must be evicted, thereby placing in the casket with them as well, the self who loved them, who laughed with them, and who admired them.

While love (Eros) idles in narcissism, jealousy (Thanatos) repeats the end in advance. That's why Swann adopts Odette's bad taste to become her as his jealousy leads to their breakup. He eviscerates his love, like an autopsy, until he sees its truth.[8] In fact, he longs for apathy as much as a prisoner does his release. And that's why the grandmother has herself photographed: to ease his eventual loss. Norman Bates, for example, kept his mother's corpse tied to a chair, and wore her clothes to deny her death. And he turned out okay, didn't he? When you internalize your lovers, as Swann does his, you follow in his footsteps.

Internalization is inevitable, for even the child, to deny the external, plays at "fort-da." The departed mother is made internal, blurring the man-woman border until, even if the beloved is of the opposite sex, desire is *homo*sexual, for narcissism projects you into the beloved. At first, the sexes don't differ. Though opposites attract, they begin in a primal repression that *engenders* opposed sexes. Thus, love nurtures the inner transvestite, not just the inner child, for this child lies on a vague sexual border. This is why, for a man, a woman embodies the repressed narcissistic child that his love disavows. Often, he dreams that he feels what she does, as if he lived in her world, for she *is* his inner child, his fragile alter-ego, his libidinal ghost. And that's why Albertine's death affects the hero so much: her corpse mirrors his death now *and* in the future. Since love is based on identification, she cannot be so easily replaced.

For instance, Ray Bradbury's story, "I Sing the Body Electric" reflects a dystopia in which a factory-ordered copy can replace a real mother. But, because love *is* narcissism, this factory would have to replace your heart as well—for, as Freud says, narcissistic love consists in loving oneself, what one was, what one would like to be, or someone who was once part of oneself. By this twisted logic, by loving a woman, however, the narcissistic man loves himself *as* a woman *for* a man like himself. He sings the transgender-body electric!

To grasp this, note how Swann acquires Odette's tastes, how he eternalizes her *in* a preconscious ideal, makes her an "ideal ego," and how, by masochistically *becoming-woman*, he invests her with a phallus. Now, she becomes his "Blue Angel," his masculine Marlene Dietrich in top hat and tailcoat, for as lovers grow more jealous, the beloved grows more masculine. In the end, he can't become-woman without woman becoming something else.

Mourning is also masochistic since a *self-attack* follows internalization. In other words, love mixes strife and reparation: the romantic strophe of falling *in* love leads to an anti-romantic antistrophe of falling *out* of it. Thus, love is awful for some. Lovers are like fleas that suck the life from them. They can only rid themselves of love by scratching. With each scratch or self-reproach, love ebbs.

But reproach is the joy of attacking the internal beloved. When the lover sings the blues, for instance, he calls himself "a no good dog, a scoundrel, and a cheat," but he also says ironically: "if I'm so bad, you must be worse for loving me." The ideal now under fire, the lover displaces every internal limit onto her. This saps his superego and lets him venture outside of himself, to live the life that a *strong* ego would block. Thus, the true *bon vivants* are those who suffer to kill their ideals, to suck the love-poison out. Thus, mourning is ambivalent.

That's why, when he mourns, the hero kills his grandmother internally not *only* to detach himself, but, using Deleuze's words, to set up a "new man devoid of sexual love" as well.[9] He mourns so that her survival can melt into nothingness. This is a paradox. He dreams that she lives, but this involuntary memory is undercut because it cannot hold or console him as she once did.

Under these circumstances, what is guilt's role in mourning? Guilt is a mode of time, a reprieve that not only extends life's lease upon the mourner, but also infests guilt with a certain pride, for mourners flaunt what the truly guilty hide. Hence, Robin Hood flouts the law, while Jack the Ripper is nowhere to be found. Mourners feel superior *in* humility—two opposed attributes, as if behind every Mother Teresa lurks a Marie Antoinette. This veiled attack upon an ideal, which makes it seem innocent, is a misdirection that makes even the Whore of Babylon seem like Mary Poppins.

Mourning *is* a dying process, as Proust indicates, it's time's irreversibility: "Doubtlessly, it's because memories do not always stay true, that love is not eternal, and because life is made up of a perpetual renewal of cells" (*RTP* 2051; III, 606). Cells, such as these, are renewed with different outlooks that see the world with *different eyes* before and after this process, which slowly parts us from this world like a Robinson Crusoe on a sinking island. Thus, without death—no ideal. Only from the standpoint of the last living man or woman does the pre-apocalyptic world seem as perfect as it does for the mourner.

Returning to the main question, how do the Combray and the dead grandmother memories differ? In the Combray memory, nothing splits the present from the past, unlike that of the grandmother, which only lets the past be recovered *as lost*. While Combray goes beyond its material encasings, in the grandmother memory, this is blocked, returning him to an empty present since he can't go back to the old days. His failure to do so returns him to himself, alone in the present, but more aware of the future. Thus, guilt stops resonance.[10]

His withdrawing libido fuels his progress. His mourning repeats *while it differs* and fragments *while it multiplies*. Thus, his death is of a "slowly dying cell," not of a final exit—a repetition, not an end. That's why the hero can't feel guilt deeply. He merely uses it to explore time.[11] Thus, his guilty rituals bring joy, a satisfying pain—the joy of forgetting by enacting, not of remembering by comprehending—not a love of pain, but a love of violence, not the violence called "crime," but the mock-institutional one called "law" that is subverted by being vulgarly repeated. Nowhere is this clearer, Deleuze insists, than in Kafka's masochistic humor. Note the scorn in "Before the Law" of the man who seems to say: "What—you mean that the law isn't instantly accessible to everyone? Well then, I'll just wait here to die just to *prove* that the law is a farce." Indeed, what would happen if a criminal were to go to a public square and, while flagellating himself, say "the law is punishing me, oh, punish me more you *great* and *just* law!" Wouldn't its absurdity be seen? After all, its power comes from *being eternally above you*. But shrink it to a worldly repetition and it ends.

Repetition is entropic. Everyday neurotics endure pain, not because they love it, but because they feel more alive, more *temporal* by repeating it. Lovers will seek out bad marriages to relive divorce. And workers will unconsciously sabotage their jobs to relive being fired. All in all, these self-destructors seek an irreversible comic-tragedy, not pain. They become colder and more *in* the present. Hence, there's an answer to Hamlet's rhetorical question: "who would bear the whips and scorns of time, the oppressor's wrong, the proud man's contumely, the pangs of dispriz'd love, the law's delay, the insolence of office, and the spurns that patient merit of the worthy takes?" Everyone! It's not a dread of "something after death" that makes us "bear those ills we have." Instead, we joyfully reenact scorns, wrongs, harsh criticisms, heart-breaks, injustices, oppressions, and failures *just to feel their absurd power*.

For instance, the sadistic ritual at Montjeuvain is a cruel scene in which the daughter repeats her father's death just to harden her heart. It's as if she were pondering a shipwreck whilst standing calmly on the shore. She remains cold. Serenely, outside the sickly-sweet walls of sentiment, she enjoys imagining her father's pain. This inverted-law flouts ethics *out of a Kantian principle*. No doubt, Kant would be horrified to see his "disinterested-interest" abused and to see his aesthetics undercut his moral law. But this isn't *just* an anti-moral law. Ironically, it *also* purges the Kantian "pathological" or sensible inclination (but to another end). This anti-law is deeply ambivalent, in the Freudian sense, for the daughter profanes her father *because* she loves him. She pains him *because* she can only grieve this way. And, in this way, she denies her loss.

With this loss comes an anger-grief mixture that breeds a passion to destroy, not only those who caused loss, but the lost object itself. Freud saw such rituals at work in the child's "fort-da" game—an act making the child active towards his loss. His mother's flight reenacted, he is free to remake *the self-other split*. The stage is set for a drama in which he "has command of all the characters" (*DR* 30; 18). Though these rituals occur in time, their *symbol* mirrors a twofold event—one in the act; the other, in its image. Though he recalls his grandmother in time, the hero's memory of her stays as eternal as a dream. It changes, but *never in tandem with* linear time.[12] In fact, as he repeats, the disavowed image complexifies. It unfolds by counter-actualizing. Three paradoxes follow this:

Repetition is subject to an *indefinite proliferation paradox* (*LS* 41; 28). With it, the hero feels a conflict: the grandmother is dead, or alive but living elsewhere; she has forgotten him, or is buried in an unknown place. All can't be true. Yet his dream explores each. And, just as the dreamer's symbolic game complicates thought, so too does a masochistic one—the real mother's loss is mastered symbolically, for unlike it, the game's iteration can be reversed.

Repetition is subject to a *neutrality paradox* (*LS* 46; 32). Though time follows its course, from eternity, the *same* mother can grow older *and* younger or be present *and* absent at once. It's renewable. Not only do the New Year and Plato's reminiscence enact reversibility, but the child's reel-game does as well. In mourning, he masters the painful end and thereby works through survival and nothingness—symbolic survival masks real nothingness.

Repetition is subject to an *impossible object paradox*: the existing-nothingness, the changing-eternal, and the living-dead (*LS* 49; 35). The lost object is recalled and denied. Like Doctor Frankenstein, it is symbolically revived, as it is in the "reel game," only to be profaned by an *active* death. The nostalgic ideal ruined, now placed below the real, Platonism is reversed. Thus, the hero recalls his grandmother only to kill her *once and for all*: what he lost passively the first time, he loses actively the next in fantasy. Perhaps he was ill-prepared for the first loss, but now, in the symbolic one, he *is* prepared. Now, he sees that time's force goes beyond memory, which becomes not only eternal, but internal to art, for fortune favors the dying: she rewards downfall with poetic triumph.

Returning to the main point, it's clear now that, by repeating them, the hero not only embraces shame, but a joyful pain that accompanies falling out of love as well, for nothing affects life as deeply as those endless hours when the world seems empty since the one who made it meaningful is gone. Nothing can so forcefully move you, as much as this, into life's ever new segments.

Where are these forced movements in Proust's novel? When Charlus has himself beaten, he makes shame joyful and repetitive, eternal and symbolic. Escaping the guilt of "never again," he adopts the symbolic one of "once more"—as if asking his superego, "Please, sir, may I have another?" This is his "playful guilt."[13] Examples abound. While animals avoid pain, humans adopt it to find what's beyond mere introspection, for an animal, when beaten for biting its master, will avoid that act. But a human will bite the feeding hand *once more* just to feel its drama. Does this not blunt religious notions of guilt? By making humans like animals, moralists err. In fact, the reverse is true. Punishment only draws us to evil, for this masochism *is* the revolving-door between heaven and hell, a Dantean ring-toss game in which paradise and purgatory trade circles.

Proust's characters play this game in their *tragic* repetition—a joyful tragedy Aristotle depicts and Deleuze calls the death instinct's three powers: a positive principle, a disguising power, and an "immanent meaning in which terror is closely mingled with the movement of selection and freedom" (*DR* 30; 19). In tragedy, Oedipus repeats his questioning until he sees his act in terror. Once exiled, he lives freely. By the same token, the hero's grandmother memory trumps involuntary ones. Quickly fading, it lacked freedom and selection. *Terror*, however, persists since it bears his earthly errency. Though the Combray memory undergoes repetition and disguise, it still lacks the sense of exile needed for *terror and freedom*. With deathly forgetting, he *selects* a past, as if redacting a text. So, unlike the Combray memory, he *works-through* the grandmother one to break free of the past. Thus, his final discovery isn't memory, but repetition—a selection and freedom defying the imperfect mixtures that thwart his will.

Imperfect mixtures

Though Freudian death instinct seems to end your burdens by returning you to matter, for Nietzsche, this is the will to nothingness. But Deleuze's death instinct, which involves the Stoics' mixtures and Lucretius' infinites, surmount this. For the Stoics, partial mixtures alter, while "the total and liquid mixture... leaves the body intact" (*LS* 109; 89). And, for Lucretius, the mind gets tangled in phantasms that promise infinite pleasure, but that give only "bitterness and torment" (*LS* 321; 277). But, if this imperfect mixture upsets, then the mind compensates. Several examples from Lewis Carroll demonstrate this: the frustrated Alice finds the "drink me" bottle and fears it may be poison: *the fear of imperfect mixtures*; the part object is the "eat me" cake that promises to shrink her, thus allowing her to enter the garden: *the hope for infinite pleasure*; the pool of tears, as a perfect mixture, holds out the risk of "being drowned in my own tears": *the desire to blend*. To escape imperfect mixtures, we concoct a political panacea, for the opium of the people is now *the antidepressant of the people—* an emotional-economic equilibrium that dulls life (Bartleby's "I would prefer not to"). So, no more revolutions, only boredom! This is how the technocrat has killed time. But once disrupted, it can pass. Two steps lead to this end:

First, cannibalistic mixtures disrupt bodies, unlike blending ones or the "liquid mixture wherein everything is exact in the cosmic present" (*LS* 156; 131). Deleuze and Guattari list this perfect mixture's forms: "the simple Thing, the Entity, the full Body, the stationary voyage, Anorexia, cutaneous Vision, Yoga, Krishna, Love, Experimentation" (*TP* 187; 151). Each one seeks mixture.

Second, in these perfect mixtures, the passions dwindle, for they only swell in partial encounters such as Klein's "bad object," or Spinoza's "inadequate idea." From whence comes this bad object? When someone rejects your friendship, for instance, or passes you over for a job, you call him "bad." But if you knew all his neurological responses, his physical mixture, he wouldn't seem so bad. This is the mechanical world (the monster of energy) that makes you *active*.

Deleuze reads Klein's good/bad object through this lens. The breast, the first frustrating object, withdrawn before it satiates, makes the infant feel like an imperfect mixture. Despite good intentions, this object is destroyed: to introject it the teeth must first grind it. This ends with an alienating, unequal mixture. For instance, when your home burns down, you dwell on the now-lost past, a regret that sets up a lost dimension. Memory now begins. This romanticized "good object" (or virtual object) stabilizes the world since it seems to repair the harm caused by a defying bad object. But when infants replace cannibalistic drives, which try to save the bad object, by introjecting the Other as-good-object, they end up destroying their object. That's why, when he equates the totem meal with identification, Freud swaps a preservative-drive for a psycho-sexual one.[14]

But this identification-substitute resists differently. The sexual drives feed off a limitless, Bramecidian banquet, like the one where Alice refuses to be presented to the pudding, who, in turn, says: "I wonder how you'd like it, if I were to cut a slice out of *you*." This humor reveals a real anxiety that comes with greed—a bad object that threatens revenge for every cannibalistic act. To avoid this, Deleuze makes *his* type of desire *ambient*. Lenz's walk, for instance, links his body to "celestial machines." He naturalizes desire. The lesson is clear: desire with these machines or let imaginary frustration dominate.

Moreover, the phantasm displaces the object: it delays pleasure and gives it a phallic aim. Alice noted this when she was crowned queen—but at what price: "Queens have to be dignified, you know!" The rule silences her: "Speak when you're spoken to." But, as Alice observes, "if everybody obeyed that rule... and if you only spoke when you were spoken to, and the other person always waited for *you* to begin, you see nobody would ever say anything." Indeed, that's just what an ideal does: subjugating you, it makes you reflect.

For Deleuze, desire is a corporeal flow, not an ideal, for men can lock you away, can deprive you of food, but as long as you live, you'll inhabit these flows. Nature is inalienable. On the other hand, there is the castration complex: the fear that you will lose the power to reach the object of pleasure. Lucretius' false infinite is at the heart of this fear. This complex has several causes: a) the mind's unlimited lust, b) desire's insatiability (unlike that reached by eating), c) desire's incorporeal aims without physical quantity, d) and a belief that only physical possession can squelch desire. But those who desire in this way soon find out—as do the candy-crazed children in Charley's chocolate factory—that, if pursued, such desirable aims will only shift to a new object.

What is this object? It is born of a fear-pleasure mixture that, according to Lucretius, those who gaze at clouds sometimes feel. That is to say, the mind projects its fears everywhere, locating them in objects that are, in themselves, morally neutral. A stranger, for example, can be hated because he unconsciously resembles a violent parent before which even grown men feel like rebellious children, for any protest against it only makes protesters more angry—as did

Lacan's infamous outburst after May '68: "As revolutionaries, what you long for is a master, You'll get one..."[15] This stung deeply. But this anger, more than anything else, reveals the *master*-as-phantasm which many resist, for they seek to be what they think that they fight: an infantile good object. Utopia, equality, or even a second-coming—no matter how the fantasy is masked, it always demands that those who "unjustly" have-it-all be destroyed and that their riches return to the social body. Their justice is greed. Like the infant, they seek the good object's total absorption.

Jealousy and greed haunt all such ideal aims. The drives must aggress more to conquer inertia. Imperfect mixtures in the depths, which defy intentions, begin within this greed.[16] And this equilibrium-frustration pendulum sets up a good-bad object dichotomy and a longing for the infinite leads you "to know bitterness and torment" here below (*LS* 321; 277). These illusions bring about a desire-as-lack that measures all your little pleasures against an unattainable, infinite one. But what's the alternative? It lies upon the surface.

From the Depths to the Surface

The destructive depth and restorative surface replace the mind-body dualism: The drives, which "our man deciphers... with his wounds," are mirrored on *the surface that records* them. That is, sexual drives, mirrored on *the restoring surface*, create *the illusion* of unity. But, like Kafka's "Great Wall of China," it can be asked, "how can a wall protect if it is not a continuous structure?" Quite simply, the nomads "kept changing their encampments" so as to have a "better general view of the progress of the wall."[17] Do we not also associate ideas unconsciously to build the Great Wall protecting our egos?

Perhaps we're moving too fast. So let's start with definitions. The body *is* the active forces that alter. Consciousness *is* the reactive forces that stabilize. The restorative ideal *is* the *good intentions* to repair, which go awry. The surface *is* that which records the unintended. The last two are Eros and Thanatos.

Deleuze also splits the destructive drives off from the death instinct, making corporeal destruction a *critical* one as Oedipus does with the Sphinx. His mental attack replaces a physical one. This counter-actualized destruction turns into thought: the labors of Hercules becoming those of Sherlock Holmes.

This twofold split is now fourfold: productive/destructive on the horizontal axis, corporeal/incorporeal on the vertical. They are opposed on each side: the corporeal-productive vs. the corporeal-destructive; the incorporeal-productive vs. the incorporeal-destructive. Vertically: Alice *destroys* the Red Queen by shaking her, but *restores* the White Queen by helping her with her shawl. Horizontally: Alice questions, and Humpty Dumpty, a *body without organs*, repairs "jabberwocky" via his schizophrenic grammar. And that's why Sade's cruelty, on the lower level, mirrors and fuels his questioning on the upper one— why the ruin of *Justine* mirrors the ultra-rational "Yet another Effort, Frenchmen." This fight has two battlefields: the one fought on the corporeal field is mirrored in the incorporeal war room.[18]

EROS (Restorative Ideal)   THANATOS (Recording Surface)
Infinite Pleasure   Body without Organs

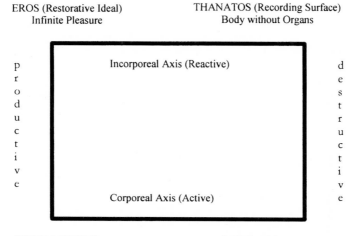

p   Incorporeal Axis (Reactive)   d
r   e
o   s
d   t
u   r
c   u
t   c
i   t
v   i
e   v
                                   Corporeal Axis (Active)   e

SEXUAL DRIVES   DESTRUCTIVE DRIVES
Intensive Depths   Destructive Depths

Above the depths, lies a two-part surface: Klein's reparation feeds the idyllic; Nietzsche's critique, the apocalyptic.[19] One is beauty; the other, sublime.

What does this surface do to time? By living in a limited present, without a surface, Alice cracks: "I know who I *was* this morning, but I think I must have been changed several times since then." But a brash Humpty Dumpty defies change: "Yes, all his horses and all his men.... They'd pick me up again in a minute, *they* would!" Assured that his words and acts are reversible, this cracked egg becomes a body without organs. But his mixture is neither Christian apotheosis, nor Freudian death instinct, for such twins succumb to the same Nietzschean critique. Instead, his zygotic, organless body mirrors a liquefied time as his incorporeal Ur-Language does a suspended one.

What are depths and surfaces? The depths, as an instinctual present, drives good-object-absorption. But it also terrifies. It becomes a bad object that, like a Punch and Judy show, avenges every attack. The surface, as a *negative* pleasure, could be called a "Captain Ahab complex": a non-suicidal, sublime fatigue. Thus, worldly-lust/otherworldly-nirvana is misplaced. Instead, we have three options: masochist reparation, sadist fatigue, and the eternal return.

Infinite pleasure-seeking only ends in bitterness: we find, like Midas, that when we destroy objects, we destroy ourselves, for every pleasure entails loss; every party, its hangover; every orgy, its regrets; and every triumph, its anti-climax. After the frenzy, regret sets in: "My God, what a waste!" Thus, sex is life-denying. Rather than uniting, these drives tear us apart. But, despite this *certain* failure, they still makes us strive for a hermaphrodite state. Though futile, we still seek it. Though every infant knows the suckled breast must run dry, Eros makes reparation—*the first effort to go from the depths to the surface.*

But what is reparation? It's the overcompensated plenitude of the beloved's flesh that seemingly heals castration's scars. That's why, for the hero, Albertine, as if bathed in a soft glow, seems more corpulent for reflecting his disavowal. Thus, a modern cupid wields, not an arrow, but an unfocused camera. By making love endure, this disavowal, the kind Dante idealizes Beatrice with, builds *a second metaphysical stairway from the depths to the surface.*

The destructive drives take *the third path*—mixing the Stoic fire with the Freudian death instinct—which works by symbolizing destruction. At first, inner sense slowly decays. In time, this libidinal grinding away, this slow death, melts away. But this ontological abortion is strangely pro-life, for, as passion cools, life grows more beautiful—a natural beauty normally blocked by human ugliness. But Thanatos depersonalizes. Its apocalyptic images expand the mind. That's why the sea's cold infinity and the desert's granular liquidity fascinate. This *pure culture of the death instinct* mutes the inner sense, not ascetically, as Freud would have it, but *nomadically*, since those who practice it live a negative aesthetics of space, sea, and desert. Think of the body without organs as libidinal Liquid Drain-o. Freeing flows by stopping drives, a surface forms as Erato's lyrical moon eclipses Eros's passionate sun.[20]

This way from the corporeal to the incorporeal has three steps: inner sense (self-consumption), repression (that stops this sense), and the verb (language). The last is impenetrable. It's no wonder, then, that when Humpty Dumpty asserts mastery over words, he sees how tricky they are, especially verbs: "They've a temper, some of them—particularly verbs, they're the proudest—adjectives you can do anything with, but not verbs." To master them, he must endure a primary repression, which leads to the surface, by naming his shape: "*my* name means the shape I am." How brash! Language reflects acts, but with a difference: verbs don't act—they merely record. One act has many bodies, but only one word. Thus, Mr. Dumpty's "impenetrability" can mean "that we've had enough of that subject, and it would be just as well if you'd mention what you mean to do next, as I suppose you don't intend to stop here all the rest of your life." Bodies differ, but each has a certain oomph of verbal impenetrability.

On this verbal level, the aggregate of persons, places, and things would splinter without the verb, without the surface on which events spread. This is the "verbal representation," which is the "affirmative power of the disjunction (univocity, with respect to that which diverges)" (*LS* 281; 241). The verb translates bodies into problems (the *chaosmosis* that Humpty Dumpty's riddles or that James Joyce's *Finnegan's Wake* produce). Resonance occurs because reparation drives us to order verbal chaos. Such puzzles fascinate. Hence, the hero's interest in place names, for they return words to a primal, twisted tongue. And that's why he's in Albertine's grip, for she envelops as many possible worlds as places do names. But when she dies, he forsakes his self-destructive love for a world-destruction. In his work, you see, enacted, what Deleuze calls a shift from destructive drives to the monstrosity of the death instinct.[21]

Monstrosity

Just as Kant's categorical imperative squelches passion, thought does so for a total critique, not for the sake of good or evil, but for a suspended judgment in the face of a natural-human monstrosity. But such rational violence is only for the morally sensitive, for comics only joke so cruelly because they aren't brutes.[22] That's why, at Montjeuvain, Vinteuil's daughter stays *neutral*. She only pretends to defile her father. She is violent, not because she lacks feeling, but because she has too much of it. Through cruelty, Proust says, she flees her normally sensitive soul: "it is in the skin of the wicked in which they implicate their partners, to have the momentary illusion of flight from their scrupulous, tender souls to a world of inhuman pleasure" (*RTP* 136; I, 179). Such sadists mime evil. This categorical imperative raises passion to a fit of reason without sublimating it. This force drives us to question everything like Dostoyevsky's underground man, but with a Nietzschean hammer.

But this cruelty isn't that of a bitter critic. The anger normally heard in a philosophical symposium is still *too* fanatical. Yes, philosophy must be critical, but it must also be joyful. Rational cruelty doesn't attack piecemeal, however. It serves intellectual revolution, not rational reform. Its negative plateau bears a negative pleasure. For example, Hamlet, waxing philosophically, thinks like a mad calculator that plots out every path. And Sade, in *One Hundred and Twenty Days of Sodom*, does nothing more than coldly list every horror. Advocating every devil, his critical power is superior to practice: as a pure sadist, he saves monstrosity by *not* acting, for only thought guarantees that no mental cop (of remorse) can raid his personal dungeon.[23]

But here's the real secret: ironically, sadists are pious Spinozists aspiring to the eternal. They long to return to nature's perpetually destroying substance, to be as indifferent as Vesuvius. For them, *diabolus sive natura* replaces *deus sive natura*. Then again, the masochist obeys the Spinozist maxim: "He who loves God cannot endeavor that God should love him in return."[24] For the masochist only loves cold idols. Together, their theater of cruelty parallels nature's apathy.

Moreover, this critical negativity blocks the paranoia often linked with the destructive drives. Alice, for example, grows as a *result* of eating the cake. She cries because she feels *persecuted*. Thought is a *result*. But the resentful bar *results*, for in anger, lust, greed, or hatred, the mind slumbers. Drowned in passion, the vengeful seek to punish; the greedy, to acquire; the hateful, to prove others inferior. In passion, thought's surface melts. Like them, Kant focuses on *intentions*, not on results. The Good is an intention, but a sadist's *evil* is nature's vicious immanence—a pure result. The good categorical imperative upholds reparation (intention: restoration); its evil twin, thought (result: castration).

Unlike crime, however, sadism is aristocratic. It makes vulgarity more noble than nobility itself! Imagine an old aristocratic couple in a sadistic scene: "My dear sir, if it doth please thee, beateth me with thy most gracious whip." Their pretentious words oppose their vulgar sense. This irony *desexualizes* Eros, thereby swapping transcendent sublimation for an immanent *being of sensation*. Thus, sadism surpasses the law to a higher, more perverse principle.

But why should sadism be a higher law? This theater of cruelty shocks us out of *offense-and-apology* and replaces it with a wonder that can only be stopped by orgasm, which a plateau, or an endless "working-through," impedes.

This repetition sustains it, unlike moral fear, which fixes its ends (as did medieval thinkers). Against this, Deleuze pits a playful monstrosity.[25]

Of course, conscience is still important. After all, freedom or mutual respect couldn't be secured without it. But without the initial freedom to criticize, no one could critique the modern prejudices that would *actually ban* freedom and mutual respect. In effect, sadistic irony, places the so-called "greater good" of tradition into question: Slave owners justified slavery, early capitalists justified child labor, early churches justified burning heretics, perhaps early man justified walking on all fours. Clearly, those who speak to the future must defy the "goods" of the present. They must dance with the devil to kill a few false gods.

But what happens to this devil's advocate when he grows a conscience? He dies. Sometimes thought must play hypothetically. But this grows tiresome and regret returns. For Klossowski, only repetition bars such orgasmic meltdown:

> Monstrosity is the zone of this being *outside of oneself, outside of conscience*; the monster can maintain himself in this zone only by the reiteration of the same act. The "voluptuous harshness"... is no longer something sensuous: the "harshness" presupposes a distinction between thought and moral conscious; the "voluptuousness" alludes the ecstasy of thought in the representation of the act reiterated "in cold blood"... opposed to its functional analogue, orgasm.[26]

This endless iteration, without an orgasmic end, occurs for the sake of problems, not for pleasure. Hence, above pleasure, Deleuze places the negative joys of Thanatos—fully cerebral joys that belong to the soberness of age. After all, the dying realize what they'll soon lose, while hedonists take life for granted.[27]

As a final point: Nietzsche can only critique on this plateau. But when it overpowers him, he sinks into the depths.[28] Then, headaches, pain, *ressentiment* and *bad conscience* haunt him. Then, he succumbs, in his depression, to the illness he finds in society. Like him, the world allows you but a few moments to think. Every demand on your time, every person who wants to chat, every paper that needs signing—not to mention the need to work—all, in the end, keep you from thinking. Despite these obstacles, Nietzsche seems to uphold thought without letting *personal* fury drive it. Indeed, his vigor often moves his readers to *do* philosophy. But, in the end, he could not hold on to this impersonal force without reverting to his grudge against Wagner or Lou Solomé. Of course, he'd be the first to admit that he's all too human. Clearly, he yields to an illness (depression and mania), which, I suggest, returns him to introjection and projection's destructive *depths*, thereby cracking his thought plane. In this way, he spans the gap between the *death instinct* and the *destructive drives* that finally drove him mad.

In this chapter, we've seen how Deleuze makes death produce not only time and thought, but freedom and ethics as well. He restores death to life, the body to thought, mourning to joy, paradox to logic, and monstrosity to ethics. In the end, the death instinct isn't the end, but the conflagration the Stoics depict. And, from chaos comes a resonance and a forced movement that makes us think.

Conclusion

We've seen time's *results* in its intermittencies. And, in its gaps, distances arise, complications unfold, and contradictions emerge. But now that the door closes on its ontological aspects, the study of paradoxes has ended. It's time to sum up.

Consider a world in which you lack identity. A tall man would see you as short; a short one, as tall. Now relative, preset harmony ends. To defy this state, your mind must project an ideal self: replacing lost wealth with true wealth unrelated to money; lost love, with a true love unrelated to affection. Doesn't this deny the present? After all, *if* you were idealized in the past, *then* wouldn't you ignore the present? This happens when the present changes incorporeally.

Consider Swann's anonymous letter. He seeks its truth: Who wrote it? And is it true? This forces him to unfold a complicated, obscure, solutionless problem. Nevertheless, he imagines a vague image. In effect, this gives rise to an Other that *is* complexity (the One equals Being) from which he extracts *possibility* (the One below Being). That's why an anonymous realm makes you draw signs *from* complex-necessity *into* the realm of possibility.

Consider what would happen if the true world vanished. Friends, no longer agreeing upon words, would become strategists of signs. But in such a world, how would they learn? Learning would arise from an *open work*, a blind spot that Elstir's paintings, Swann's jealousy, or Cottard's diagnoses produce. Given the choice between a despotic signifier (truth) and a floating signifier (experiment), the artist can only pick the latter. But several things block this. Not only must he give up passivity, thereby swapping the superego's orders for initiative, but he must also seek a subliminal muse rather than merely aping others.

The hero faces a barrier to creativity. First, he's too internal or neurotic since he seeks failure because he writes *for others* when he asks for Norpois's approval. Finally, he fetishizes the literary profession when he tries to *be* one of the great writers. Such roadblocks set up an aim that makes him mediocre. In effect, he doesn't realize how writing transmits signs poetically, to produce an affect, not to dialectically engage readers. He fails to write when he thinks writing is interpretation. He only starts to write when he experiments.

Consider the mystery of memory. Do our general ideas stem empirically from our actual past, ideally from our innate mind, or Platonically from some time before birth? On one hand, some believe in "clear ideas" that are only reached after reflection. On the other hand, the past *itself* seems unclear and in need of selection. Both fail to analyze ideas adequately. What's meant by "recall" is merely a subjective act that posits equality between moments. And when they cohere in this way, they support the idea of a subject.

Nevertheless, three obstacles bar this clear and distinct, subjective reflection: first, when the thinker uses a general concept, it ceases to be general (the concept "animal" differs in a horse and in a human); second, the general concept is more vague than a thing (the rose is more vivid than its abstract image); third, a general concept only arrives after many misrecognitions (the comic or tragic actor must repeatedly err until he comes to a moment of recognition). These three obstacles to clarity and distinctness show that, in fact, the clear is actually obscure. Therefore, recollection doesn't extract an equal moment from the past. Instead, it enforces equality. Thus, there must be a virtual or unequal *pure past* that doesn't let itself be recalled in this way. Given this situation, Proust tries to recover this *past that one cannot recall*.

Consider what occurs to the hero when he realizes that his grandmother is dead. Vast distances in time are felt, his masochism grows, and, eventually, he becomes an artist. But without this slow death, he would neither come to his insights about art, nor would he think. Therefore, memory and resonance aren't enough to produce thought. Sure, they bring about ecstatic encounters, like the tea and madeleine episode, but they don't engender the insights that come with painful experience. Therefore, the hero must delve into life's mixtures, live its chaos, and test its intermittences. In the end, he comes to a monstrous result. For instance, the more the novel progresses, the more sadism and masochism occur: Charlus has himself beaten, the hero taunts Albertine with his letters, and Berma is sidelined. Evil becomes a principle used to test these intermittences. And, in the end, they reveal their force through their unintended results.

These five *considerations* have been examined in the last five chapters. These are time's pure "results." And, though these forces of time are not time itself, they express it indirectly. They show how you can sense it and how you can alter it. For instance, nostalgia and forgetting, otherness and possibility, the clear-actual and the obscure-virtual, not to mention the destructive depth and the creative surface, all show how time affects your sensibilities and how these affects can be used. This has been the role of part two.

This part has gone beyond the intensive, continuous sense of time and has shown what happens when events are envisaged: time breaks into segments— into days, weeks, and years. Large gaps appear. These *results* of time no longer cohere. But without them, time would neither move, nor have any force. This second part has shown us why.

General Conclusion

Proust at Last

To sense time's force, to perceive its signs, and to open himself up to its folds, the hero must take up a line of flight. But this line is torn between the depressive and schizoid positions—between resonance and forced movement. That is, there are two ways to take flight: to fly toward possible worlds (those distant lands and exotic women of which the hero dreams), or to fly toward unknown worlds (the unknowable lesbianism and expanses of empty time). Love and jealousy, Eros and Thanatos, idealization and destruction, are all poles to which Proust's pendulum swings. They underlie the incredible forced movements that drive his line of flight. But, beyond all these things, there's also the profound technique Proust develops: profanation—the heart of his destructive humor—the lever that moves this whole machine.

How? It plays off guilt and weakens it; destroys envy and rivalry, the accursed legacy of depressive Platonism; overcomes the stagnation and the fixity that impedes thought and creativity; and weakens the effect of the Other's judgment. All these change his sensitivity to time. In short, the *aim* of Proust's system is to bring about this sensitivity; its *means* is the line of flight; its *problem* is the schizoid and depressive positions; and its *solution* is profanation and humor. In this way, it opposes the abstractness of traditional philosophies of time. All the episodes examined in this book add to this:

We've seen how guilt extends time by a line of flight. The hero feels this when his father lets his mother sleep in his room or when he lets him go to the theater. We've seen how this brings about a new sense of time: not the inner, intensive one the hero feels when he anticipates a kiss, but the extended and historical one he senses when he realizes how much his friends have aged.

We've seen how this force of time thwarts interpretation and calls for thinking through signs instead. That is, by asking what a sign does, not what it means, Cottard and Norpois use natural and deceptive signs. With insight, but little taste, Cottard must diagnose through signs. This is his non-interpretation, for unlike Madam Verdurin, who symbolically expresses grief over the musician's death, Saint-Loup, as a soldier, must think strategically to read the deceptive signs that his foe lets slip. Thus, the sign is always an encounter. And the hero must confront disappointing signs if he is to learn to become a writer. He sees this learning at work in Swann, who must read signs of remorse on Odette's face—or in Charlus, whose attacks elicit signs—a kind of non-language, which each of these characters reads.

We've seen how these signs come with the explication and the complication of worlds. Combray-in-a-teacup complicates a whole spatiotemporal region into a single bloc of becoming. But the hero does not truly know this involuntary memory's nature (a fragment of time in a pure state) until he reencounters it in the waiting room. He finds that these time-fragments get their intensity from repetitions like those of a musical phrase. Like life, the phrase returns in different scenes and with different accompaniments, but each time it draws the whole past along with it. Likewise, Vinteuil's little phrase delves into an artistic vision, differing each time, yet forever in search of a pure artistic fragment—a melody, or a little patch of yellow. This fragment has an aesthetic aspect, which the hero finds in the complicated angles of Elstir's paintings. It has a sexual aspect, which the hero finds in Charlus's uncertain sexuality. It has an amorous aspect, which Swann finds in the anonymous letter that accuses Odette of lesbianism. These are the transversal aspects that cause fragmented part objects to resonate across time and space.

We've seen how profanation destroys the phantasms that enslave the hero—phantasms such as the Freudian "primal scene," which the hero evokes when he wrestles with Gilberte in the garden. Vinteuil's daughter casts off this kind of phantasm when she threatens to spit on her dead father's portrait. And the Verdurins abolish it by ridiculing the president of the republic after they hear that Swann dines with him. And it's this kind of phantasm that the hero expels when he forsakes his romantic fantasies and, instead, seeks to profane the body of the Putbus's maid. In each case, a phantasm denies them a world of inhuman pleasure. This is the pleasure that the hero feels when he's among his hawthorn trees. But as soon as he falls in love with Albertine, he's cut off from this natural world of becoming. Only when he sees her asleep, can he recapture it in her silent, meaningless flesh. Only then does the world become *his*. Not until she dies, does he finally escape from the depressive position in which she had entrapped him. If only Swann had outlived Odette, perhaps then he too would have found the schizoid realm of art that his depressive love had blocked.

We've seen how this depressive position can make us sense the nostalgic illusion of distance. When the hero dreams of exotic places and women, when he's forced to give up Gilberte, when Swann idealizes Odette using Zipporah's portrait, and when Saint-Loup alone sees beauty in Rachel, there's a depressive Platonism at work that makes places seem distant, loves more ideal, and faces more beautiful. Certainly, the hero engages in these idealizations in the beginning when he uses art as a window into possible worlds, or when he imagines that Albertine cheats on him. But he saves these ideals by staying home and relying on his spies to report her transgressions rather than constantly staying near her. He prefers this distance for the same reason that he prefers having the partition between him and his grandmother: through it, he retains the type of beauty only distance can preserve. He knows what happens when beauty is seen directly because he has seen Rachel at close range. Only his love-struck friend sees her distantly. By imagining other places and times, the hero feels separated from them. These are his closed vessels. And because they cannot be reached in an instant, even by train, they become segmented places surrounded by the fog of empty space and time. But, still, they resonate.

We've seen how the schizoid position gives birth to unknowable worlds, not the unified worlds that he imagines through art, but those fragmented ones that he finds through Albertine's lesbianism. By pointing out how the dancing girls arouse each other, Cottard enflames the hero to imagine this unknowable lesbian world. He can imagine the sensations that occur between a man and a woman by a simple reversal in his mind, but he cannot imagine what this arousal between women could be like, for he lacks a woman's skin. This is the secret behind the band of girls. Their nebulous mixture seems to be an unknowable viewpoint on a world that bars him. It's fragmented because it's disguised. Just as Charlus disguises his real tastes behind a mask of virility to hide his member-ship in the homosexual underground. And, perhaps Albertine's love for the hero is also a disguise. Through Charlus and Albertine, the hero learns the art of deception subliminally. That is, he learns how to manipulate symbols to mask his true feelings. But this shifting symbolic mask only brings about more fragmentation. With the Dreyfus trial, society suddenly shifts. By continuing to praise Swann after he was exiled from the group, Cottard faces rebuke and finds that signs have changed. Time breaks with these symbols. Though they disguise the underlying flux of becoming (just as Saint-Loup's family cares more about symbolic appearances than they do about his emotions when they ask the hero to make him renounce Rachel) the symbol also aids displacement, just as, by not being able to travel on them both on the same day, the two ways come to symbolize division. Sometimes they show their underlying violence, as they do when the hero imagines that he hears a fight in the adjacent shop, but realizes that pain's sound is also that of pleasure. These are the violent divisions that drive the forced movements in Proust's novel.

We've seen how these forced movements produce a slow demolition of life and a sense of death. Beaten down by time, Swann loses interest in faces and sees the world's true beauty. And, having destroyed the selves who loved her one by one, the hero forgets Albertine in stages. These fatalistic strategies aren't brought about by a desire to die, but by a desire to live purely, with a cold, realistic vision. After the hero stops trying to replace Albertine by becoming her, he releases all the libidinal energy that was bound up with her. He now gives it over to the creation of his future novel. By investing in art-as-a-superior-viewpoint, he finds that style is not a personal expression, but the shared vision of a future people. It mixes incompatible realities, such as the living-dead grandmother, and mixes it within a complex metaphor as Elstir's paintings do— by setting up a resonance between them. In the end, the hero finds that the two ways really do meet in the face of Swann's granddaughter. She's the ultimate metaphor, mixing parallel worlds that, though they were once separate, are now joined by the decay of society. This is the secret of the transversal: the slow death of the body, physical and social, brings about the mixture of different and parallel series. Like Wagner and Vinteuil's little phrase, they start to sound alike since time deafens even the most attentive listener. That is its force.

What philosophical changes does this reading of Proust suggest? It suggests that, where once representation and the abyss were opposed, it now faces a formless time; that, the "meanwhile" of empty time was once what recollection would fill, it now replaces recognition; that, where thought was once other-worldly, worldly ruin now drives thought; and that, where creation was once the expression of personal genius, it now confronts a complicated blind spot. Ultimately, the shift from the depressive consciousness of time to a more schizoid one, which I've depicted in this book, could not only renew our thoughts about time, but could bring about a new sense of its force as well.

Notes

General Introduction: The Story of N

1. Bernard Groethuysen, "De quelques aspects du Temps. Notes pour une phenomenology du Récit," *Philosophie et histoire* (Paris: Éditions Albin Michel, 1995), 218.
2. Ibid.
3. Ibid.
4. Ibid.
5. Ibid., 221.
6. Ibid., 223.
7. Ibid., 224.
8. Ibid., 224-225.
9. Ibid., 225.
10. Ibid., 227-228.
11. "Boulez, Proust and Time: 'Occupying Without Counting,'" trans. T. Murphy (*Angelaki* 3.2, 1998), 72. "Occuper sans compter: Boulez, Proust et le temps" *Deux Régimes de fous* (Paris: Les Editions de Minuit), 278.

Chapter 1: A Sort of Magnifying Glass

1. Modern art "has no problem of meaning, it only has a problem of use" (*PS* 176; 146).
2. Plato, "Timaeus," *Collected Dialogues*, Edited by E. Hamilton & H. Cairns, New Jersey: Princeton University Press, 1961, 47a; Stephen Gaukroger, *Descartes: An Intellectual Biography* (Oxford: Oxford University Press, 1997), 368; Immanuel Kant, *Critique of Pure Reason*, trans. N. K. Smith (New York: Palgrave, 2003), 74; Edmund Husserl, *Ideas: General Introduction to Phenomenology*, trans. W. R. B. Gibson (London: Collier Macmillan Publishers, 1962), 218.
3. For Spinoza, the mind's power "will vary in proportion to the variety of states which its body can assume," *The Ethics, Treatise on the Emendation of the Intellect and Selected Letters*, trans. S. Shirley (Indianapolis: Hackett Publishing Co., 1992), 76 (II, Pro. 14). For example, a stickleback becomes "less aggressive in red or blue light." Rémy Chauvin & Bernadette Muckensturm-Chauvin, *Behavioral Complexities*, trans. J. Diamanti (New York: International University Press, 1980), 134-135.
4. G. W. Leibniz, *Philosophical Writings*, trans. M. Morris & G. H. R. Parkinson. Ed. G. H. R. Parkinson (New York: The Everyman Library, 1995), 212; Kant depicts this nexus: "transitions can be empirically known only as changing determinations of that which is permanent," *Critique of Pure Reason*, 217.
5. Ibid., 205; time's internal genesis is an "intensive quantity rather than schema," which is "related to Ideas rather than to concepts of the understanding" (*DR* 40; 26).
6. Ibid., 77. However, no representation, not even a line, can represent time because "representation is above all the eviction of time," because "one stops time in an image, in a present representation." Instead, it is "the crack that forces thought... the empty form of time as a death instinct, as an ontological problem." Véronique Bergen, *L'Ontologie de Gilles Deleuze* (Paris: L'Harmattan, 2001), 228 & 229 (my trans.).
7. Ibid., 214.
8. Deleuze, "Boulez, Proust and Time,'" 70. "Occuper sans compter," 274.
9. Charles Darwin, *The Origin of Species by Means of Natural Selection or The Preservation of Favored Races in the Struggle for Life* (London: Senate, 1994), 426.

10. Gilles Deleuze, *Bergsonism*, trans. H. Tomlinson & B. Habberjam (New York: Zone Books, 1991), 33. *Le bergsonisme*, (Paris: Presses Universitaires de France, 1966), 24. Intuition is "a complex process that is a goal of knowledge, not a starting point." Bruce Baugh, "Transcendental Empiricism," *Man and World*, 25 (1992), 141.

11. Deleuze, *Bergsonism*, 32. *Le bergsonisme*, 24; *Critique of Pure Reason*, 206.

12. Plato, "The Sophist," *Collected Dialogues*, 254a; For Deleuze, "when Plato formulated his method of division, he too intended to divide a composite into two halves.... But the whole problem lay in knowing how to choose the right half." *Bergsonism*, 32. *Le bergsonisme*, 24; Plato, "Timaeus," *Collected Dialogues*, 47c.

13. Spinoza, *The Ethics*, 72 (II, Pro 13, L. 1).

14. Immanuel Kant, *Groundwork of the Metaphysic of Morals*, trans. H. J. Paton (New York: Harper Torchbooks, 1956), 70. The law "does not tell us what we must do" Gilles Deleuze, *Essays Critical and Clinical*, trans. D. W. Smith & M. A. Greco (Minneapolis: University of Minnesota Press, 1997), 32. *Critique et clinique* (Paris: Les Editions de Minuit, 1993), 46.

15. Renunciation increases "the strength and severity of conscience." Gilles Deleuze, "Coldness and Cruelty," *Masochism* (New York: Zone Books, 1989), 84.

16. Deleuze, *Kant's Critical Philosophy: The Doctrine of the Faculties*, trans. Tomlinson & Habberjam (Minneapolis: University of Minnesota Press, 1984), 37. *La philosophie critique de Kant* (Paris: Presses Universitaires de France, 1962), 55.

17. Gilles Deleuze, *Essays Critical and Clinical*, 33. *Critique et clinique*, 47. Bergen claims that "Deleuze inextricably links the Kantian liberation of time's empty form to that of the practical, moral law," *L'Ontologie de Gilles Deleuze*, 245 (my trans.). The law's real transcendent enemy is the mental phantasm, not the life of the body.

18. Plato, "The Republic," *Collected Dialogues*, 546a.

19. Pleasure (freedom from pain) should not spur morality: "the pursuit of happiness cannot possibly produce morality." Immanuel Kant, *Critique of Practical Reason*, trans. T. K. Abbott (New York: Prometheus Books, 1996), 144.

20. Ibid., 155; Deleuze, *Essays Critical and Clinical*, 33. *Critique et clinique*, 47.

21. Spinoza, *The Ethics*, 81 (II, Pro 23); Gilles Deleuze, *Spinoza: Practical Philosophy*, trans. R. Hurley (San Francisco: City Lights Books, 48), 48 & 49.

22. Intensity is diminished "from empirical consciousness to pure consciousness" Kant, *Critique of Pure Reason*, 201.

23. Kant, *Critique of Practical Reason*, 142; Deleuze, *Kant's Critical Philosophy*, 37. *La philosophie critique de Kant*, 55.

24. Franz Kafka, *The Trial*, trans. W. Muir, E. Muir, E. Butler (New York: Schocken Books, 1984), 213; The law is "repressed desire," "Coldness and Cruelty," 85.

25. Ibid., 211; To submit is pleasant: "by the closest adherence to it... we may hope to partake of its pleasures" Deleuze, "Coldness and Cruelty," 88.

26. Sigmund Freud, *Jokes and their Relation to the Unconscious*, trans. J. Strachey (New York: Penguin Books, 1991), 187. The joke's pleasure strips out spatiotemporal measure: an hour spent laughing can't be adequately measured subjectively.

27. Immanuel Kant, *Critique of Judgement*, trans. J. H. Bernard (London: Collier Macmillan Publishers, 1951), 115; For Bergen, in pure, non-schematized time, "the sublime totally breaks the link between the form of objectivity and the I think's unity," *L'Ontologie de Gilles Deleuze*, 249 (my trans.). In fact, time bursts "in a pathos beyond all logic" Deleuze, *Essays Critical and Clinical*, 34. *Critique et clinique*, 48. And time's forces "cannot be penetrated by logical reasoning." Keith Ansell-Pearson, "Time, Space Forced Movement, and the Death-Drive: Reading Proust with Deleuze," *Pli, The Warwick Journal of Philosophy*. Vol 15 (2004), 171.

28. Deleuze & Guattari say of the oedipal saga: "The whole first part is imperial, despotic, paranoid, interpretive, divinatory. But the whole second part is Oedipus's wandering, his line of flight, the double turning away of his own face and that of God" (*TP* 156; 124). *Time as pathos* lacks the *order of time's* "despotic regime of significance and interpretation" (*TP* 157; 125) ordering things. And the *time as pathos* is "the postsygnifying passional regime" (*TP* 158; 126) in time's intensive contours.

29. J. C. F. Hölderlin, "Remarques sur *Œdipe*." *Œdipe le tyran de Spohocle*, trans. Lacoue-Labarthe (Paris: Christian Bourgois Éditeur, 1998), 225 (my trans.); Deleuze cites Hölderlin's emptiness of pure time, fractured I, and "passion of the self" (*DR* 118; 87); "Pure consciousness" Kant, *Critique of Pure Reason*, 201. This schizophrenia is an intensive change "stripped of all shape and form" (*AO* 25; 18).

30. In the "Anticipations of Perception," Kant limits intensity to pure intuitions.

31. Deleuze, *Kant's Critical Philosophy*, 19-20. *La philosophie critique de Kant*, 31; The empirical selves are "diverse and without relation to the identity of the subject" Kant, *Critique of Pure Reason*, 153. Only through the ideal foci ("I think") can empirical selves be synthesized.

32. Nietzsche, *The Will to Power*, 288; Kant depicts this as a logical march toward unity from the soul to the world, to God. *Critique of Pure Reason*, 325.

33. See chapter six, note 18. Daniel Smith depicts how Maïmon surmounts Kant's duality in "Deleuze's Theory of Sensation: Overcoming the Kantian Duality," *Deleuze: A Critical Reader*, (Oxford: Blackwell Publishers, 1996).

34. Henri Bergson, *The Creative Mind: An Introduction to Metaphysics* (New York: Citadel Press, 1992), 51-52; Ibid., 52; Ibid., 37.

35. Gilles Deleuze & Félix Guattari, *Kafka: Towards a Minor Literature*, trans. D. Polan (Minneapolis: University of Minnesota Press, 1986), 46. *Kafka, pour une littérature mineure* (Paris: Les Editions de Minuit, 1975), 84.

36. Bergson, *The Creative Mind*, 83. Non-interpretation is physical. To learn, you must "consider a substance" (*PS* 10; 4). If signs are physical, then Jean-Jacques Thomas wrongly reduces them to "inherently totalizing codes," while arguing that the second half of *Proust and Signs* sees "signs as fragments that rule out holistic approaches." "Poststructuralism and the New Humanism," *SubStance* #68, (1992), 62. Deleuze's signs are not those of Saussure. Although Proust anticipated many of the insights of structuralism, Guattari writes, he did not succumb to their "reductionist abuses." *L' Inconscient machinique: Essais de schizo-analyse* (Paris: Encres, 1979), p 241 (my trans.).

37. Ibid., 81.

38. Ibid., 51.

39. Ibid., 50-51.

40. Ibid., 65; Ibid., 67; Kant, *Critique of Pure Reason*, 82.

41. "These forces are not necessarily time, but they are intertwined and united with those of time." "Boulez, Proust and Time'" 72. "Occuper sans compter," 278.

Chapter 2: The Two Sexes Will Die, Each on its Own Side

1. "Affirmation—as a substitute for uniting—belongs to Eros; negation—the successor to expulsion—belongs to the instinct of destruction" Freud, *On Metapsychology: The Theory of Psychoanalysis*, trans. J. Stranchy (London: Penguin Books, 1991), 441.

2. Alfred de Vigny, *Oeuvres completes*, 2 vols. (Paris: Gallamard, 1986). Vol. 1, 141.

3. Franz Kafka, *The Complete Stories*, (New York: Schocken Books, 1971), 150.

4. Plato, *The Republic*, 505a; "If men knew what the Good was... they would not need laws" Deleuze, "Coldness and Cruelty," 81; The law is above the Good: "Imitation has no place in morality... they can never entitle us to set aside their true original, which resides in reason." Kant, *Groundwork of the Metaphysic of Morals*, 76. Freud rediscovered the fragment in denegation: "There is no stronger evidence that we have been successful in our efforts to uncover the unconscious than when the patient reacts to it with the words 'I didn't think that', or 'I didn't (ever) think that.'" *On Metapsychology*, 442. Stephen Frosh says that "fragments are split shards of experience, kaleidoscopic patterns with no real objects in the background, here the image, there the image of the image, nowhere the substance." "Psychoanalysis, Psychosis, and Postmodernism" *Human Relations*, Vol. 44, No. 1, (1991), 93.

5. Franz Kafka, *The Trial*, 1.

6. Ibid., p 210.

7. Deleuze says "to love supposes the guilt of the beloved" (*PS* 160; 132); The law's formless formality is "an excessive formlessness" (*DR* 122; 91). Kant says of the supersensible "absolutely nothing is known except freedom (through the moral law)... and moreover all supersensible objects to which reason might lead us... have still no reality for us," and for him this "guards against the *empiricism* of practical reason, which founds the practical notions of good and evil merely on experienced consequences." Kant, *Critique of Practical Reason*, 90.

8. Kant, *Critique of Judgement*, 115.

9. Plato, "Symposium," *Collected Dialogues*, 211c.

10. Rather than a lost animal totality, Proust's hermaphrodite is the "partitioning of the two sexes in one and the same plant" (*PS* 163; 135).

11. Plato, "Symposium," *Collected Dialogues*, 189d-e, 190b; Ansell-Pearson rightly calls the primal scene an "original term... that would always remain in its place, so acting as a point and power of attraction." "Time, Space, Forced Movement," 177. This "original term" is projected and "exists only as a virtual object," 180.

12. Ibid., 191d; Ibid., 193a.

13. Frustration is love and hatred's "common origin" (LS 223; 191).

14. Depression splits time in two, "but not at all in the Proustian manner" (*LS* 184; 158).

15. This demolition is a "flight of the past" that creates a "fantastic past." (*LS* 187; 159). Ideas are "recovered *in* absence and *in* forgetfulness" (*LS* 240; 205).

16. For Deleuze, the superego's voice opposes and uses aggressive drives (*LS* 226; 194).

17. Sigmund Freud, *On Sexuality: Three Essays on the Theory of Sexuality and Other Works*, trans. J. Stranchy (London: Penguin Books, 1991), 198.

18. Coitus "in its deferred action operated like a second seduction." Sigmund Freud, *Three Case Histories*, trans. Rieff (New York: Touchstone, 1996), 204.

19. Plato, "Phaedo," *Collected Dialogues*, 75b.

20. Plato is Christianized when we have become simulacra (*LS* 297; 257).

21. The superego's voice is extracted from the sounds of depth (LS 225; 193).

22. For Deleuze, the divided parent is the phantasm of "divorced parents" (*LS* 238; 204); Klein depicts the depressive position: "father or mother enjoys the desired object of which he is deprived" But when separated, "the primitive combined parent figures lose in strength." *Envy and Gratitude and Other Works 1946-1963* (New York: The Free Press, 1975), 79; For Deleuze, direction-change is *ressentiment* "we are all guilty towards ourselves." *Nietzsche and Philosophy*, 142. This castration anxiety creates indebtedness echoed in a mother's anguish and inflicted by a father (*LS* 240; 206).

23. Deleuze & Guattari liken Proustian society-life to that of gangs (*TP* 443; 358). For Alphonso Lingis, the schizoid isn't a "retreat into psychosis," but "a regression to the primary process nomadism of a libido without transcendent ideal, without the negativity of the law, without the regulation of alterity of exteriority." "Oedipus Rex: The Oedipus Rule and its Subversion," *Human Studies* 7: 91-100 (1984), 94.

24. Freud separates sadism fused with sex from "*sadism* which has made itself independent" *Metapsychology*, 382, and from sadism that, Deleuze says, "depends on the schizoid position" (*LS* 224; 193). I argued that the sadism's perversion surpasses mere sublimation towards thought because morality limits sublimation, *Deleuze and the Three Syntheses of Time*, (New York: Peter Lang, 2006), 50-53.

25. Aggression is intensity because, in a body without organs, "*everything is passion and action*," and "communication of bodies in depth" (*LS* 224; 192); But Klein confuses part and whole because, for her, "schizoparanoid partial objects are related to a whole," though they only appear "in a final depressive stage (the complete Object)" (*AO* 52-53; 44). Furtos & Roussillon depict this: "The mother is no longer divided (good or bad), but complete, and fully absent or fully present; this is the birth of the whole but lost object that creates the desire to recover it fully, or the desire of lack that opens the phantasm." "'L'Anti-Oedipe' Essai d'explication," 821 (my trans.).

26. For Deleuze & Guattari, the phallus "makes the two sexes communicate in a common absence—*castration*" (*AO* 350-351; 295).

27. Amazonians don't negotiate for men, as Deleuze & Guattari explain, because they lack alliance paranoia. They see two types: "an Oedipal or filliative homosexuality," secondary to "group homosexuality," which is "non-oedipal" (*AO* 194-195; 165).

28. But Julia Kristeva misreads Deleuze's position on Proust's homosexuality, claiming that he "has internalized Freud's revelation." *Time and Sense: Proust and the Experience of Litterature*, trans. R. Guberman (New York: Colombia University Press, 1996). She confuses Freud's filiative homosexuality with Proust's alliance or group homosexuality with which Deleuze & Guattari combat Freud.

29. Jean-Paul Sartre, *Being and Nothingness: A Phenomenological Essay on Ontology*, trans. H. E. Barnes (New York: Washington Square Press, 1956), 478.

30. When asleep, Albertine's transversals vanish (*PS* 169;141); normally, the hero's logos-driven mind separates parts (PS 159; 132). Though the hero imprisons her "to deny the unknown Albertine," Mark D. Seem says, "difference can never be subjugated, made 'prisoner,' or possessed by a totalizing act of Logos." "Liberation of Difference: Towards a Theory of Antiliterature," New Literary History 5(1), October 1973, 132. In fact, Guattari sees how the hero, by this denial, keeps from totally falling in love: "the hero will keep himself from falling into a certain type of love, of an amorous fascination and of contemplative dependence." *L' Inconscient machinique* (Paris: Encres, 1979), 263 (my trans).

31. Gilles Deleuze & Claire Parnet, *L'abecedaire de Gilles Deleuze* (Paris: Vidéo Editions Montparnasse), J come joi.

32. Ibid.

33. Ibid.

34. Charlus's language becomes physical by mingling "sonorous elements with the body's olfactory, gustatory, or digestive affects" (*LS* 111; 91). Non-language is not the "Anti-system" as Charles Levin thinks. It is not "an unmediated desire, an absolute unconscious, a pristine nonmeaning, a pure power, a negative being, a non-entity." "Carnal Knowledge of Aesthetic States," *Canadian Journal of Political and Social Theory* (Winter/Spring 1987), 93. I argue that Charlus's language is a third term—neither a pure anti-system of the body, nor a system of language (social mediation), but between

them: a language-becoming-body and a body-becoming-language. Deleuze calls this a sign's immanent use since it does not refer "to a transcendent signification," but to worldly signs that seem disappointing, cruel, and stupid (*PS* 12-13; 6).

35. Deleuze, "Coldness and Cruelty," 82; Plato, "Phaedo," *Collected Dialogues*, 59a; Philosophy has a schizoid language: "there are songs and cries, veritable songs in philosophy, concepts are veritable songs, and cries are in philosophy. Suddenly Aristotle says: you have to stop! Or another says, no, I'll never stop! Spinoza: what is a body capable of? We don't even know what a body is capable of!" Deleuze & Parnet, *L'abecedaire de Gilles Deleuze*, O comme Opera.

36. These rivalry bonds develop in "competitive distrust of the rival as much as an amorous striving towards the object" Deleuze & Guattari, *What is Philosophy?*, 4. *Qu'est-ce que la philosophie?* (Paris: Les editions de minuit, 1991), 9.

37. Guattari writes of the hero: "To come to a kind of *becoming-woman*, which is the essential spring of his creation, he must destroy all that attached him to the world of women." *L' Inconscient machinique* (Paris: Encres, 1979), 249.

38. For Deleuze, an assemblage/desire is "an aggregate of the skirt, of the sunray, of a street, of a woman, of a vista, of a color... constructing an assemblage, constructing a region." Deleuze & Parnet, *L'abecedaire de Gilles Deleuze*, D comme Desir.

39. Blocs of becoming are neither memories, nor fantasies, but "components of deterritorialization passing from one assemblage to another" (*TP* 377; 306).

Chapter 3: The Original Sin of Women

1. Visiting Andrée, he says: "The memory of Albertine had become so fragmentary that it no longer caused me any sadness and was no more now than a transition to fresh desires, like a chord that announces a change of key" (*RTP* 2055; III, 612).

2. Ladenson, *Proust's Lesbianism* (New York: Cornell University Press, 1999), 53.

3. Sigmund Freud, *On Sexuality*, 376, 375.

4. Sigmund Freud, *On Metapsychology*, 84.

5. Ibid., 83.

6. Elisabeth Ladenson, *Proust's Lesbianism*, 54. Love and repressed narcissism are linked because the pure past comes from the same source: the past as love.

7. For Deleuze, Gide's logos-homosexuality differs from that of Proust (*PS* 165; 186). See: André Gide, *Corydon* (Champaign: University of Illinois, 2001).

8. "It is not immodesty that leads them to such pleasures, but daring, fortitude, and masculinity... which is proved by the fact that in after years they are the only men who show any real manliness." Plato, "Symposium" *Collected Dialogues*, 192a. Greek homosexuality's consequence: imitation is prized over difference and repetition.

9. This method severs "the authentic from the inauthentic" (*LS* 293; 254). This perversity parallels the fracturing of moral aims.

10. Lagace's jealousy study found only one jealous of a lesbian lover. *The Work of Daniel Lagache: Selected Papers 1938-1964*, trans. E. Holder (London: Karnac Books, 1993). Proof that jealousy is homosexual: jealousy of a rival of one's own sex. Furthermore, if homosexuality weren't repressed, there would be no jealousy.

11. Freud, *On Sexuality*, 372.

12. Freud, *On Metapsychology*, 83.

13. Just as the "finite self thinks the infinite," as Blanchot writes, this feminine narcissism, I claim, makes the mind think "more than it thinks." *The Infinite Conversation*, trans. S. Hanson (Minneapolis: University of Minnesota Press, 1993), 53. Life and time are given force by the "outside" of love (and time), not by logos.

14. Under jealousy, self-as-ideal-love replaces beloved-as-lost-ideal. The first extols virtue (the Platonic Good lovers still embrace as the "best"), the second fosters a universal harmony. Leibniz's other worlds are "less well-founded 'pretenders'" (*LS* 300; 260). We would lack a faculty of reason without the outside chaos that it tries to discover. Thus, the force of reason comes from this outside. Reason is reparation.

15. G. W. Leibniz, *Theodicy: Essays on the Goodness of God the Freedom of Man and the Origin of Evil*, trans. E. M. Huggard (Illinois: Open Court, 1998), 68; Kant, *Groundwork of the Metaphysic of Morals*, 89. Harmony-reason (modern, multiple) and ideal forms (ancient, one) deny chaos. There are many ways to achieve harmony (perfect lies are harmony), but only one way to be ideal (perfect truths).

16. Ibid., 80; this "leads to a broadened chromatic scale." *The Fold*, 82. *Le pli*, 112. Restoring order is the attempt to find coherent examples. But the law that drives this search is *itself* formless. By analogy, her "other nature" is the formless law that makes all empirical examples fail. Thus, the search is an indefinite postponement.

17. Plato, "Philebus" *Collected Dialogues*, 24d.

18. Plato, "Theatetus" *Collected Dialogues*, 176e. This is the "something unmeasured," which is a "reserve of familiar discourse" Blanchot, *The Infinite Conversation*, 211. The "outside" is a void "into which its immediate certainties slip," "Maurice Blanchot: the thought from Outside," *Foucault/Blanchot* (New York: Zone Books, 1990), 16. Lorraine writes that " 'feminine' activity involves touching the corporal... an 'outside' which... threatens stable formations." Tamsin Lorraine, *Irigaray and Deleuze: Experiments in Visceral Philosophy* (Ithaca: Cornell University Press, 1999), 232. But this "unmeasured," Platonic misery is the source of thought, that which drives it.

19. Jean-Paul Sartre, *Being and Nothingness*, 438. I've argued: "Pure consciousness is unreflective consciousness in so far as it has no object to reflect on outside itself. As long as it remains at this level, consciousness remains internal to itself, but as soon as it distances the pain, or projects it into an object, it realizes an external world." "Deleuze *in utero*: Deleuze-Sartre and the Essence of Woman" *Angelaki* 7.3 (2002).

20. Suffering is an exploration undertaken by "neuropaths and psychopaths" (*DR* 142; 107).

21. In time, repetition traverses media while it "reunites different objects" (*PS* 63; 49). For Deleuze, this painful repetition in the novel's "meanwhile" has more *lived* significance than the grand theories at its end. Roger Shattuck, however, concluded that "Deleuze is blind" because he insists that the novel is fragmented, despite the so-called "synthesis" at the end, *Proust's Way* (New York: W. W. Norton and Company, 2000), 165. The "meanwhile" reveals the forces of thought; philosophy merely records results.

22. Kant's practical law demands that "we absolutely must proceed in a certain manner." In the third critique, the sublime lacks such an aim: "*boundlessness* is represented, and yet its totality is also present to thought." *Critique of Practical Reason*, 46, *Critique of Judgment*, 82. The first *sets up* a rule, the second *voids* it.

23. Friedrich Nietzsche, *Basic Writings of Nietzsche*, trans. W. Kaufmann (New York: The Modern Library, 1992), 516. Memory needs repression because "man must constitute himself" through it (*AO* 225; 190).

24. Lucretius, *On the Nature of Things*, trans. J. S. Watson (New York: Prometheus Books, 1997), 236; Ibid., 244. This infantile sexuality becomes a Supreme Being.

25. Birth, death, and sexual difference are problems (*DR* 142; 107); they symbolize the origins of language, of fire, and of the first metals. Unhappy events are "inseparable from the myths which render them possible" (*LS* 322; 278).

26. Deleuze praises Lucretius for speaking about nature, not about the gods (*LS* 323; 278). He avoids a "One" or a "Whole," which "are the myth of a false philosophy totally impregnated by theology." Naturalism, Lucretius says, "is the sensation of finite compounds" that don't form a whole (*LS* 323; 279).

27. Spinoza, *The Ethics*, 107 (III, Pro 3); Ibid., 114 (III, Pro 18); The finite is sensual the finite is the sensual object, the infinite is a mental object (*LS* 324; 279).

28. For Bergson, dreams imply "a corruption of pure memory" (*PS* 74; 59). For another reading of Deleuze, Proust, and Bergson see: Jean-Claude Demoncel, *Le symbole d'Hécate: philosophie deleuzienne et roman proustien* (Paris: Édition HYX), 1996.

29. While discerning clear and confused memory, Bergson says, "certain confused recollections... may overflow the usefully associated images, making around these a less illuminated fringe which fades away into an immense zone of obscurity." *Matter and Memory*, trans. N. M. Paul & S. Palmer (New York: Zone Books, 1991), 85; A mediated memory: "a likeness of attitude in a diversity of situations." Ibid., 161.

30. For Deleuze, rather than repeating his childhood love for his mother, the hero "replays with his mother Swann's passion for Odette" (*DR* 28; 17).

31. A narcissistic wound is restored in "the domain of Images" (*LS* 253; 218).

32. As a schizoid work, such "confessions of guilt are merely a sort of joke" (*AO* 51; 43). Serge Doubrovsky, on the other hand, interprets the *Recherche* in light of the Oedipus complex: *La place de la madeleine: Écriture et fantasme chez Proust* (Paris: Mercure de France, 1974).

33. For Deleuze & Guattari, in Kafka's work (as in Proust's) women "are part sister, part maid, part whore. They are anticonjugal and antifamilial" *Kafka*, 64. *Kafka, pour une littérature mineure*; 117. But, the underworld is confused with the oedipal: "the sister is presented as a substitute for the mother, the maid as a derivative of the mother, the whore as a reaction-formation." Ibid., 66.

34. This is how Proust's characters evade oedipal guilt: "Mlle Vinteuil associates her father's photograph with her sexual revels. The narrator puts family furniture in a brothel" (*PS* 170; 141). Transgression plays no role in this, contrary to what Mark D. Seem says: "This repeated act of transgression is central to the entire Proustian discourse, a discourse directed against laws," "Liberation of Difference," 130. While transgression affirms the laws it breaks and "impurity is only known by contrast," as Gorges Bataille writes, I claim that, for Deleuze, profanation side-steps the law. *Literature and Evil*, trans. A. Hamilton (New York: Marion Boyers), 1985.

35. To transgress isn't to profane: "Oedipal incest... works to transgress this law... Schizo-incest corresponds... to the immanent schizo-law... a progression instead of a transgression" *Kafka*, 67. *Kafka, pour une littérature mineure*, 122.

36. Ibid., 67, 122; Kafka ties segments to women: "Elsa... is so linked to the banking segment that she knows nothing of the trial... the washer woman is linked to the segment of the subordinate functionaries... Leni is linked to the segment of the lawyers" Ibid., 63; 117. This same analysis applies to Proust's novel.

37. Konrad Lorenz, *On Aggression*, trans. M. K. Wilson (New York: Harcourt Brace & Co., 1966), 20; The novel's women "operate within a territory beyond which they will not pursue you" *Kafka*, 68. *Kafka, pour une littérature mineure*, 123.

38. Betrayal is deterritorialization that "comes from the fact that K has already moved into another segment, marked by Olga, whose arrival Frieda caused." Ibid., 68.; 124

39. Deleuze & Guattari depict this as a categorical imperative to betray (*TP* 158; 126).

40. Deleuze & Guattari, *Kafka*, 34. *Kafka, pour une littérature mineure*, 61-62.

Chapter 4: A World of Inhuman Pleasure

1. They liken this desire to "the fetishist view of stocks and lacks" (*AO* 87; 73). Stanley Aronowitz says, "just as capitalism transforms labor from its concrete into an abstract, quantified object to be exchanged for money, so desire loses its concrete self expression when it is represented" "Anti-Oedipus & Molecular Politics," *New Political Science* 1(4): 19-24 (Fall 1980), 21-22.

2. Proper names, Deleuze says, imprison all history (*PS* 142; 118). But the Combray memory disappoints because "the true container is not the cup, but the sensuous quality, the flavor." (*PS* 144; 119). Though the hero thinks that he *imagines* Combray's viewpoint, in fact, disavowal draws it from the *real*. Unlike Lacan's "foreclosure" (the symbolic expelled into the real), this "disavowal," for Deleuze, "is not an hallucination, but rather an esoteric knowledge" (*LS* 283; 243); though it exceeds the hero's grasp, this knowledge is its *real* nucleus, for neither symbol, nor fantasy can explain Combray's timeless nature, but intensity can since, through it, "thought comes to us" (*DR* 188; 144); before its energy sources (intensities) are found, "the organism can be said to nourish itself but not to breathe" (*TP* 67; 51). Ignoring objects, it seeks *energy sources* because "the signs by which an animal 'senses' the presence of water" are not "the elements its thirsty organism lacks" (*DR* 100; 73).

3. Deleuze & Guattari depict sexed molecules as hard and soft (*TP* 338; 276). Deleuze defines becoming-woman by a relation of movement and rest (*TP* 339; 276). The "class" of woman or of man would be an ideal, but the most concrete form of being is the extreme particular, therefore. Becoming is nothing more than this extreme "*haecceitas*."

4. The mother Platonically defined "is not something other than a mother" Deleuze & Guattari, *What is Philosophy?*, 30. *Qu'est-ce que la philosophie?*, 34.

5. René Spitz, *The First Year of Life: A Psychoanalytic Study of Normal and Deviant Development of Object Relations* (Connecticut: International Universities Press, 1965), 81; Deleuze & Guattari also depict this infantile face-experience (*TP* 208; 169).

6. This is not a "phenomenological field or split in a structural field." (*TP* 210; 171).

7. Faces are seen everywhere, even "a utensil becomes a face-landscape" (*TP* 215; 175).

8. The interpreter unfolds possible worlds (*PS* 167; 138). Swann's passion dies: "the appearance of the neurotic black hole, centered on Odette's faciality, leads to the ruin of all his hopes." *L'Inconscient machinique* (Paris: Encres, 1979), 245.

9. The loss of the possible is a world "without potentialities or virtualities" (*LS* 356; 306).

10. *The Ethics*, 86 (II, Pro 34).

11. There is no "false" without the Other that is "the tribunal of all reality" that can "debate, falsify, or verify that which I think I see" (*LS* 361; 311).

12. Without the Other, transitions vanish (*LS* 356;306-307); Deleuze says Albertine is a world: "At the heart of what universe was she perceiving me?" (*LS* 357; 308).

13. Deleuze challenges Sartre, who reduces the Other to an object or to another subject (*LS* 356; 307). For Constantin Boundas, Deleuze replaces Sartre's Other with an otherwise-Other that is "the transcendental field against... which egological and personological consciousness will have to be constituted." "The fate of transcendental empiricism," he concludes, "depends upon our ability to think this otherwise Other." "Foreclosure of the Other: From Sartre to Deleuze," *Journal of the British Society for Phenomenology*. 24:1 (Jan. 1993); For Spinoza, "the individual actually existing thing," not an image, "constitutes the actual being of the human mind." *The Ethics*, 70 (II, Pro 11).

14. An adequate idea is of bodies that are discerned "in respect of motion and rest, quickness and slowness, and not in respect of substance." *The Ethics*, 72 (II, Pro 13, L. 1); Emotions, such as envy, are inadequate ideas: "If anyone thinks that there is between the object of his love and another person the same or a more intimate bond of friendship than there was between them when he alone used to possess the object loved, he will be affected with hatred towards the object loved and will envy his rival." Ibid., 124., (III, 35).

15. Spinoza, *The Ethics*, 39 (I, Pro 13); For Deleuze & Guattari, Spinoza "gave infinite speeds to thought in the third kind of knowledge" *What is Philosophy?*, 48. *Qu'est-ce que la philosophie?*, 49-50.

16. Deleuze & Guattari, *What is Philosophy?*, 48. *Qu'est-ce que la philosophie?*, 50.

17. Jacques Lacan, *The Four Fundamental Concepts of Psycho-Analysis*, trans. A. Sheridan (New York: W. W. Norton & Co., 1978), 53. They identify the part object with Lacan's object *a* as a desiring-machine, with *the real*, which is not a fantasy or a need, but "a real production" (*AO* 34; 27).

18. Lacan, *The Four Fundamental Concepts of Psycho-Analysis*, 57-58.

19. Not expressing a need, *the active* symbolizes: "the activity as a whole symbolizes repetition, but not at all that of some need that might demand the return of the mother, and which would be expressed quite simply in a cry." Ibid., 62; For Freud, the child repeats "everything that has made a great impression" to master excitation, *On Metapsychology*, 286; Deleuze & Guattari condemn Melanie Klein's interpretation of part objects for reducing them to parental images "totalized in Oedipus," thereby reducing to nothing "the logic of partial objects" (*AO* 54; 46). Elsewhere, I argue that part objects are pre-oedipal intensities "such as feeding, bathing, cleaning, stroking, or any action the infant undergoes *without* understanding its source." *Deleuze and the Three Syntheses of Time*, 36. These affects predate oedipal whole objects.

20. The extensive equalizes and suppresses the intensive (*DR* 300; 233).

21. For Deleuze & Guattari, the "impossible real" is productive (*AO* 62; 53).

22. Lacan, *The Four Fundamental Concepts of Psycho-Analysis*, 59; For Deleuze, Spinoza's substance-attribute combines modes without making them whole: "The attributes are types or genuses of BwO's, substances, powers, zero intensities as matrices of production. The modes are everything that comes to pass: waves and vibrations, migrations, thresholds and gradients, intensities" (*TP* 190; 153); I play on "unconscious," not the repressed father as God, but a differential unconscious.

23. Spinoza, *The Ethics*, 32 (I, Ax.5).

24. Leibniz, *Philosophical Writings*, 180. Spinoza, *The Ethics*, 34 (I, Pro 8). If qualities were conceptually opposable, then they would limit a substance (negation). Spinoza's ontology forbids such conceptual distinction.

25. Ibid., 31 (I, Def. 5).

26. Ibid., 52 (I, Pro 30).

27. Encountering Being "in act" is a machine that creates the whole, not a Spinozist principle (*PS* 195-196;163); Kant, *Critique of Pure Reason*, 202; Attributes are non-hierarchical because "substance is equally designated by all the attributes" (*DR* 59;40).

28. Deleuze & Guattari, *What is Philosophy?*, 189. *Qu'est-ce que la philosophie?*, 179; Non-human sexes communicate transversally, by "the transversal insect" (*PS* 202; 168); Lacan depicts the unified real: "there is no absence in the real" and "The real is without fissure" *The Seminar of Jacques Lacan: Book II, The Ego in Freud's Theory and in the Technique of Psychoanalysis 1954-1955*, trans. S. Tomaselli (New York: W. W. Norton & Company, 1988), 313, 97. The same is true for Spinoza: "Being cannot be

divided into parts" and each mode "contains in itself perfection to the degree that it expresses reality." Only imaginary negation/privation blocks the real: "the privation in question is a term applicable in respect of our intellect only, and not of God's" Spinoza, *The Letters*, trans. S. Shirley (Indianapolis: Hackett Publishing Co., 1995), 207, 133, 134. Sexual difference is a mental lack, cut off from the real.

29. Marcel Proust, *Marcel Proust on Art and Literature 1896-1919*, trans. S. T. Warner (New York: Carroll & Graf Publishers, 1957), 19.

30. Ibid., 20.

31. Deleuze depicts this potentially infinite sexual division (PS 211; 175).

32. Unlike Kant's disjunctive syllogism, Deleuze & Guattari's is "inclusive" (*AO* 90; 76).

33. Judge Schreber is a trans-positional subject because he passes through qualitative states (*AO* 91; 77); his "I feel" is a disjunction, not a fantasy (AO 25; 19).

34. Pierre Klossowski, Deleuze & Guattari say, sets up an Antichrist, "the passage of a subject through all possible predicates" (AO 92; 77), to counter Kant's God. He says, "all changes perpetually until all combinations are exhausted and the cycle recommences" *The Baphomet*, trans. S. Hawkes & S. Sartarelli (New York: Marsilio Publishers, 1988), 111. This mirrors Nietzsche's eternal return: "every possible combination... would be realized an infinite number of times" *The Will to Power*, 549. This eternal return is the transpositional subject.

35. Henri Michaux, *The Major Ordeals of the Mind and the Countless Minor Ones*, trans. R. Howard (London: Secker & Warburg, 1974), 126; Deleuze & Guattari, *What is Philosophy?*, 70. *Qu'est-ce que la philosophie?*, 69.

36. These "disjunctive syntheses" occur on the body without organ's "slippery surface" (*AO* 18; 12); these intensive passages are "passive transitions that explicate for us the emotions of Pleasure and Pain." Spinoza, *The Ethics*, 110 (III, Pro 11, Schol.)

37. Ibid., 105 (III, Pro 2, Schol.)

38. Deleuze, "Coldness and Cruelty," 119. Deleuze depicts profanation (*PS* 170; 141); Evil is an experiment only if it clashes with the Good because "the strongest effects on the senses are caused by contrasts." Georges Bataille, *Literature and Evil*, trans. A. Hamilton (New York: Marion Boyars, 1985), 142; Thus, the sadist strips the other person of otherness, but not to cause suffering (*LS* 371; 320).

39. Nietzsche, *The Will to Power*, 550.

Chapter 5: A Passionate Astronomy

1. For Leibniz, the whole universe is sensed, past, present, and future, "by observing in the present the things that are distant." *Philosophical Writings*, 189; The monad's relational accidents create spatiotemporal relations.

2. Ibid., 133.

3. Deleuze, *The Fold*, 68. *Le pli*, 92.

4. Leibniz, *Philosophical Writings*, 187-188.

5. For Deleuze, "communication can result only from machines," not from preset harmony (*PS* 196; 164); Leibniz applied intermediate attributes to world creation.

6. Deleuze says that these selves seek suicide "to repeat/prepare their own end," and then when they are reborn as a loveless self, "to repeat/remember their life" (*PS* 146; 121).

7. Deleuze, *The Fold*, 70. *Le pli*, 95.

8. By applying a Kantian principle to Leibniz, Deleuze merges the "anticipations of perception" and the *Monadology*: The monad becomes a photosensitive plate through which intensive rays pass and leave behind a conceptual trace. That's why he claims that,

in Leibniz's philosophy, "difference ceases being extrinsic and palpable (in this sense it vanishes) in order to become intrinsic, intelligible or conceptual, in conformity with the principle of indiscernibles." *The Fold*, 65-66. *Le pli*, 88; While God chooses predicates for all possible individuals, only some are actualized.

9. Deleuze, *The Fold*, 70. *Le pli*, 95.

10. Libidinal energy becomes that of disjunctive inscription (*AO* 19; 13).

11. Sigmund Freud, "Project for a Scientific Psychology." *The Standard Edition of the Complete Psychological Works of Sigmund Freud: Volume 1 (1886-1889)*, trans. J. Stranchy (London: Vintage Books, 2001), 357.

12. For Deleuze & Guattari, "memory has a punctual organization" (*TP* 361; 294).

13. Deleuze says in a note that Proust read Leibniz (PS 196; 188).

14. Deleuze upholds a self-other: "I find in the sphere of what belongs to me the mark of something that I do not possess... that last is distinguished from all the others because it is extrinsic, a body not being *in* my monad." *The Fold*, 107. *Le pli*, 143-144

15. Deleuze depicts the two natures: "a first Nature, constituted by all their respective zones of clarity..." the second nature is "a meeting with the other... produced at the level of the body." *The Fold*, 107. *Le pli*, 144.

16. Every monad's clear zones contain other bodily monads, which themselves "possess crowds of tertiary monads." Deleuze, *The Fold*, 108. *Le pli*, 145.

17. Leibniz, *The Theodicy*, 370; "As if we should mean by Adam the first man, whom God set in a garden of pleasure whence he went out because of sin, and from whose side God fashioned a woman. All of this would not sufficiently determine him and there might have been several Adams separately possible or several individuals to whom all that would apply." Leibniz, *Discourse on Metaphysics, Correspondence with Arnauld, Monadology*, trans. Montgomery (La Salle: Open Court, 1994), 129.

18. Jean-Paul Sartre, *The Emotions: Outline of a Theory*, trans. B. Frechtman (New York: Citadel Press, 1993), 88; Deleuze depicts this face-event as a "frightening possible world" expressed in a face that "bears no resemblance to the terrifying thing," but "implicates it, it envelops it as something else" (*LS* 357; 307).

19. The face separates "my consciousness and its object" (*LS* 360; 310).

20. Spinoza, *The Ethics*, 34 (I, Pro 8, Proof); for Deleuze, the unseen springs from Others who "introduce the sign of the unseen in what I do see" (*LS* 355; 306).

21. Deleuze says that the Other pushes you into the past (LS 360; 310).

22. By seeing Albertine asleep, the hero avoids "being carried away by the beloved's viewpoint" (*PS* 169; 141); by eliminating the Other "the *difference of the sexes* is disavowed" and an androgynous *double* supplants it (*LS* 371; 319); now, an associative chain breaks and "a Viewpoint superior to the subject" unseats it (*PS* 194; 161).

23. Without Kant's synthesis, "I should have as many-colored and diverse a self as I have representations of which I am conscious to myself" *Critique of Pure Reason*, 154.

24. Poulet says space is a place, "space is not a communicating milieu" *Proustian Space*, trans. E. Coleman (New York: John Hopkins University Press, 1970), 43.

25. Like a Monad's clear-obscure zone, places emerge in obscure space: "Whatever places are... the mind conceives, behind them, below them, all around them, a bare anonymous reality, abstract, totally devoid of characteristics, which presents itself as the impersonal ground where places stand and distribute themselves." Ibid., 40-41.

26. Ibid., 47.

27. Ibid., 42; Ibid.

28. Ibid., 41.

29. Ibid., 42-43.

30. Sartre, *Being and Nothingness*, 372.

31. Poulet favors Leibniz over Bergson: "if the Proustian world greatly differs from the Bergsonian one, it resembles, on the contrary, some others where quality also predominates; for instance, the world of Leibniz" Poulet, *Proustian Space*, 40; Deleuze criticizes Poulet for this (*PS* 149; 184). Ansell-Pearson argues that Deleuze and Poulet share "the appreciation of the fragment." But I argue that Poulet's fragments differ from those of Deleuze because the latter's fragments resemble the infinite attributes of a Spinozist substance while Poulet, he says, "locates in the novel only a *discontinuity of essences*, a non-Spinozist world... without the unity of substance." "Time, Space Forced Movement, and the Death-Drive," 164-165.

32. Deleuze credits Blanchot for finding "a world in fragments" (*PS* 149; 184).

33. The fragment has two wholes: "the severed finger refers back to the hand," and "the first atom contains... the universe." Blanchot, *The Infinite Conversation*, 307.

34. Ibid., 155; Denis Diderot, *Rameau's Nephew and Other Works*, trans. J. Barzun & R. H. Bowen (Cambridge: Hackett Publishing Company, 2001), 280. Roger Shattuck thinks that the "constant decoding" of interpretation makes Deleuze overlook Proust's humor: "Deleuze fails to bring out... a parade of gaffes... Marcel is forever getting his signals switched," *Proust's Way*, 66. For Deleuze, however, interpretation isn't about getting signals right. In fact, humor is at the heart of this type of interpretation, which he calls a "humoristics": "As soon as Proust manipulates the laws, a dimension of humor intervenes that I see as essential and that raises a problem of interpretation... Interpreting a text... always comes back to evaluating its humor" *Two Regimes of Madness: Texts and Interviews 1975-1995*, trans. A. Hodges and M. Taormina (New York: Semiotext(e), 2006), 41. *Deux Régimes de fous: Textes et entretiens 1975-1995* (Paris: Éditions de Minuit, 2003), 40.

35. For Blanchot, becoming is not "not the fluidity of an infinite (Bergsonian) *durée*," but a "knowledge of the tearing apart." *The Infinite Conversation*, 157.

36. Franz Kafka, *The Trial*, 128.

37. Nietzsche says that the ego hems in "like a horizon." *The Will to Power*, 281.

38. *The Infinite Conversation*, 161. The fragment drives this passive synthesis, this intimate force, in Proust's novel: "By fragments, by successive approximations... this abstract machinery never stops transversing and driving the processes of the *Recherche*. The little phrase will finally be revealed for what it is: one of the essential motors of the Proustian machine." *L'Inconscient machinique* (Paris: Encres, 1979), 253 (my trans.).

39. Starting with chaos, which Blanchot depicts as a "metaphoric site that organizes disorganization," but which "does not serve as its matrix" Ibid., 160; an open work, like *Finnegans Wake*, is "unable to give unitary form to the world" Umberto Eco, *The Open Work*, trans. A. Cancogni (Cambridge: Harvard University Press, 1989), 156.

40. Roger Shattuck thinks that the "constant decoding" of interpretation makes Deleuze overlook Proust's humor: "Deleuze fails to bring out... a parade of gaffes... Marcel is forever getting his signals switched," *Proust's Way*, 66. For Deleuze, however, interpretation isn't about getting signals right. In fact, humor is at the heart of this type of interpretation, which he calls a "humoristics": "As soon as Proust manipulates the laws, a dimension of humor intervenes that I see as essential and that raises a problem of interpretation... Interpreting a text... always comes back to evaluating its humor" *Two Regimes of Madness: Texts and Interviews 1975-1995*, trans. A. Hodges and M. Taormina (New York: Semiotext(e), 2006), 41. *Deux Régimes de fous: Textes et entretiens 1975-1995* (Paris: Éditions de Minuit, 2003), 40.

41. Harold Rosenberg, *The Tradition of the New* (New York: DaCapo, 1994), 135.

42. For Rosenberg, "judgment is an inseparable part of the recognition of the individual." Ibid., 136. Deleuze says "guilt is experienced socially," not morally (*PS* 162; 134).

43. Ibid., 143.

44. Leibniz, *Discourse on Metaphysics*, 231-232.

45. Leibniz, *Philosophical Writings*, 183. Though memory and reason both seek a maximum unity, memory clearly connects the past by recording while logic does so by combining parts into a whole. Thus a person's metamorphoses cannot be deduced by logical syllogism—memory's logic attaches parts, but ultimately neglects wholes; Rosenberg, *The Tradition of the New*, 152.

46. "A practical remembrance," for Leibniz, is "open to moral qualities, to chastisement and to recompense even after this life, for immortality without remembrance would be of no value." *Discourse on Metaphysics, Correspondence with Arnauld, Monadology*, 133. For Deleuze, time as a whole gathers around an act with the moral qualities Leibniz depicts, an "image of a formidable... action = x" (*DR* 146; 110).

47. Charles Péguy depicts this type of point: "a problem in which a whole world collided, a problem without issue... suddenly ceased to exist... the whole world had passed what seemed like a physical crisis point" quoted in (*DR* 244-245; 189).

48. This telescope "does not reduce distance," but extends it (*PS* 173; 144); like these distances, mathematical *group theory* has its "adjunct fields" (*DR* 233; 180).

49. Deleuze splits events (solutions-problems), which "double our history" (*DR* 244; 189).

Chapter 6: The Birth of the World

1. Deleuze & Guattari, *What is Philosophy?*, 60. *Qu'est-ce que la philosophie?*, 59.

2. Gilles Deleuze, *Expressionism in Philosophy: Spinoza*, trans. M. Joughin (New York: Zone Books, 1992), 174. *Spinoza et le problème de l'expression* (Paris: Les Editions de Minuit, 1968), 157; Deleuze & Guattari, *Kafka*, 45. *Kafka, pour une littérature mineure*; 82.

3. Long & Sedley, *The Hellenistic Philosophers: Volume 1, Translations of the Principle Sources, With Philosophical Commentary*, (Cambridge: Cambridge University Press, 1987), 336. This instant is a *total mixture* because, as the Stoics say, "nothing stops a single drop of wine from tempering the sea." Ibid., 290; Ibid., 334; Deleuze calls this the instant "which perverts the present" (*LS* 193; 165). And Plato calls this instant, "the time at which it will be when it makes the transition... the instant." Plato, "Parmenides" *Collected Dialogues*, 156d.

4. Plato, "Parmenides" *Collected Dialogues*, 152b-c.

5. Long & Sedley, *The Hellenistic Philosophers*, 338.

6. For Deleuze, the sign has two aspects: "an implicated order of constitutive differences" and "the extended order" in which they are canceled out (*DR* 294; 228).

7. Long & Sedley, *The Hellenistic Philosophers*, 260. Learning occurs in the unconscious, "between nature and mind" (*DR* 214; 165).

8. Charlus retains "all the souls that compose him in the 'complicated' state," as Deleuze writes, he "has the freshness of a world" (*PS* 58-59; 45).

9. Boethius writes, "if anything binds and unites itself to the centre, it is gathered together in singleness and ceases to be broken up and dissipated. In a similar way what departs further from the supreme Mind is bound in greater bonds of fate, and a thing is free from fate to the extent that it draws closer to the Pivot of things." Boethius & Cicero, *Cicero: On Fate* (De Fato) *& Boethius: The Consolation of Philosophy* (Philosophiae

Consolationis) *IV.5-7, V,* trans. R. W. Sharples (Warminster: Aris & Phillips, 1991), 109. This type of cause is echoed in Spinoza's "adequate ideas."

10. Ibid., 107.

11. Deleuze, "Statements and Profiles" (*Angelaki* (8.3) 2003), 91-92. This *a priori* Other disrupts the world's necessity by introducing possibilities into it (*DR* 334; 260).

12. Jean-Paul Sartre, *The Psychology of Imagination* (New Jersey: The Citadel Press, 1985), 127-128.

13. Without the Other, there would be no notions "of form-ground, profile-unity of the object, depth-length, horizon-focus" (*DR* 360; 281).

14. "The primary process," as a "a discharge of excitation... may establish a 'perceptual identity'. The secondary process, however, has abandoned this intention" and has established "a '*thought* identity'." Thus, Freud concludes: "thinking is no more than a circuitous path from the memory of a satisfaction... to an identical cathexis of the same memory which it is hoped to attain once more through... motor experiences." *The Interpretation of Dreams* (London: Penguin Books, 1991), 761-762.

15. The two series, Deleuze says, "coexist in relation to Combray in itself as the object = x" (*DR* 160; 122). But this x is a sensible reality, not an identity. Bruce Baugh says that the sensible is "the reality of a specific actualization falls outside of the concept; the concept determines the equivalency among actualizations (they are all actualizations of the same concept), the sensible is the ground of their difference." "Transcendental Empiricism: Deleuze's Response to Hegel," *Man and World*, 25 (1992), 134. Thus, Combray must be the underlying sensible reality, not the concept.

16. Deleuze's essences are not Platonic because they "do not allow any posting of an essence as 'what the thing is'"(*DR* 248; 191). André Colombat says that Proust's essences "will permit Deleuze to affirm his own theory of language by linking it to the thought of the simulacra that will definitively reverse Proustian neo-Platonism." *Deleuze et la literature*, (New York: Peter Lang, 1990), 99 (my trans.).

17. Kant, *Critique of Pure Reason*, 183.

18. Salomon Maïmon uses the principle of exhaustion, which swayed Deleuze, to find what he calls "Ideas of the understanding," the rules that create objects by a *progressive determination*. In this quote, Maïmon depicts how the circle is created: "For example, the understanding prescribes to itself a rule with the following condition: from a given point, draw an infinite number of equal lines, because of which (by the linking of their ends) the concept of a circle must be produced. The possibility of this rule, and also by following this concept, can be raised in the intuition (by the movement of a line around a given point) and therefore equally in its formal completion (of the unity in the diverse). But its material completeness (of the diverse) cannot be given in the intuition, because one can never draw more than a finite number of equal lines between them. Therefore, this is not a concept of the understanding that corresponds with the object, but only an Idea of the understanding, of which one can always be approached to infinity in intuition by successive addition of lines, and consequently a limit-concept." *Essai sur la philosophie transcendantale*, trans. J.-B. Scherrer (Paris: J. Vrin, 1989), 72 (my trans.).

19. Freud, "Project for a Scientific Psychology," 330-331.

20. Richard Rorty, "Matter and Event", in L. Ford & G. Kline, ed., *Explorations in Whitehead's Philosophy* (New York: Fordham University Press, 1983), 91-92.

21. For Deleuze, "eternal objects are... pure Virtualities that are actualized in prehensions." *The Fold*, 79. *Le pli*, 108. James Williams lays out four differences between the eternal objects of Deleuze and of Whitehead: *The Transversal Thought of Gilles Deleuze: Encounters and Influences* (Manchester: Clinamen Press, 2005), 96.

22. "The *Law of Continuity* states that nature leaves no gaps." Leibniz, *New Essays on Human Understanding* (Cambridge: Cambridge University Press, 1996), 307.

23. *The Concept of Nature* (Cambridge: Cambridge University Press, 1995), 76, 77.

24. Deleuze, *The Fold*, 80. *Le pli*, 109.

25. Cicero's *On divination* states that "time is like the unwinding of a rope." Long & Sedley, *The Hellenistic Philosophers*, 338. Deleuze cites this (*LS* 169; 144).

26. Deleuze, *The Fold*, 80. *Le pli*, 109.

27. For Deleuze, Proustian reminiscence "proceeds from a mood, from a state of soul, and from its associative chains, to a creative or transcendent viewpoint—and no longer, in Plato's fashion, from a state of the world to seen objectivities" (*PS* 134; 110). John Hughes writes that style is a machine that produces "unconscious feeling and thought in the reader, while also articulating for consciousness... the virtual viewpoint which they express," *Lines of Flight* (Sheffield: Sheffield Academic Press, 1997), 24.

Chapter 7: Between the Two Routes Transversals Established Themselves

1. This blind spot or empty square is at the heart of a serial method in which "one series has the role of the signifier, and the other the role of the signified" (*LS* 52; 38).

2. René Descartes, *Discourse on Method and Meditations on First Philosophy*, trans. D. A. Cress (Indianapolis: Hackett Publishing, 1993), 19; Kant, however, thinks that the "I" is purely intellectual, but expresses an indeterminate empirical intuition of the self. Hence, the "I" floats above the empirical series; Time in the subject "makes the determined Self represent the determination to itself as an Other" *Essays Critical and Clinical*, 30. *Critique et clinique*, 43-44; For Deleuze, the double (the outside) "is not the emanation of an 'I', but something that places in immanence an always other or a Non-self." *Foucault*, trans. S. Hand (Minneapolis: University of Minnesota Press, 1995), 98. *Foucault*, (Paris: Les Editions de Minuit, 1986), 105.

3. So, like the *Las Meninas*, our observations are unequal to this "function" since, unlike us, this painting includes its own pre-subjective "individuating viewpoint" (*PS* 194; 162). Combray's individuating viewpoint, for instance, creates its own truth by the processes Colombat depicts: "part object machines, drives, which produce the truths of lost time... resonance machines, Eros, which produce the truths of time regained... forced movement machines, Thanatos, which produce the truths of lost time as the condition for the artwork's form." *Deleuze et la littérature*, 172. These machines create observing functions. For Foucault, persons vanish in this void: "In the midst of this dispersion... is an essential void: the necessary disappearance of that which is its foundation... And representation, freed finally from the relation that was impeding it, can offer itself as representation in its pure form." *The Order of Things*, 16.

4. Sartre, *Being and Nothingness*, 349; For Sartre, "The Other is... the condition of my being-unrevealed." Ibid., 359; Kafka, *The Trial*, 222.

5. Nietzsche's *internalization*: "All instincts that do not discharge themselves outwardly *turn inward.*" "The Genealogy of Morals" *Basic Writings of Nietzsche*, 520.

6. Félix Guattari, *Molecular Revolution: Psychiatry and Politics*, trans. R. Sheed (New York: Penguin, 1884), 17. For Deleuze, a transversal makes them communicate "according to the landscape's own dimension" (*PS* 201-202; 168).

7. Sigmund Freud, *Group Psychology and the Analysis of the Ego*, trans. J. Stranchy (New York: W. W. Norton & Company, 1959), 50 & 51.

8. Guattari, *Molecular Revolution*, 13.

9. Ibid., 13-14; For Deleuze, the transversal is "without unifying or totalizing objects and subjects" (*PS* 202; 169). This is why Guattari writes: "One must not consider human subjectivity as something undifferentiated and empty that will be filled and animated

from the exterior" but as "trans-subjective and trans-objective abstract machines." *L'Inconscient machinique* (Paris: Encres, 1979), 242-243 (my trans.).

10. For Merleau-Ponty, the transversal is a self-unfolding: "a body... offers itself to..., opens upon... an immanent spectator, is a charged field." *The Visible and the Invisible*, trans. A. Lingis (Evanston: North Western University Press, 1968), 264; Deleuze says, "it was Merleau-Ponty who showed us how a radical, 'vertical' visibility was folded into Self-seeing, and from that point on made possible the horizontal relation between a seeing and a seen." This transversal-fold's twisting "defines 'Flesh', beyond the body proper and its objects." *Foucault*, 110. *Foucault* (French), 117.

11. Deleuze's transversal is "the formal structure of the work of art" that proposes new linguistic conventions; he attributes this to Eco (*PS* 201; 168).

12. Gilles Deleuze, *Francis Bacon: The Logic of Sensation*, trans. D. W. Smith (New York: Continuum, 2003), 178. *Francis Bacon: logique de la sensation* (Paris, Aux editions de la difference, 1981), 27; Ibid., 35; 27 (French). Sensation "is the opposite of the facile and the ready-made, the cliché." Ibid., 34; 27 (French).

13. Ibid., 34-35; 27 (French).

14. Maurice Merleau-Ponty, *Phenomenology of Perception*, trans. C. Smith (New York: Routledge, 1962), 197-198.

15. A new linguistic convention (a "formal structure") is transversal, which "unites Proust's book to those he preferred, by Nerval, Chateaubriand, Balzac" (*PS* 202; 168); Guattari, *Molecular Revolution*, 17.

16. Ibid., 22.

17. Deleuze & Guattari, *What is Philosophy?*, 109. *Qu'est-ce que la philosophie?*, 104.

18. For Deleuze & Guattari, philosophy and art "contain their sums of unimaginable sufferings that forewarn of the advent of a people" *What is Philosophy?*, 110. *Qu'est-ce que la philosophie?*, 105.

19. Freud, *On Metapsychology*, 291.

20. Ibid; Ibid.

21. Ibid., 421.

22. Guattari, *Molecular Revolution*, 22; Ibid.; language becomes musical (*TP* 132; 104); Ibid; Deterritorialization creates a "new earth" (*AO* 384; 321).

23. *On Metapsychology*, 42. For Freud, an artist "turns away from reality because he cannot come to terms with the renunciation of instinctual satisfaction." Ibid., 41.

Chapter 8: As if there were in Time Different and Parallel Series

1. Leibniz, *Discourse on Metaphysics*, 126.

2. Time unfolds theatrically because, like Oedipus, the hero is blind to his "blocked representation" (*DR* 25; 15). He repeats it until the moment of Aristotelian recognition.

3. For Deleuze, our grasp of word is finite since writing "gives them an existence *hic et nunc*" (*DR* 22; 13). By passing into existence, it changes. Nature lacks memory since its objects "neither possess nor collect in themselves their own moments" (*DR* 24; 14). As Hayden notes, in a natural blockage, "the concept itself is forced into place in space and time, causing it to pass into existence in the form of a dispersion of definite individuals." *Multiplicity and Becoming: The Pluralist Empiricism of Gilles Deleuze*, (New York: Peter Lang, 1998), 10. Deleuze allows concepts to be self-alienated into nature, but rejects Hegel's sublimating-synthesis that reduces nature to a dialectic.

4. Discrete extension is "repetition in existence," not one of equivalence (*DR* 22; 13).

5. Repetition emerges from the difference within "the order of the symbol" (*DR* 28; 17).

6. Self-consciousness is "the faculty of the future" (*DR* 25; 15), not of the present.

7. Bergson, *Matter and Memory*, 134.

8. We must seek virtual memory "in impassive Being, and gradually we gave it an embodiment, a 'psychologization'" *Bergsonism*, 57. *Le bergsonisme*, 52.

9. *Bergsonism*, 71-72. *Le bergsonisme*, 69-70.

10. Actualization occurs on the clear-confused threshold: "clear because it is distinguished or differenciated, and confused because it is clear" (*DR* 276; 213); from Descartes to Leibniz, the problem shifts: "no longer posed in terms of whole-parts (from the point of view of logical possibility), but in terms of a virtual-actual (actualization of differential relations, incarnation of singular points)" (*DR* 276; 213-214).

11. For Bergson, even "our recollection still remains virtual" because it must be lost or obscure, for "if, when once realized, it did not retain something of its original virtuality, if, being a present state, it were not also something which stands out distinct from the present, we should never know it for a memory," *Matter and Memory*, 134. Bergson's virtual-obscurity becomes actual; Leibniz depicts monadic contracting as a period "a swoon ... a deep, dreamless sleep" and "in such a state the soul does not sensibly differ at all from a simple Monad." *Philosophical Writings*, 182.

12. Essential and empirical forgetting are distinct (*DR* 183; 140); Thus, for Nietzsche, memory "has as its precondition a '*positing* of equality,'" *The Will to Power*, 274.

13. "These would be screen memories that have *pushed ahead* or been *displaced forward.*" Freud, *The Psychopathology of Everyday Life*, 84.

14. Bergson, *Matter and Memory*, 167.

15. The death instinct creates unequal worlds, one of "the excessive and the unequal" (*DR* 151; 115). This is how Thanatos (the unequal) "gives repetition to Eros" (*DR* 29; 18).

16. Infantile amnesia (repression) "consists in a simple withholding of these impressions from consciousness" Freud, *On Sexuality*, 90.

17. Ibid., 91; Freud, *The Psychopathology of Everyday Life*, 83.

18. In dreams, Bergson says, consciousness would "keep in view the totality of its past" *Matter and Memory*, 167. The hero does this as well.

Chapter 9: The Strange Contradiction of Survival and Nothingness

1. Cowardice, cruelty, baseness, and stupidity "are structures of thought" (*DR* 196; 151); Freud separates destructive instincts that serve procreation from the death instinct, the defusion that serves thought: "We perceive that for purposes of discharge the *instinct of destruction* is habitually brought into the service of Eros... and we come to understand that instinctual defusion and the marked emergence of the death instinct call for particular consideration." *On Metapsychology*, 382; "Eros" is fusion; the death instinct, defusion. Thanatos is "the desexualization of Eros" (*DR* 149; 113).

2. Sandor Ferenczi portrays this traumatic progression: "Not only emotionally, but also *intellectually*, can the trauma bring to maturity a part of the person." *Selected Writings*, (London: Penguin Books, 1999), 301.

3. For Freud, this force empowers the categorical imperative: "its dictatorial 'thou shalt.'" *On Metapsychology*, 396. And Deleuze calls this dictatorial harshness "forced movement," or "a machine that produces the effect of withdrawal" (*PS* 192; 160).

4. The incorporeal surface theme recurs in three books: first, as a temporal "horizon" (*PS* 191; 159). Second, as "the pure line of the Aion and the death instinct" (*LS* 243;

209). And third, as the body without organs is "a surface for the recording of the entire process of production of desire" (*AO* 17; 11).

5. Pierre Klossowski, *Roberte Ce Soir and The Revocation of the Edict of Nantes*, trans. A. Wainhouse (New York: Marion Boyars, 1989), 19.

6. In sleep, "we tend to scatter ourselves over AB in the measure that we detach ourselves from our sensory and motor state" Bergson, *Matter and Memory*, 162.

7. Eros generates a never-lived past by which we "penetrate this pure past in itself" (*DR* 115; 85). Forced movement creates an essential forgetting by "extracting Thanatos from Eros and abstracting time from all content" (*DR* 150; 114).

8. Jealousy destroys love and thereby leads to an understanding if it (*PS* 86; 69).

9. "Coldness and Cruelty," 128. Freud depicts this ambivalence: "Just as mourning impels the ego to give up the object by declaring the object to be dead and offering the ego the inducement of continuing to live, so does each single struggle of ambivalence loosen the fixation of the libido to the object by disparaging it, denigrating it and even as it were killing it." Freud, *On Metapsychology*, 267. Deleuze also portrays masochism as a process whereby fathers are abolished: "*It is not a child but a father that is being beaten.* The masochist thus liberates himself in preparation for a rebirth in which the father will have no part" "Coldness and Cruelty," 66.

10. Guilt blocks resonance because it "gives the present sensation the power to avoid the embrace of the earlier one" (*PS* 29; 20).

11. The masochistic ritual lacks shame. Freud's melancholic patients are proud of their shame: "Feelings of shame in front of other people... are lacking in the melancholic" because he "finds satisfaction in self-exposure." *On Metapsychology*, p 255.

12. Deleuze depicts this externalization in which "the masochist reaches towards the most mythical and the most timeless realms" "Coldness and Cruelty," 66.

13. Deleuze & Guattari, *Kafka*, 34. *Kafka, pour une littérature mineure*, 62.

14. For Melanie Klein, "persecutory anxiety, therefore, enters from the beginning into his relation to objects in so far as he is exposed to privations.... This relation is at first a relation to a part-object, for both oral-libidinal and oral-destructive impulses from the beginning of life are directed towards the mother's breast in particular" *Envy and Gratitude and Other Works 1946-1963*, (New York: The Free Press, 1975), 62; This anaclitic process, Freud says, occurs when intensity surpasses a certain level: "sexual excitation arises as a concomitant effect, as soon as the intensity of those processes passes beyond certain qualitative limits." *On Sexuality*, 124. In short, the organism's capacity (like the stomach's capacity) limits self-preservative drives.

15. Elisabeth Roudinesco, *Jacques Lacan*, trans. B. Bray (New York: Columbia University Press, 1994), 342.

16. Klein says that frustration spurs greed: "I suggest that such an alteration in the balance between libido and aggression gives rise to the emotion called greed... Any increase in greed strengthens feelings of frustration and in turn the aggressive impulses.... It could be conceived that in periods of freedom from hunger and tension there is an optimal balance between libidinal and aggressive impulses. This equilibrium is disturbed whenever, owing to privations from internal or external sources, aggressive impulses are reinforced" *Envy and Gratitude*, 62

17. Franz Kafka, *The Complete Stories*, 235-236.

18. André Colombat organizes this square differently: "1) the alimentary model of the ungrounded with two depths, 2) the constitution of a good object of the heights with which the ego tends to identify, 3) the recording of the surfaces by the phallus image and 4) the passage of the physical surface to the metaphysical surface. The first three can be

linked to two of the three Kleinian positions that are 1) the paranoid-schizoid position (the simulacra world for Deleuze), 2) the manic depressive position (the world of the idol in the heights) 3) the oedipal position (evocation of the father/reparation of the mother's body, the double good intention)." *Deleuze et la literature*, 160-161. Reorganizing this list, I call the "two depths" the sexual and destructive drives, "the good object" Eros, and "the metaphysical surface" Thanatos.

19. Behind all thought, lurks an apocalypse. Unlike the otherworldly "eternal ideal," the apocalypse eternalizes ideas, not ideally, but *actively*. That's why Pierre Fedida says, "Gilles Deleuze makes the first position [paranoid-schizoid] corresponds to a descent to the ungrounded depths—the swallowing up of the body in an abyss where destructions and mixtures are produced—and he acknowledges the depressive position of the *heights*—the dimension and the place of the *good object*." "Le philosophe et sa peau," *L'arc* 44 (1972), 67 (my trans.). The heights is a *reaction* to the fall into the depths (the apocalypse) and the surface is an *action* that supplants the depth-height.

20. Freud, *On Metapsychology*, 394; André Green depicts this pure culture of the death instinct: "This is the quest of non-desire for the Other, of non-existence, non-being; another way of acceding to immortality. The ego is never more immortal than when it claims that it no longer has any organs or body." *Life Narcissism Death Narcissism*, trans. A. Weller (London: Free Association Press, 2001), 222; Deleuze calls this surface-forming process a mouth-brain struggle (*LS* 280; 240). The mouth consumes (thing-presentations) while the brain thinks (word-presentations).

21. The ego becomes narcissistic, turns to a metaphysical surface, but against the solid terrestrial plane. Beyond the destructive mixtures, it turns to verbal flows: "beginning with a sexual pair, and retracing the path of the divine creation" (*LS* 256; 220).

22. This is Sade's sadism: a speculative prison-cell-monstrosity that frees his critical faculty—for he was a great social critic as well. Because he showed mercy even during the sadistic French Revolution, his sadism, like Proust's, is gentle. In fact, Deleuze insists that apathy maximizes "sadistic projection." "Coldness and Cruelty," 118. According to Ansell-Pearson, "there is no contradiction here between the suspension of ethics... and the affirmation of ethics" *Germinal Life*, p104.

23. Deleuze defends perversion against the charge of criminality (*LS* 283; 243).

24. Spinoza, *The Ethics*, 211 (V, Pro 19); Masoch loves theater (suspended medium). And Sade loves calculating (endless irritation). This gives thought critical force. Leclercq writes that Sade is a Spinozist because it is "marked by the univocity of beings that embrace all bodies," *Gilles Deleuze, immanence, uvivocité et trnscendantal* (Belgium: Éditions Sils Maria, 2003), 75 (my trans.).

25. They define the plateau, like Gregory Bastson, as "a piece of immanence" (*TP* 194; 158); Monstrosity is repetition's creative power. Freudian sublimation, however, creates thought-preferences, "interpretations" that fall short.

26. Klossowski, *Sade my Neighbour*, trans. A. Lingis (London: Quartet, 1992), 32.

27. Deleuze & Guattari don't directly argue for sexual freedom, not even a delayed or intensified pleasure (*TP* 194-195; 157). Though sexuality seems immanent (an intensive body), sex depends on taboos. But Deleuze's "joy" is like the feeling Proust said would come with the news of the world's end: everything would be beautiful.

28. Deleuze depicts Nietzsche's "apparently manic-depressive episodes" (*LS* 230; 198).

Bibliography

Ansell-Pearson, Keith. *Germinal Life: The Difference and Repetition of Deleuze.* New York: Routledge, 1999.
———. "Time, Space Forced Movement, and the Death-Drive: Reading Proust with Deleuze," *Pli, The Warwick Journal of Philosophy.* Vol 15 (2004).
Aronowitz, Stanly. "Anti-Oedipus & Molecular Politics." *New Political* Science 1(4): 19–24 (Fall 1980).
Bataille, Geroges. *Litterature and Evil.* Translated by A. Hamilton. New York: Marion Boyars, 1985.
Baugh, Bruce. "Transcendental Empiricism: Deleuze's Response to Hegel," *Man and World*, 25 (1992).
Bergen, Véronique. *L'Ontologie de Gilles Deleuze.* Paris: L'Harmattan, 2001.
Bergson, Henri. *The Creative Mind: An Introduction to Metaphysics.* Translated by M. L. Andison. New York: Citadel Press, 1992.
———. *Matter and Memory.* Translated by N. M. Paul and S. Palmer. New York: Zone Books, 1991.
Blanchot, Maurice. *The Infinite Conversation.* Translated by S. Hanson. Minneapolis: University of Minnesota Press, 1993.
Boethius and Cicero. *Cicero: On Fate* (De Fato) *& Boethius: The Consolation of Philosophy* (Philosophiae Consolationis) *IV.5–7, V.* Translated by R. W. Sharples. Warminster: Aris & Phillips, 1991.
Boundas, Constantin V. "Foreclosure of the Other: From Sartre to Deleuze." *Journal of the British Society for Phenomenology.* 24:1 (Jan. 1993).
Carroll, Lewis. *Alice's Adventures in Wonderland.* Woodbury: Bobley Publishing, 1979.
Chauvin, Rémy and Bernadette Muckensturm-Chauvin, *Behavioral Complexities.* Translated by J. Diamanti. New York: International University Press, 1980.
Colombat, André. *Deleuze et la literature.* New York: Peter Lang, 1990.
Darwin, Charles. *The Origin of Species by Means of Natural Selection or The Preservation of Favored Races in the Struggle for Life.* London: Senate, 1994.
Deleuze, Gilles. *Bergsonism.* Translated by H. Tomlinson and B. Habberjam. New York: Zone Books, 1988. (*Le Bergsonisme.* Paris: PUF, 1966).
———. "Boulez, Prousy and Time: 'Occupying Without Counting'." Translated by T. S. Murphy. *Angelaki* (3.2) 1998. ("Occuper sans compter: Boulez, Proust et le temps" *Deux régimes de fous:Textes et entretiens 1975-1995.* Paris: Éditions de Minuit, 2003, pp. 272–279).

————. "Coldness and Cruelty." *Masochism.* New York: Zone Books, 1989. (*Présentation de Sacher-Masoch: Le froid et le cruel.* Paris: Éditions de Minuit, 1967).

————. *Desert Islands and Other Texts: 1953-1974.* Translated by M. Taormina. Edited by D. Lapoujade. New York: Semiotext(e), 2004. (*L'île Déserte et autres texts: Textes et entretiens 1953-1974.* Paris: Éditions de Minuit, 2002).

————. "Description of a Woman: For a Philosophy of the Sexed Other" Translated by K. W. Faulkner. *Angelaki* (7.3) 2002. ("Description de la femme: Pour une philosophie d'Autri sexuée" *Poésie 28* (1945): 28–39).

————. *Difference and Repetition.* Translated by P. Patton. New York: Columbia University Press, 1994. (*Différence et répétition.* Paris: PUF, 1968).

————. *Empiricism and Subjectivity: An Essay on Hume's Theory of Human Nature.* Translated by C. Boundas. New York: Columbia University Press, 1991. (*Empirisme et subjectivité: Essai sur la nature humaine selon Hume.* Paris: PUF, 1953).

————. *Essays Critical and Clinical.* Translated by D. W. Smith and M. A. Greco. Minneapolis: University of Minnesota Press, 1997. (*Critique et clinique.* Paris: Éditions de Minuit, 1993).

————. *Expressionism in Philosophy: Spinoza.* Translated by M. Joughin. New York: Zone Books, 1992. (*Spinoza et le problème de l'expression.* Paris: Éditions de Minuit, 1968).

————. *The Fold: Leibniz and the Baroque.* Translated by T. Conley. Minneapolis: University of Minnesota Press, 1993. (*Le Pli: Leibniz et le Baroque.* Paris: Éditions de Minuit, 1988).

————. *Foucault.* Translated by S. Hand. Minneapolis: University of Minnesota Press, 1995. (*Foucault.* Éditions de Minuit, 1986).

————. *Francis Bacon: The Logic of Sensation.* Translated by D. W. Smith. New York: Continuum, 2003. (*Francis Bacon: Logique de la sensation.* Paris: Éditions de la Différence, 1981).

————. *Kant's Critical Philosophy: The Doctrine of the Faculties.* Translated by H. Tomlinson and B. Habberjam. Minneapolis: University of Minnesota Press, 1984. (*La philosophie critique de Kant: Doctrine des facultés.* Paris: PUF, 1963).

————. *The Logic of Sense.* Translated by M. Lester with C. Stivale, edited by C. Boundas. New York: Columbia University Press, 1990. (*Logique du sens.* Paris: Les. Éditions de Minuit, 1969).

————. *Nietzsche and Philosophy.* Translated by H. Tomlinson. New York: Columbia University Press, 1983. (*Nietzsche et la philosophie.* Paris: PUF, 1962).

————. *Proust and Signs: The Complete Text.* Translated by R. Howard. Minneapolis: University of Minnesota Press, 2000. (*Proust et les signes* Paris: PUF, 1964).

————. *Spinoza: Practical Philosophy.* Translated by R. Hurley. San Francisco: City Lights Books, 1988. (*Spinoza: Philosophie pratique.* Paris: Éditions de Minuit, 1981).

————. "Statements and Profiles" Translated by K. W. Faulkner. *Angelaki* (8.3) 2003. ("Dires et profiles" *Poésie 36* (1946): 68–78).

————. *Two Regimes of Madness: Texts and Interviews 1975–1995.* Translated by A. Hodges and M. Taormina. New York: Semiotext(e), 2006. (*Deux Régimes de fous: Textes et entretiens 1975–1995* Paris: Éditions de Minuit, 2003).

Deleuze, Gilles and Claire Parnet. *L'abecedaire de Gilles Deleuze.* Paris: Vidéo Editions Montparnasse.

Deleuze, Gilles and Félix Guattari. *Anti-Oedipus: Capitalism and Schizophrenia.* Translated by R. Hurly, M. Seem, H. R. Lane. Minneapolis: University of Minnesota Press, 1983. (*L'Anti-Oedipe.* Paris: Éditions de Minuit, 1972).

———. *Kafka: Toward a Minor Literature.* Translated by D. Polan. Minneapolis: University of Minnesota Press, 1994. (*Kafka: Pour une literature mineure.* Paris: Éditions de Minuit, 1975).

———. *A Thousand Plateaus: Capatalism and Schizophrenia.* Translated by B. Massumi. Minneapolis: University of Minnesota Press, 1987. (*Mille plateaux.* Paris: Éditions de Minuit, 1980).

———. *What is Philosophy?* Translated by H. Tomlinson, G. Burchell. New York: Columbia Press, 1994. (*Qu'est-ce que la philosophie?.* Paris: Éditions de Minuit, 1991).

Demoncel, Jean-Claude. Le symbole d'Hécate: philosophie deleuzienne et roman proustien. (Paris: Édition HYX, 1996).

Descartes, René. *Discourse on Method and Meditations on First Philosophy.* Translated by D. A. Cress. Indinapolis: Hackett Publishing Company, 1993.

Diderot, Denis. *Rameau's Nephew and Other Works.* Translated by J. Barzun and R. H. Bowen. Cambridge: Hackett Publishing Company, 2001.

Doubrovsky, Serge. *La place de la madeleine: Écriture et fantasme chez Proust.* (Paris: Mercure de France, 1974).

Eco, Umberto. *The Open Work.* Translated by A. Cancogni. Cambridge: Harvard University Press, 1989.

Faulkner, Keith W. *Deleuze and the Three Syntheses of Time.* New York: Peter Lang, 2006.

———. "Deleuze *in Utero*: Deleuze-Sartre and the essence of Women" *Angelaki* (7.3) 2002.

Ferenczi, Sándor. *Selected Writings.* Edited by J. Borossa. New York: Penguin Books, 1999.

Fitzgerald, F. Scott. *The Great Gatsby.* London: Penguin Books, 1950.

Foucault, Michel. "Maurice Blanchot: The Thought from Outside" *Foucault/Blanchot.* Translated by B. Massumi. New York: Zone Books, 1990.

———. *The Order of Things: An Archaeology of the Human Sciences.* New York: Vintage Books, 1973.

Fredida, Pierre. "Le philosophe et sa peau." *L'arc* 44 (1972).

Freud, Sigmund. *Group Psychology and the Analysis of the Ego.* Translated by J. Stranchy. New York: W. W. Norton & Company, 1959.

———. *The Interpretation of Dreams.* Translated by J. Stranchy. London: Penguin Books, 1991.

———. *Jokes and their Relation to the Unconscious.* Translated by J. Strachey. New York: Penguin Books, 1991.

———. *On Metapsychology: The Theory of Psychoanalysis.* Translated by J. Stranchy. London: Penguin Books, 1991.

———. "Project for a Scientific Psychology." *The Standard Edition of the Complete Psychological Works of Sigmund Freud: Volume 1 (1886-1889) Pre-Psycho-Analytic Publications and Unpublished Drafts.* Translated by J. Stranchy. London: Vintage Books, 2001.

———. *The Psychopathology of Everyday Life.* Translated by A. Tyson. London: Penguin Books, 1991.

———. *On Sexuality: Three Essays on the Theory of Sexuality and Other Works.* Translated by J. Stranchy. London: Penguin Books, 1991.

————. *Three Case Histories*. Translated by P. Rieff. New York: Touchstone, 1996.

Frosh, Stephen "Psychoanalysis, Psychosis, and Postmodernism" *Human Relations*, Vol. 44, No. 1, (1991).

Furtos, J. and R. Roussillon, "'L'Anti-Oedipe" Essai d'explication" *Revue esprit*, 1972.

Gaukroger, Stephen. *Descartes: An Intellectual Biography*. Oxford: Oxford University Press, 1997.

Gide, André. *Corydon*. Trans. R. Howard. Champaign: University of Illinois, 2001.

Green, André. *Life Narcissism Death Narcissism*. Translated by A. Weller. London: Free Association Press, 2001.

Groethuysen, Bernard. "De quelques aspects du Temps. Notes pour une phenomenology du Récit" in *Philosophie et histoire*. Paris: Albin Michel, 1995.

Guattari, Félix. *L'Inconscient machinique: Essais de schizo-analyse*. Paris: Encres, 1979.

————. *Molecular Revolution: Psychiatry and Politics*, Translated by R. Sheed (New York: Penguin, 1984).

Hayden, Patrick. *Multiplicity and Becoming: The Pluralist Empiricism of Gilles Deleuze*. New York: Peter Lang, 1998.

Hölderlin, J. C. F. "Remarques sur *Œdipe*." *Œdipe le tyran de Spohocle*. Translated by P. Lacoue-Labarthe. Paris: Christian Bourgois Éditeur, 1998.

Hughes, John. *Lines of Flight: Reading Deleuze with Hardy, Gissing, Conrad, Woolf*. Sheffield: Sheffield Academic Press, 1997.

Husserl, Edmund. *Ideas: General Introduction to Phenomenology* Translated by W. R. Boyce Gibson. London: Collier Macmillan Publishers, 1962

Joyce, James. *Finnegans Wake*. New York: Penguin Books, 1976.

Kafka, Franz. *The Complete Stories*. New York: Schocken Books, 1971.

————. *The Trial*. Translated by W. Muir, E. Muir and E. M. Butler. New York: Schocken Books, 1984.

Kant, Immanuel. *Critique of Judgement*. Translated by J. H. Bernard. London: Collier Macmillan Publishers, 1951.

————. *Critique of Practical Reason*. Translated by T. K. Abbott. New York: Prometheus Books, 1996.

————. *Critique of Pure Reason*. Translated by N. K. Smith. New York: Palgrave Macmillan, 2003.

————. *Groundwork of the Metaphysic of Morals*. Translated by H. J. Paton. New York: Harper Torchbooks, 1956.

Kierkegaard, Søren. *Fear and Trembling/Repetition*. Translated by H. V. Hong and E. H. Hong. New Jersey: Princeton University Press, 1983.

Klein, Melanie. *Envy and Gratitude and Other Works 1946–1963*. New York: The Free Press, 1975.

Klossowski, Pierre *The Baphomet*, Translated by S. Hawkes & S. Sartarelli. New York: Marsilio Publishers, 1988.

————. *Roberte Ce Soir and The Revocation of the Edict of Nantes*, Translated by A. Wainhouse. New York: Marion Boyars, 1989.

————. *Sade my Neighbour*. Translated by A. Lingis. London: Quartet Books, 1992.

Kristava, Julia. *Time and Sense: Proust and the Experience of Literature*. Translated by R. Guberman. New York: Colombia University Press, 1996.

Lacan, Jacques. *The Four Fundamental Concepts of Psycho-Analysis*. Translated by A. Sheridan. New York: W. W. Norton and Company, 1978.

————. *The Seminar of Jacques Lacan: Book II, The Ego in Freud's Theory and in the Technique of Psychoanalysis 1954-1955*. Translated by S. Tomaselli. New York: W. W. Norton & Company, 1988.

Ladenson, Elisabeth. *Proust's Lesbianism*. New York: Cornell University Press, 1999.

Lagache, Daniel. *The Work of Daniel Lagache: Selected Papers 1938-1964*. Translated by E. Holder. London: Karnac Books, 1993.

Leclercq, Stéfan. *Gilles Deleuze, immanence, uvivocité et trnscendantal*. Belgium: Éditions Sils Maria, 2003.

Leibniz, G. W. *Philosophical Writings*. Translated by M. Morris and G. H. R. Parkinson. Edited by G. H. R. Parkinson. New York: The Everyman Library, 1995.

———. *Theodicy: Essays on the Goodness of God, the Freedom of Man and the Origin of Evil*. Translated by E. M. Huggard. Edited by A. Farrer. Chicago: Open Court, 1998.

———. *Discourse on Metaphysics, Correspondence with Arnauld, Monadology*. Translated by Dr. Montgomery. La Salle: Open Court, 1994.

———. *New Essays on Human Understanding*. Cambridge: Cambridge University Press, 1996.

Levin, Charles. "Carnal Knowledge of Aesthetic States," *Canadian Journal of Political and Social Theory* (Winter/Spring 1987).

Lingis, Alphonso. "Oedipus Rex: The Oedipus Rule and its Subversion," *Human Studies* 7: 91–100 (1984).

Long, A. A. and D. N. Sedley. *The Hellenistic Philosophers: Volume 1, Translations of the Principle Sources, With Philosophical Commentary*. Cambridge: Cambridge University Press, 1987.

Lorenz, Konrad. *On Aggression*. Translated by M. K. Wilson. New York: Harcourt Brace and Company, 1966.

Lorraine, Tamsin. *Irigaray and Deleuze: Experiments in Visceral Philosophy*. Ithaca: Cornell University Press, 1999.

Lucretius. *On the Nature of Things*. Translated by J. S. Watson. New York: Prometheus Books, 1997.

Maïmon, Salomon. *Essai sur la philosophie transcendantale*, Translated by J.-B. Scherrer. Paris: J. Vrin, 1989.

Merleau-Ponty, Maurice. *Phenomenology of Perception*, Translated by C. Smith. New York: Routledge, 1962.

———. *The Visible and the Invisible*. Translated by A. Lingis. Evanston: North Western University Press, 1968.

Michaux, Henri. *The Major Ordeals of the Mind and the Countless Minor Ones*. Translated by R. Howard. London: Secker and Warburg, 1974.

Nietzsche, Friedrich. *Basic Writings of Nietzsche*. Translated by W. Kaufmann. New York: The Modern Library, 1992.

———. *The Will to Power*. Translated by W. Kaufmann and R. J. Hollingdale. New York: Vintage Books, 1968.

Plato. *Collected Dialogues*. Edited by E. Hamilton and H. Cairns. New Jersey: Princeton University Press, 1961.

Poulet, Georges. *Proustian Space*. Translated by E. Coleman. New York: John Hopkins University Press, 1970.

Proust, Marcel. *À la recherché du temps perdu*. Paris: Gallimard, 1999.

———. *Marcel Proust on Art and Literature 1896–1919*. Translated by S. T. Warner. New York: Carroll & Graf Publishers, 1957.

———. *Pleasures and Regrets*. Translated by L. Varese. London: Peter Owen, 1986.

———. *Remembrance of Things Past*. Translated by C. K. Scott Moncrieff, T. Kilmartin and A. Mayor, 3 vols. New York: Vintage Books, 1981.

Rorty, Richard "Matter and Event" L. Ford and G. Kline, ed., *Explorations in Whitehead's Philosophy*. New York: Fordham University Press, 1983.

Rosenberg, Harold. *The Tradition of the New*. New York: DA Capo Press, 1994.

Roudinesco, Elisabeth. *Jacques Lacan*. Translated by B. Bray. New York: Columbia University Press, 1994.

Sartre, Jean-Paul. *Being and Nothingness: A Phenomenological Essay on Ontology*. Translated by H. E. Barnes. New York: Washenton Square Press, 1956.

———. *The Emotions: Outline of a Theory*. Translated by B. Frechtman. New York: Citadel Press, 1993.

———. *The Psychology of Imagination*. New Jersey: The Citadel Press, 1985.

Seem, Mark D. "Liberation of Difference: Towards a Theory of Antiliterature," *New Literary History*, vol. 5.1 (1973).

Shakespeare, William. *The Complete Dramatic and Poetic Works of William Shakespeare*. Chicago: International Press, 1926.

Shattuck, Roger. *Proust's Way*. New York: W. W. Norton and Company, 2000.

Smith, Daniel W. "Deleuze's Theory of Sensation: Overcoming the Kantian Duality." *Deleuze: A Critical Reader*. Oxford: Blackwell Publishers, 1996.

Spinoza, Baruch. *The Ethics, Treatise on the Emendation of the Intellect and Selected Letters*. Translated by S. Shirley. Indianapolis: Hackett Publishing Co., 1992.

———. *The Letters*. Translated by S. Shirley. Indianapolis: Hackett Publishing Co., 1995.

Spitz, René. *The First Year of Life: A Psychoanalytic Study of Normal and Deviant Development of Object Relations*. Connecticut: International Universities Press, 1965.

Thomas, Jean-Jacques. "Poststructuralism and the New Humanism." *SubStance* #68, (1992).

Vigny, Alfred de. *Oeuvres completes*. 2 vol. Paris: Gallimard, 1986.

Whitehead, Alfred North. *The Concept of Nature*. Cambridge: Cambridge University Press, 1995.

Williams, James. *The Transversal Thought of Gilles Deleuze: Encounters and Influences*. Manchester: Clinamen Press, 2005.

Index